The Three Miracles

To Diane,
Hope you'll enjoy
the book!

Mark Mulligan

Chapter One

There she was in my rear view mirror. All alone, standing there in the driveway, waving goodbye as I slowly pulled our black Nissan X-Trail out onto the street.

She'd been in a great mood all morning. Come to think of it, Adela had been in a really great mood for several months straight. And on this July morning, without even asking her to do it, she had packed my suitcase for me, carefully folding my shirts while I put new strings on my Taylor guitar.

This wasn't going to be one of my typical northbound runs across the border to play a gig at some bar up in Arizona or southern California. I was Nashville bound! A year after my first visit there, ten brand-new songs were written and ready to go for what I anticipated would be my strongest album yet.

In the past, Adela would've already gotten a sneak preview of an upcoming project, usually from hearing me bang out freshly-written tunes while she sliced vegetables or swept the kitchen floor. This time though, she hadn't heard a single one. The first time she'd pop my finished CD into the stereo and hit "play," she'd hear ten fully produced songs exactly as I'd been hearing them in my head. Even the title of the album, *A Bar Down in Mexico*, would be a surprise to her.

After all the ups and downs we'd been through, I had an inexplicable urge to do things differently than I'd done them in the past. Maybe because, much like Adela, "different" is how I was feeling.

Different from the guy who, seven long years before, had sat on the edge of the bed during his honeymoon, confused and exhausted from arguing, wondering what he had done to upset his beautiful new bride so much. After all, hadn't he simply asked her to join him in a jacuzzi? What could have possibly been the problem? Was she actually upset that a few strangers who were in it happened to be female? It was a cruise ship, for God's sake!

Different from the guy who realized right then that he had seen plenty of warning signs of this increasingly extreme jealousy during their three years of dating, but had chosen to ignore them. "I won't be this way once we're married," she'd assured him more than once.

Different from the guy who began to feel handcuffed as he stood in front of a microphone night after night, guitar in hand, trying to provide for his family while fully aware of the hell he would face if asked to sign a CD for an even semi-attractive female. Or, God forbid, if he happened to glance anywhere within a twenty-five foot radius of a blonde, brunette, redhead, or for that matter, bald woman.

Different from the guy who prayed time and time again to simply hear the words, "I trust you," come from Adela's mouth one day.

And very different from the guy who, two years before, sat across the table from his father at an Applebee's Restaurant in Phoenix, worn-out and depressed, announcing that he was going to divorce his wife.

"I've tried everything, Dad. Believe me, for years I really have. I've asked her time after time to go to counseling with me. But she doesn't want to go. She thinks it's my problem," I explained, knowing how much a divorce would disappoint my Catholic parents. After all, divorce just didn't happen in my family. My parents had been married for nearly fifty years at this point. And my grandparents? They were married seventy-one years!

Dad listened carefully to every word.

"Mark, there are two bad qualities that are almost impossible for people to ever change," he answered. "One is stinginess. When people are tight with their money, they'll always be tight."

He continued. "The other is jealousy. When someone doesn't trust you no matter how trustworthy you are, there's nothing you can do about it. No matter what you do to earn that trust, they'll just demand more "proof" from you the next time. It's an addiction that needs to be fed, but every time you feed it, it just grows stronger." I could tell, Dad wished he was wrong. But he wasn't. We both knew it.

Several days later I was back in Mexico, packing my bags.

Adela knew I wasn't bluffing. She'd heard it in my voice over the phone, one week before when I called her just before a private party I was about to perform at in the States. I'd already given her three days and a make-it-or-break-it choice to go forward in our marriage and attend joint counseling, or call it quits. My final offer was about to expire, in the days leading up to that difficult conversation with my dad.

"Your three days are up, Adela. No more denying this, and no more putting it off. It's now or never. We can't go on like this any more. I can't live my life constantly defending myself against things I haven't done. I've told you before, I'm willing to seek help if it's both of us together. But me going alone is pointless. The choice belongs to you. What's it going to be?"

I waited for a response for what seemed like an eternity. Just when I began to think we'd been disconnected and was about to curse billionaire

Carlos Slim's notoriously inept TelMex international phone service, the silence was broken by Adela's voice.

"I don't have a problem, Marcos. I don't need anyone's help," she replied coldly. "I'm not going."

I was stunned. Had she not understood me when I said this was a make-it-or-break-it decision? After eleven years of residing in Mexico, was my Spanish still that bad?

This was unbelievable. Here I'd offered, like countless other times before, to visit the counselor of *her* choice. Anybody! A Catholic priest. A psychologist. A friend. I didn't care if it was the trash collector, as long as we could finally start dealing with the one problem that kept rearing its ugly head over and over, no matter how many times we tried to tell ourselves things were fine.

How could Adela *not* realize that this really mattered to me? Shouldn't that have mattered to her? How could I possibly live my life, do my job, and raise my kids while constantly defending myself from ridiculous accusation after accusation? Bill Clinton's legal defense team faced fewer charges than I did, for Pete's sake!

OK, I admit, I certainly was no angel before meeting Adela. After getting married, I had been faithful, but no, I hadn't been perfect. Did I ever notice when a female happened to be attractive? Yes. Last time I checked, I'm a guy! And for the record, shocking as this may sound, guys do happen to notice when women are attractive! Had I ever innocently said something flirtatious over the years? OK, like millions of happily-married, monogamous men who have done the same, I plead guilty. But did I really deserve to be treated as if I were some unfaithful deviant out there hitting on girls or carrying on secret relationships? Or even wanting to?

More than anything, I wondered how a woman so beautiful could let herself become tormented by fictional issues like the ones her jealousy repeatedly brought up. How could someone who was such an otherwise wonderful, giving, caring wife and mother let this happen to herself? Was her jealousy purely emotional, or could it be a medical issue too? Could clinical depression be a factor? Where's Dr. Phil when you need him?

At the moment, none of my questions mattered. She wasn't interested in seeking help, so that was it. The deal was sealed.

"OK, Adela. You win. But you know what this means. I'll be home in a few days to pack up my stuff. I'm gone."

Click.

I hung up the phone, reeling in shock from what had just transpired. The shock quickly turned to anger.

You idiot! All these years of being faithful… for what? You may as well have cheated on her a thousand times. You stupid idiot!

I had just begun to berate myself when a thought suddenly hit me. *I had a show to play.* My gear was already set up, and in less than an hour I'd have a crowd of people to entertain. Like it or not, I would have to flip a switch and instantly become the life of the party. You know, that cheerful, laid-back, smiling "trop-rock" singer without a care in the world.

By this point in my career, I rarely drank alcohol during my show. I guess I'd learned some lessons after routinely treating my body like a shot glass onstage in my early years, when too many forgotten lyrics led to too many forgotten nights. These days, I usually chose to hold off until after the last song had been sung before imbibing. But on this particular evening, I already had a stiff Captain Morgan and Coke in my hand by the time I took the microphone. A few songs later, that one was followed by another, then another. Sometime in the second set, I lost count.

Adela's response kept popping back into my head between songs, and even during songs while I was trying to sing. Though no one realized it, that guy up there with his guitar singing "Don't Worry, Be Happy" was expending every ounce of energy he had just to hide the anger behind his forced smile. Add unspecified quantities of alcohol to the equation, and things quickly became more confusing than ever.

Later that night, unbeknownst to anyone else and for the first time ever in my marriage, I found myself in a parking lot, making out with a complete stranger.

Meanwhile, four hundred forty-two miles away, Adela was tucking her two-year-old son into bed.

"Buenas noches Marcos," she whispered, kissing his forehead softly before slipping out the bedroom door and returning to her room.

Adela took the phone from the kitchen and placed it beside the bed, in case her husband called to talk things out as he always seemed to do after a fight. She turned out the light, crawled into bed, and began to cry.

"What have I done?" she asked herself over and over again. She wiped away her tears and tried to sleep. As the hours went by and the phone never rang, reality sank in and she knew.

He's not bluffing. This is really it.

****

It took only a couple sessions for our first marriage counselor, a Catholic priest named Padre Jorge, to realize that our issues required a different kind of help than he was qualified to offer. He handed us a business card with a phone number scribbled on the back, hugged us both, and wished us luck as we walked out his parish office door. Something tells me that our little time spent together made him feel much better about his decision to live a celibate life.

A few days later, we found ourselves sitting across the table from another man we had just met, again sharing the most intimate details of our marriage. The more we shared, the more his questions became directed at Adela.

"Adela, tell me. Was your father an alcoholic?"

"Did you often see him drunk?"

"How did he behave when he was drunk?"

Question after question and answer after answer, Adela squirmed uncomfortably in her seat as she was forced to deal with an interrogation she was unprepared for. But I wasn't about to let her back out now. It had been a long road to get her to join me here. A road we had almost gotten lost on.

"Adela, when was the first time you suspected your father was being unfaithful to your mother?"

"Tell me what you saw that day."

No doubt, her father certainly had done his part in making these questions and every other one on the list so difficult to answer. Especially the very last one.

"Adela, do you love your father?"

I felt sorry for Adela as I watched her struggle with her answers, trying to guard secrets that had never been shared publicly. But I didn't intervene or say a word. I just listened.

****

Adela's mother was a saint. Etelvina, or "Doña Telma" as she was known to everyone, was strong and wise, despite not having had a high school or even grade school education. With a husband who spent nearly every peso of his income on booze, she somehow found a way to keep her four daughters and one son in line, and she always kept their humble home in Guaymas' working-class Fatima neighborhood spotless. With no budget, she could make a great meal out of just about anything. And when she did have a few pesos to buy the necessary ingredients, homemade banana-leaf tamales were her specialty. She was patient, loving, and always had a smile on her face, even though she had been dealt a difficult hand in life.

Her children, their friends, the neighbors, and even strangers all respected her. Everyone except for one man, who unfortunately happened to be her husband. Jose Juan Lerma, known to his fellow construction workers simply as "Bigotes," was the stereotypical macho Mexican male. Never once in their entire marriage had he taken his wife out of town, given her a Christmas gift or birthday card, surprised her with flowers or danced with her. In fact, about the sweetest thing he'd ever done for his wife was allow her to give him a foot massage, which she routinely did without complaining.

Before I met Adela, her father's free time was spent drinking with his buddies. When he'd return from carousing, he'd often pull up a chair on the porch next to the family pet, a pig, and crack open another quart of beer. Bigotes loved to get the pig drunk, and being the loyal drinking buddy he was, the smelly animal happily obliged. Soon Bigotes would start to sing, and the intoxicated beast would join in with strange noises that only a drunken pig can make. They made quite a duo, until one day the family got hungry and ate the pig. And you thought Fleetwood Mac ended on a rough note!

The rest of the family never got as close to Bigotes as the pig did. Few people ever had. Since he was a small boy, he'd survived all alone on the dusty streets of Choix, Sinaloa. Like his wife, he had never attended school, and couldn't read nor write. Life was work. Hard work. And when the work was done, there was drinking. Hard drinking.

That would never change, until one day when Adela's brother Jorge came home with news for his father. After dreaming of one day going to college, Jorge had been forced to abandon further education and get a job at a cement factory. When Bigotes heard this, he got angry.

"¿Por qué?" asked Bigotes. Why would his only son make a decision like that?

"Somebody has to support this family," young Jorge responded. "And you can't, not drinking the way you do."

Bigotes hung his head in shame. Until the day he died, he never touched alcohol again.

****

Some wounds take a lifetime to heal. Others never do. There were things Adela had seen in her young life that she never intended to share with anyone. Horrible things. Traumatic experiences at the innocent age of five can scar you permanently and shape your life forever.

"Mark, the bad news is that there's nothing that you can do to solve this," the doctor told me during a difficult session, after asking Adela to give us a moment alone.

"And the good news," he continued, "is that there's nothing you can do to solve this."

I didn't understand.

"This isn't about you, about anything you've done or haven't done. As you and I have talked about, Mark, your wife really needs the medication we've discussed at earlier sessions. Not because of the difficult experiences she's shared with me here, but because of a simple chemical imbalance. Her depression is not by choice. But it may be exacerbating normal degrees of jealousy and leading to extremes like the ones you've experienced."

I didn't like what I was hearing. I'd always been somewhat suspicious of doctors who prescribe Prozac as if it were aspirin. Can't people just cheer the hell up? Sounds a lot easier to me, and cheaper.

"This wasn't her choice, Mark, it was the hand that was dealt to her" he continued. "But she *can* choose to treat it, like many other people out there suffering from similar imbalances. I've gotta hand it to you, you've been better at handling her issues than most guys. A Mexican husband would have dumped her years ago!" he chuckled.

Political correctness still hasn't caught on in Mexico.

"I don't want to leave her. I still love her," I answered quietly, wondering if she could hear me through the door. "I can handle it if we argue now and then. We're married, and we have a kid, so I expect that. I just want to bring it back to some kind of manageable level, if there is such a thing. Where I can l do my job without feeling like I'm betraying my wife because there happens to be a girl in the crowd. Where I can look around a room and not be terrified of a decent-looking woman walking in. Where I won't be accused of secretly wanting to have affairs with people I've never even met."

(I could've mentioned the worst case of all, when Adela had seen me reading a tabloid article about Rosie O'Donnell... I repeat, *Rosie O'Donnell...* and suggested that I somehow desired her. Yes, Rosie O'Donnell, in case you missed that. But like any other reasonable person hearing something so ridiculously far-fetched, he surely would've thought

I was exaggerating. To Adela's credit, the article about Miss O'Donnell contained no photos.)

"Be patient with her Mark," he answered reassuringly. "These sessions have been really good for her. Things are going to change if you just hang in there and show her some support. Let me call Adela back in here, and share with both of you where I think we should go from here."

****

I kept trying not to look in my rear view mirror, but I just couldn't help it. There she was, still standing in the driveway, still waving as I inched further down the street. Only then did it dawn on me just how long I'd actually be gone. Following Nashville, I had a series of shows to perform at in Indiana, Arizona and the Pacific Northwest before I'd be back home. A lot of miles lay ahead of me. And that rear view mirror wasn't making this moment any easier.

After all, it had been only days since Adela and I had returned from a wonderful trip a couple hours up the coast to Kino Bay. It was one of our best vacations ever, as a matter of fact. The entire *gringo* side of the family had come down from the States, excited to spend time with Adela, Marcos, me, and seventeen-month-old Luis Antonio, the unexpected product of our successful marriage counseling sessions!

That big, joyful Mulligan family reunion would turn out to be unlike any other before, all because of Adela. Something about her was different on that trip, something no one could explain. She smiled. She laughed. She was happy. She played with nephews and nieces, and had more fun than ever before just hanging out with everyone, sharing stories about her family while patiently listening to recycled tales about our own. It was hard to believe this was the same girl who had seemingly shied away from our family in the past.

"Don't tell anyone, but Adela is my new favorite aunt," one of my nieces whispered to my mom.

"Mine too!" another confided. Yes, that trip had opened doors that I'd never dreamed would ever open. For Adela, a new leaf had been turned. She knew it, and everybody else did too.

****

I couldn't take it anymore. I stopped and slammed the car into reverse, nearly crashing into our open gate as I backed into the driveway. Engine running, I got out and ran to Adela. I reached out to embrace her, only to find teardrops running down her face. She tried not to let me see her cry.

"Why do we always have to say goodbye?" she asked, hugging me tightly. "I know you have to go, but I don't want you to. Can't you stay a little longer?"

"Shh, don't worry," I assured her, wiping her tears away. "When I get back from this trip, you and me, we've got nothing but time. I promise, Adela. Nothing but time."

I looked at her one more time. Then I got back into the car, pulled out of the driveway and was gone.

Chapter Two

"Let's make a record!"

There it was, that big Kenny Royster smile, just a few feet away on the other side of the small glass window. Perched on his producer's chair, 48 tracks of Radar technology and seemingly endless channels of preamps at his fingertips, he fidgeted with some last minute adjustments before turning to me, flashing a thumbs up. "Ready?"

On my side of the window, inside a tiny isolation booth where I would sing my "scratch" vocals along with the band so they could track their parts, I nervously wiped the sweat from my hands.

****

I had arrived at Nashville the night before, setting my guitar down in my hotel room and immediately calling Adela to let her know I had arrived.

"*Suerte Marcos, te amo,*" she said, wishing me luck and telling me she loved me.

"I'll talk to you tomorrow as soon as I'm done with the session," I assured her. "I've already bought a few phone cards with ten bucks of credit on each, so I can call you every day!" The way I blew through international calling cards, I wouldn't doubt if the NSA were tracking me.

"Don't worry about that Marcos. I know you're busy. Just call me when you can, do what you need to do, and come home with a great record. I can't wait to hear it. *Te amo.*"

I have to admit, even though things had greatly improved for us following our marriage counseling, I wasn't yet accustomed to this kind of attitude coming from my wife. Was it too good to be true? Would I merely set myself up for a letdown, as had happened so many other times I had gotten my hopes up? There was good reason to be hesitant in accepting that these changes and improvements were actually permanent. Only distance could be our true test. After all, it was trips like this one where jealousy and trust issues had erupted in the past. Would it happen again? This experience in Nashville was going to answer some big questions for both of us.

****

"Here we go," I thought, the studio suddenly growing silent.

"ONE..."

Dennis Holt's voice boomed in my headphones, so clearly you'd think he was in the same booth as me, instead of sitting behind his drum kit in a separate isolation room.

"TWO..."

I wondered if Kenny, Dennis, and the rest of the band could hear my heart pounding through that microphone inches in front of me. Or if they had any idea what question had been running through my head ever since walking in the front door of Direct Image Recording.

What in the world am I doing here?

Really, hanging out with producers like Kenny and guys who had performed with the likes of Kenny Chesney and other huge major label artists, what *was* I doing here? The question was familiar, one I'd first asked myself fifteen years earlier, when I first saw a classified ad in the newspaper advertising a recording studio in my hometown of Phoenix, Arizona.

"Thirty bucks an hour," the voice on the other end of the line had answered.

"How 'bout twenty?" I groveled.

Next thing I knew I was recording my first album, a country-flavored, eleven-song cassette called *The Things I Love*, produced by a fellow named Jim Gerkin and recorded in a bedroom in his house. It featured an electric guitar player I never met, who traded session work on two tracks for a case of beer while I was out of town. Jim also brought in a pedal steel player who had played for Lyle Lovett on the road, lending some badly needed credibility to the project. Aside from vocals, I played piano and rhythm guitar, and also did my own leads. Not exactly Clapton-esque stuff, but hey, when it came to lead guitarists, I was all I could afford.

Jim also cut me a deal on recording fees in exchange for what turned out to be informal "counseling" sessions, where I'd crack open a beer and listen to him gripe about his impending divorce. This happened so often that at one point, I believe he actually owed *me* money.

In a shocking turn of events, the cassette's release was ignored by *Rolling Stone*. And although Jim couldn't score a pack of Chiclets with production royalties from our project, he evidently did gain something from our time together in the studio. His next job offer was as a comedy writer for the hit television show *Frasier*.

As for me, you'd think I would've learned. So why, soon after that album's release, did I find myself in the parking lot of The Tufa Tavern in Kirkland Junction, Arizona, scribbling words to what would become the title track of a second album? So much for that business degree.

Why write songs in the first place? People often ask me where they come from. A lot of songwriters have a lot of different answers. Truth is, I haven't got a clue. Perhaps you're simply driving down the interstate when a catchy lyric comes to mind, or maybe some melody suddenly pops into your head. You should really pull over, but decide instead to risk the lives of everyone else on the road by reaching over to the passenger side floorboard and fumbling around until you find any scrap of paper that could be pressed against the steering wheel and scribbled on. Another line comes to mind. Then another. Moments later, you're oblivious to the fact that you're getting simultaneously flipped off by a mom in a minivan and some dude with a *"Jesus Loves You"* bumper sticker.

Twenty-seven exits and six near-misses later, there's no more room to write. And by the time you've made it to wherever you're going, this barely legible scrap of paper has somehow avoided being relegated to the heap of other countless scrawled-on matchbooks, takeout menus and parking tickets in your car.

Days, weeks, or even months later, assuming you haven't been charged with vehicular manslaughter or eventually discovered your melody was a direct rip-off of "New Kid In Town," you're still at it. After so many rewrites, your song bears absolutely no resemblance whatsoever to the one you started to write. Even the title is different.

Not only is this song still unfinished, but in the meantime you've started three more. Sleep has become impossible. Your wife is sick and tired of being woken up night after night while you fumble around in the darkness for a flashlight, pen and paper. At some point, most likely on a lonely couch during a late-night infomercial for any given Ronco product, you actually come to hate having this song inside you and wonder why in your right mind you ever started to write it.

But none of that occurred to you as you nearly sideswiped a Kenworth, scribbling away at what promised to be your best song yet. All you knew was that one day, after months or even years of frustration, you'd be standing at a microphone in a recording studio, headphones on, drummer counting down, with a full band ready to kick into gear.

That song, along with nine or ten more, is finally on the verge of fully coming to life, with drums, bass, keyboards and electric guitars ready to breathe definition into it. Maybe this baby will turn out just like you've pictured in your head, or maybe it will be completely unlike anything you had ever imagined. As a songwriter, nothing is more exciting than that moment.

****

"*...ONE, TWO, THREE, FOUR!*" Dennis counted in.

"*Well I have worked my fingers to the bone, trying to build myself a happy home.*"

A familiar voice rang through my headphones, the same one heard on *The Things I Love* and a half-dozen more albums that had since followed. My nervous anticipation quickly evaporated, and I felt completely at ease.

"*But the more I work, the more goes to the man. So now I've got myself a better plan.*"

Finally, the album that had existed up until now only in my head, the one that Adela would be the first to hear, was coming to life. The full band kicked in.

"*I'm gonna buy me a bar down in Mexico*"

Chapter Three

"Hey man, you got a few extra bucks?" asked a grimy-looking fellow reeking of booze.

"If I had a few extra bucks, think I'd be staying in this dump?" I retorted in rather non-Christ-like fashion. I'd already been hit up for cash twice as I ran the gauntlet from Kenny's studio to the hotel, a run-down Days Inn near Vanderbilt University on West End Street.

With half my life's savings invested into airfare, lodging, band and studio time, there wasn't much left in my budget for a nice place. OK, so it wasn't the Hilton. Or even a Motel 6. So what? At least I had free breakfast and a somewhat comfortable bed. Most importantly, the hotel was close enough for me to walk to the studio over at 1700 Hayes Street rather than take a cab.

Besides, I was only going to be in my room at night. Studio sessions began at 10 a.m., and with Kenny and I trying to get a ten-song album recorded in a week, this meant that we'd be busy until 8 or 9 p.m. each night. Around that time, I'd run a couple blocks down the street to the nearest liquor store, where I'd buy Kenny a cigar and his favorite non-alcoholic beer to celebrate the day's accomplishments while we planned out the next day's sessions. It was a tradition we'd started back on the first project we recorded together, *Journey Around The Sun*.

Kenny didn't drink. And me, I had too much invested in my Nashville trip to risk showing up to even one studio session with the slightest hangover or sore throat from going out on the town. To pull off a decent performance, I had to be on top of my game, which meant getting back to my hotel room to work on vocals, map out harmonies, and rehearse along to whatever tracks we had recorded up to that point.

When I wasn't practicing, I was busy doing a million little things like preparing liner notes, approving artwork files or editing lyrics to send to my graphic designer, Tony Amato, who was preparing the album cover in Phoenix. You never knew when we were going to change a lyric, or even an entire verse or chorus, on the spot. After all, during our vocal sessions, Kenny would obsess over the most minute details of my phrasing, and we'd spend what seemed like an eternity focusing on something I never even dreamed we'd have to work out.

But nine times out of ten, by trying a different choice of words or simply changing the emphasis on a particular syllable, we'd come up with something that always left me wondering why I hadn't already thought of that. Just another reason, among many, that Kenny Royster is a Grammy Award winner.

When you work with a producer of that caliber, not to mention some of the best session players in Nashville, the bar is definitely raised, challenging you to deliver the best performance you possibly can. You have to. After all, once you record it, mix it, master it and release it, it's permanent. There's no going back to change something later. Once it's out, what you hear is what you get, forever. That's why I'd often look at the clock on my nightstand, see 1:15 a.m., and keep working. In any other hotel, angry calls would have been placed to the front desk, complaining about some guy singing and playing guitar in the wee hours of the morning. But this was the Days Inn on West End Street in Nashville. My neighbors were up watching Jerry Springer.

And so I went, back and forth between the studio and the hotel as the songs slowly took form. Monday and Tuesday were spent tracking drums, bass, keyboards and guitars, all played along to my initially recorded "scratch" vocals. Wednesday, Kenny brought in a trumpet player, Scott Ducaj, as well as an accordion player, Jim Hoke. Next thing we knew, our musical tracks were recorded and we were ready to start the actual vocal takes.

Thanks to Kenny's vocal training lessons with me during the making of *Journey Around The Sun*, we sailed through the sessions. By the time Kenny cracked open his first nonalcoholic beer on Friday night, we had all ten songs fully tracked with instruments and vocals. We were ready to mix.

"Yeah baby!" he exclaimed, grinning broadly as we listened to song after song blasting through his studio monitors.

I couldn't believe it. We hadn't even begun to mix, and the album already sounded great! The players had each nailed their parts and their performances were awesome. From festive, Latin-flavored songs like "Saint Anywhere" and "Third World Cantina," to ballads like "It's About Time" and "If I Saw You Tonight," the raw tracks were everything I'd hoped for and more.

"It's rockin', I love it!" I said excitedly, thanking him for all he had done so far.

"Wait until we mix it. Then you're *really* going to love it!" Kenny answered.

As I sipped a celebratory beer, Kenny scribbled down notes on tracking sheets, already preparing for the mixing process that awaited us. Perfectionist that he was, mixing ten songs would take several days at the very least. Add another day for mastering. Kenny had a full plate in front of him.

As for me, I'd fly out of Nashville on Saturday after our first mixing session, bound for Cincinnati, Ohio. I had a Sunday show scheduled just across the state border in Indiana. Then, I'd rejoin Kenny in Nashville on Monday, in hopes that we could have all ten songs mixed *and* mastered by the time I had to leave again to play events in Arizona and Washington.

But in the happiness of that moment, I wasn't thinking about any other shows on the horizon. I was thinking about walking through my door two thousand miles away, kissing my wife, handing her a master copy of my CD, and letting her be the first person in the world to ever listen to *A Bar Down in Mexico.*

Saturday morning I woke up, packed my duffel bag, picked up my guitar and headed for Kenny's studio to milk every last second I could with him before leaving for the airport later that day. On my way to the studio, I stopped at a payphone on West End Street and pulled out my international calling card.

"Adela, I think you're going to love it! Kenny and the band did great. I can't believe how good the tracks came out! We've just got to mix it and master it when I get back from Indiana, and we're done."

"I can't wait, Marcos. I only wish you were coming right now," she answered. "I miss you. And the boys miss their daddy."

"I miss you guys too. And I'm counting down the days 'til I get home. Give Marcos and Luis a kiss from me."

"And don't worry," I added. "I'll call you from the airport before I take off for Cincinnati and again when I get there. You don't have to worry about a thing, Adela."

Needless to say, over the years, constantly letting Adela know where I was, whom I was with, and what I was doing had become automatic. It was a way for me to preemptively defuse potential issues and avoid blowups when I was out on the road and her suspicions ran highest.

"You don't have to call me at any certain time, Marcos," she replied. "Just relax, get on the plane and go to your next show. Don't stress about calling me, just do it when the timing is right, okay?"

All week long she had sounded like this! Still, old habits are hard to break.

"OK, first thing when I get to the airport," I repeated, so accustomed to our old routine that I seemingly couldn't let go of it.

"Marcos, don't you get it?" The question was followed by a lingering silence.

"Get what?" I asked, somewhat confused.

"Haven't you noticed anything lately? Something different in Kino Bay? Something different during this whole week apart?"

The questions hung in the air, waiting for an answer. But before I could reply, Adela answered for me, in three words. Three words that I'd prayed for literally every day since our honeymoon.

"I trust you."

I couldn't believe my ears. After ten years together and approximately 2,587 days of marriage, endless ups and downs, and countless times I'd hoped to hear those very simple words. After nearly giving up on ever hearing them, there they were.

"I love you so much. And I trust you."

I stood there at the payphone, stunned.

"*You have one minute remaining on your balance,*" interrupted an annoying recorded voice. I was almost out of time, gathering my thoughts as quickly as I could.

"Adela, I swear I love you more than I ever have. You have no idea how happy I am to be your husband. All I want to do is go home and spend the rest of my life with you."

"*Te amo, Marcos. Adiós.*"

"*Adiós, Adela.*"

Chapter Four

011- 52-1622- 111- 1799 I dialed the number and waited.

Outside the door on Gary and Kathie Schmid's 55 acre Indiana farm, people were already beginning to arrive for the mid-afternoon show. My friends Larry and Maris Kalmbach had already shown up, coming all the way from Grass Lake, Michigan, and though they had just met the Schmids earlier that morning, they had bonded right off the bat. While Larry helped Gary with getting some chairs, Maris was busy at work in the kitchen.

"You get out of here and let me handle this," she said to Kathie with a big smile, helping to prepare for the hordes of friends and neighbors that would soon be descending upon the Schmid home for "Mulligan Fest," an event that could trace its beginnings all the way south of the border to some little bar called Froggys. Oh, and a Bellamy Brothers song.

****

Gary and Kathie weren't supposed to be anywhere within two thousand miles of San Carlos that night in 2005. But blame it on Gary's younger brother Ken, who instigated the whole thing after a business trip had taken him to the region back in August, 2004.

Ken had quickly fallen in love with San Carlos. To him, it was one of the most beautiful places he had ever traveled to. And this little bar he had stumbled across? Wow, it was the absolute coolest. With the aroma of wood fired brick oven pizza wafting through the air, the ice cold beer, ESPN on satellite TV and a bar full of gringos, this little place felt just like home.

When some fellow nicknamed "Mexico Mark" picked up a guitar and started singing a bunch of beach tunes in English, the night got even better. Pizza, *cerveza*, ESPN, live music, who could ask for more? But something was missing.

In twenty-six years of traveling on business for General Electric, Kenny had often invited his wife Diane to come along. But for some reason, spending her entire day alone in a hotel room in some strange town while Kenny was off visiting plants operated by GE just didn't do it for her. It had been years since a trip to Los Angeles didn't turn out so well, and after that Diane elected to stay home and let Ken travel alone.

Convincing her to give it another shot after all these years seemed impossible. But what if he wasn't inviting her to join him on a business trip? What if it was, instead, a vacation? An actual trip where they could spend time together, just the two of them, far away in some south of the border paradise?

OK, maybe it can be blamed on a slight buzz. But as Kenny walked back to his hotel along the beach that night, he pulled out his cell phone and dialed home. Even though he had learned during many years of traveling that telling your wife how much fun you're having while away from her *isn't* always a wise idea, tonight was a night to break the rules. He would tell her all about the incredible natural beauty of the Sea of Cortez, the friendliness of the people he had met, Froggys, anything and everything he could think of to convince her to come.

Diane wasn't buying it. That is, not until Ken returned home to Cincinnati and showed her photo after photo he had snapped on his trip. There are some things, like the Sea of Cortez, that words just can't describe. But pictures can. What Diane saw in the photos changed everything. Before he knew it, Kenny had convinced her. Diane was going to San Carlos!

"*But*, only if you can also convince Gary and Kathie to come too," she added. Uh-oh! Ken had a potential deal-breaker on his hands.

Even though Gary was a busy guy, getting him to come would be relatively easy. It was Kathie who would be difficult. She was terrified of flying, and since the trip from the Midwest would have to be by plane, Ken knew he had his work cut out for him. This would require a far better sales job than the one he had just pulled on Diane. How in the world could he get Kathie on a plane?

Who knows exactly what Ken said that day, but Gary awoke from an afternoon nap to hear Kathie excitedly chattering on the phone. *Man, whoever she's talking to*, he thought, *she sounds happy!*

The phone conversation continued.

What in the world is going on? Gary wondered.

Seconds later, Kathie hung up the phone. "We're going to San Carlos!" she happily informed her husband.

Before they knew it, there they were. Gary, Kathie, Kenny and Diane Schmid, a world away from midwest Indiana, enjoying drinks at Froggys, mixed in among the sea of expat and tourist faces that packed the bar that Tuesday night. Beer flowed, the dance floor was rocking, and the friendly environment was exactly like Kenny had described.

Even that same singer was back, singing his beach songs.

This was all new to Gary, Kathie and Diane. But just as Ken had felt on his first visit to Froggys, this was definitely a place they could get used to. They sat there, sipping ice cold *cervezas* and laughing among themselves at their table while I cranked out "First World Refugee", "Pacifico Blue", and "Drinking Mexico Dry" along with a few requests for cover songs from the crowd.

On typical Tuesday nights, those requests for covers were usually for songs by Van Morrison, Jimmy Buffett, The Eagles, etc. Inevitably every Tuesday, some mildly intoxicated gringo would shout *"Guacamole!"* and seconds later the crowd would be going crazy, standing room only on the dance floor and a packed house singing along. Trying to get out of Froggys without playing that tune meant risking getting shot by a crazed ex-pat.

But seldom was I asked to play the song whose title was scribbled on a soggy cocktail napkin stuffed in my tip jar, wrapped around a dollar bill.

Cool, I don't often get to play this one, I thought, kicking off the opening verse.

Over at the Schmid table, Gary turned to Kathie. "Hey, he's singing a Bellamy Brothers song!" Gary exclaimed, surprised to hear a familiar song being played. "I didn't know this guy could sing any Bellamy Brothers stuff!" Gary had no idea that The Bellamy Brothers, with their laid back, "country meets tropical," so-called *"Floribbean"* style were an early influence on my songwriting.

"If I said you had a beautiful body would you hold it against me?" I sang, remembering how my Catholic mother used to scold me for singing a lyric so sinfully suggestive.

More songs followed, then it was time to take a quick break. "Don't go anywhere, it's Tuesday night at Froggys!" I shouted out to the rowdy crowd.

After saying a few "hellos" to friends, signing a CD and selling a T-shirt or two, I made my way up to the bar to grab a glass of water for the second set. Before I got there, I ran into Gary, not one to be shy about talking with entertainers.

"Hey, pretty cool you did that Bellamy Brothers song," he said with a big smile.

"I love those guys," I replied, introducing myself. "So, you're a fan too?"

"I am!" he responded, "Actually, years ago my wife Kathie and I had a band, and we got to open up for them at a local festival."

"Really? You guys have a band?" I asked, somewhat surprised. After all, this average looking, middle aged guy didn't *look* like a rock star.

"No, not anymore," Gary quickly shot back. "These days the two of us sing at church and that's about it."

After a bit more small talk, it was time for me to get back up and sing. The Schmids ordered up another round and fell back into conversation among themselves, while in the noisy background I kicked off the another set.

"Oh oh la la, life in a beach town"

As always on a Tuesday night at Froggys, it was chaotic and loud, and when things got rowdy it wasn't always easy for patrons sitting far back among the crowd to hear what was coming across the two beat-up, 15 inch JBL speakers mounted up front.

"Hey buddy, I think the singer is talking to you!"

Gary swung around to see a stranger at the table next to him, motioning towards me. "I think Mark Mulligan wants you to go up there with him!" the stranger insisted.

Suddenly, it started getting louder as the crowd began to clap. Through the clamor the Schmids could barely make out my voice.

"We've got a couple singers in the crowd tonight who have opened for The Bellamy Brothers!"

"What?" Gary turned back to Kathy, a stunned look on his face, panicking as the crowd called for a performance from our newly announced guest stars. "Wait a minute! I can't... we can't..."

It was pointless to resist. Thirty seconds later, a sheepish Gary Schmid and his lovely wife approached the microphone.

"Dude!" he whispered to me as the crowd went crazy. "I told you, we haven't sung anywhere but in church for years!"

It was too late. The crowd was already going crazy and the microphone was now inches in front of Gary's mouth. Somehow, in the span of twenty seconds, off the top of our heads we came up with a song we thought we could spontaneously pull off.

"Can you fake your way through "Some Broken Hearts Never Mend?" Ah, a Don Williams classic. *And,* one the Bellamy's had covered.

"I think so," Gary shot back nervously, glancing at Kathie. She nodded and away we went. I led us off on the first verse. *"Coffee black, cigarettes, I start this day like all the rest. First thing every morning that*

I do is start missing you."

Suddenly, a beautiful pair of harmonies came from out of nowhere. *"Some broken hearts never mend. Some memories never end. Some tears will never dry. My love for you will never die."*

The crowd erupted! Gary and Kathie were nailing it, their voices blending gorgeously, harmonizing every syllable perfectly just as they had done more than twenty years earlier in their old band, Bitter Creek. As the song ended, the packed house was going wild. Gary and Kathie grinned widely, waving to the crowd as they turned to thank me and then scurry back to their table.

But the cheering crowd wasn't about to let Gary and Kathie disappear, not without doing another song. After all, they were just getting warmed up! Seconds later, we kicked into James Taylor's "Shower The People," and by the time we were finished, the stage had been set for a friendship that hadn't existed moments before. One that would soon take me north of the border to the farm fields of Indiana.

****

Guests continued to arrive. There would be over a hundred of them on the Schmid farm that hot July day, gathered under a huge canopy set up to shield concert-goers from the blazing sun. Most guests were already milling around by the frozen margarita machine or taking their seats, where they could cool themselves in the breeze of the electric fans Gary's son Jason had set up.

I looked at my watch. *Do I have time?* My mind raced, international phone card in hand. *Maybe just a quick hello before I head out to sing!*

Hurriedly, I dialed the 800 number on the back of the card, punched in the scratched-off code, and dialed. *011-52 1622-111- 1799*

But somewhere in between dialing those sixteen digits and waiting for Adela's phone to ring in Mexico, I made a decision I'd regret for the rest of my life. One I'd forever wish I could take back.

Why rush this conversation right now? I'll do it after the show, when we've got more time to talk, I thought to myself.

Click. I hung up, before she could ever answer the call. Setting the phone down, I raced out the door to a waiting crowd.

Moments later, I stood in front of a microphone. "Hello Moore's Hill, Indiana!"

Chapter Five

Frank Sinatra can have New York. Wayne Newton can have Las Vegas. Me, I'll take Moore's Hill, Indiana. Seems like small towns are where I've always enjoyed playing the most. Tiny dots on a Rand McNally atlas, unnoticed by stars and big shots, are often where I play for my best crowds. People in places like Blaine,Washington... Sierra Vista, Arizona... Elizabeth, Colorado... Corning, Iowa... yes, Corning Iowa... they treat you like family. And family is just what the Schmids would become to me that day.

Gary and Kathie's kids reminded me a lot of my own seven brothers and sisters. A close knit Catholic bunch, they were outgoing, fun, and totally welcoming to some visiting singer-songwriter their parents had probably forced them to listen to after returning from vacation in Mexico. I admired how they might jokingly razz their folks in public, but how in private, they spoke of their parents with great affection and respect.

"I thank God all the time that I'm part of this family," son in-law Josh confided before the show, filling me in on the positive Christian influence Gary had been on him while dating daughter Sarah Beth.

Gary had worked hard in life, he and his wife running a Cincinnati based industrial painting, heat treating and sandblasting company that had been in her family for five generations. With Jason, their oldest son, in line to eventually take over the business, Gary knew one day he'd be able to back off a bit and focus on a task of even greater importance. The job of, quite simply, being a spiritual leader to his family and helping his kids get to Heaven. One couldn't help but admire the continual effort he and Kathie put into achieving that goal. Looking at their family that July day, I had no doubt that they'd be successful.

"You have this deeper thread running through your music," Gary would say to me. "Hey, could 'Journey Around the Sun' actually be about a journey around the *Son?*" Good ol' Gary, always seeing the big picture that other people missed.

While Gary was comical and often downright goofy, younger brother Kenny was equally cheerful, yet more soft spoken, possessing a deep spiritual intellect. Both in their fifties, the two brothers shared a bond in their Catholic faith that only grew stronger as years went by. Gary and Kathie sang together on Sundays in the choir at Mass, and Kenny would eventually spend two years at the School of Faith in Kansas City, Kansas, studying to become a spiritual mentor. With his calm demeanor and ability to somehow take the complicated and make it simple, no one was more well-suited for that position than Ken Schmid. Now matter how complex the issue, he could make it understandable, even to a guy like me who couldn't comprehend the text on the back of a box of Froot Loops.

When it came to marriage, both brothers had married wonderful wives who were also hard working, great mothers. Diane and Kathie enjoyed the fact that their families, along with other relatives, could get together as often as they did for holidays and other occasions. How they managed to fit a huge, always growing number of smiling faces into their annual family portrait is a challenge I had previously suspected only Hispanics, Mormons, and the Mulligan family dealt with.

And now, finally, after weeks of "planning sessions" held at local happy hours, and spending an entire morning running around like madmen, it was time for the Schmids to enjoy this long awaited day. The rented frozen margarita machine was officially open for business, as the Schmid's youngest daughter Carly served up glass after glass to thirsty concert-goers. All proceeds from sales and tips would go to Castaway Kids, a charitable organization I had founded a couple years before, focusing on scholarships for disadvantaged kids who otherwise couldn't afford education.

And hey, though I may have technically been the "headliner," I wasn't the only musical act that day. This was Gary and Kathie's home crowd, and folks went nuts when they hopped up alongside guitar-playing Jason to belt out a few songs. By the time they had sung their last note, the three of them had the crowd on their feet, leaving amazed onlookers wondering why their old band ever did break up in the first place. If The Eagles could reunite after all those years, how 'bout Bitter Creek?

No doubt, the greenery and hayfield backdrop was a world apart from San Carlos and its blue Sea of Cortez waters. But, fun songs like "Pacifico Blue", "Saint Anywhere" and "First World Refugee" instantly transported Kenny, Diane, Gary and Kathie right back to Mexico. As I sang "A Bar Down in Mexico," I could picture them laughing and sipping *cervezas* at Froggys, where this whole mess had started.

Larry and Maris would enjoy this day too. In what seemed to be a common theme, our friendship could also be traced to bar stools at Froggys, where *Pacifico* beer-induced conversations led them to join my efforts with Castaway Kids. In the years to come, the Kalmbachs and I would drink a few more cold ones together, eventually developing the kind of friendship that would find them hopping in their RV and driving who knows how many miles across the Midwest from Michigan, just to catch this so-called "Mulligan Fest."

Unlike most others in the crowd that day, Larry and Maris knew Adela personally, not just through my music. Back in Mexico, they had invited us to a social event in their neighborhood once, meeting and spending time with the inspiration behind songs like "I Want to Love You Like That"... the girl I returned to in "Home Again"... the woman I wanted to plant a big 'ol kiss on in "Bésame Baby," etc. But other than the Schmids and a couple other friends in the crowd, no one else there knew much about Adela at all. Their only exposure to her would be through what they'd hear in my songs that afternoon. Songs sung by a guy who had just had years of prayers answered a day before, hearing three words that made him want to race for the nearest southbound plane and hop on it.

She trusted me. That's all I needed to know. We didn't need to solve the world's problems, or even fix every problem that ever existed between us. As long as I knew she believed in me, we could go forward, forgiving each other for mistakes of the past. Yes, she had hers, and I definitely had mine. But the important thing now was that our good times were just beginning.

I wanted to somehow introduce this crowd to my wife, even if it was only through my music. And even if it meant switching things up a bit from my usual playlist. "This one goes out long distance, to Mexico," I announced, performing the intro to a song rarely played at my shows. As I fingerpicked the beginning notes, I could picture in my head the moment I'd eventually be greeted by Adela at my front door.

I've taken some long roads, I know
That led towards the distance to places I just had to go
But now that I'm back here with you
There's nothing in the world that I'd rather do
Than be looking at you looking at me
Still blows my mind, it's like we're meant to be
When I look into those eyes after all we've been through
And see reflections of me looking at you

At first, Adela hadn't understood why I recorded the song at such a slow tempo. Maybe I'm overly sensitive about this stuff, but I couldn't understand why that mattered, given the fact that I had written her a song. Geez, wasn't that good enough? It's not like I was begging for glowing reviews when I gave her that gift, but with her reaction, you'd think I'd have surprised her with an iron rather than a song that came from my heart, a ballad called "Looking at You."

Until several days later when I walked in the house, that song filling the living room. There was Adela, standing just a few feet in front of our CD player, listening intently. Hearing the door open, she turned to me and smiled.

"I can't believe you wrote this beautiful song for me. Now that I understand the words, everything about it is perfect. The tempo, the music, the words, but mostly that you wrote it for me."

We've waited for such a long time
Counting down the moments
Now I can't believe that I'm
Finally looking at you looking at me

****

Maybe it was the summer heat, but the festive crowd seemed quite "charitable" that day, Carly cranking out drink after drink on behalf of Castaway Kids. So what if the machine wasn't working and the "frozen" margaritas weren't actually frozen? The crowd slugged 'em down anyway, cheering loudly each time our fundraising updates were announced from the stage. Heck, we could have put a Castaway Kid through Harvard thanks to Carly's bartending efforts.

Although she was nothing but smiles as she whipped out drinks, little did folks know the range of emotions newly-married Carly was feeling that day, participating in a festive party like Mulligan Fest while her husband was off serving in Afghanistan. They also didn't know a thing about that mysterious premonition Carly had just hours earlier, while the last details were being prepared for the day's event. One that overwhelmed her with a strange feeling. A feeling that something spiritual was going to happen that day. The feeling was strong. It was one she recognized immediately, when she looked off the deck and saw a white dove.

****

"I've loved every minute with you guys today. But I've been away from home for over a week now. And when I get home, I've got a little business to take care of with my wife!"

The crowd laughed as I continued. "In all seriousness, I've got some more places to go after this, but when it all ends, I get to see my family again. And I can't wait!"

What a day it had been so far, thanks not only to my hosts, but to the wonderful crowd that filled the seats in front of me. They had welcomed me in like family, dancing and singing and raising money for charity. They clapped along to the beach songs, laughed at the funny songs, and wiped tears away during the sad songs. In something that would never happen in Berkely, they even stood in unison on their feet to belt out a patriotic song, a local Vietnam veteran leading them at the top of his lungs in singing along to Lee Greenwood's "Proud To Be An American."

Yes, what a day. Not only did I get to perform the fun stuff I always like to sing, but also share some songs that meant a lot to me personally, especially as I remembered the events from the day before. But the day wasn't over yet.

"How many of you have been in love for a long time?"

With the exception of a couple guys who apparently considered it far too much effort to set their beers down, the entire crowd's hands shot up. Someone shouted out fifteen years. Someone else, twenty-five. Someone else, nearly fifty. I felt like an auctioneer the way the crowd was shouting out escalating numbers.

"Great job!" I answered, as hearty applause rang out for the longest married couple in the crowd. "But you've *all* got a little catching up to do to reach my grandparents. Know how long they were married? *Seventy one years!*"

"And this one goes out for them," I added, pointing to the sky.

Granddad fell in love my grandma back in '29
He knew right then she was the one, and now there they are in black and white
And as I wipe the dust off of that frame
I know that they're together once again

By the time I reached the chorus, you could hear a pin drop.

I want to love you like that
Or I don't want to love you at all

Someday I want to look back
At a picture hanging on the wall
And remember how it all began
When I took your hand and said
I want to love you, I want to love you like that

I had sung the song hundreds of times before. But today, as the chorus ended, I was doing all I could to keep my voice from breaking. How my granddad felt about my grandmother, that's exactly how I wanted to love Adela. I had told her that way back when we got engaged. *If not forever, why even mess with it?*

One day we stood up before God and everyone we knew
I gave my word, you gave your heart
And we softly said "I do"
With a promise to live faithfully
For not a day less than eternity

My thoughts suddenly turned to little Marcos and Luis, who Adela would soon be strapping tightly into car seats a couple thousand miles away.

So here we are now, me and you raising two kids of our own
We've done the best that we can do to make this house into a home
Our kids will meet someone someday
And when they think of us, I hope that they will say
I want to love you like that

****

"I'll meet you at Mom's house in just a little while, OK Eva?" Adela said, holding the phone in one arm and Luis in the other. "The kids are just about ready and I've made some really delicious *albóndigas* for all of us. *¡Nos vemos pronto!"*

Minutes later, Marcos and Luis buckled snugly in their car seats, her silver Volkswagen Derby pulled out of the driveway and began its journey toward Guaymas.

****

"Here comes something we can all sing to," I exhorted the crowd, breaking into "Brown Eyed Girl." Everybody shot up out of their chairs to dance, singing along with me until the very last *"la ti da"* as the show came to a close. It was a day I wish didn't have to end.

Before I knew it, darkness had set in and the last "Mulligan Fester" had been carted off in a golf cart to the now empty parking lot, over in the hay field. *Man, that feels good!* I thought to myself, easing my butt into a chair and kicking my tired feet up.

It was down to just us now, the Schmid family and me. There we sat, gathered in a circle, guitars in hand, tired but giddy from the wonderful day we had just experienced, sipping drinks and laughing about how the margarita machine finally started working, just minutes after the show ended.

"Just think, were it not for some Bellamy Brothers song, none of this would have happened," someone remarked. "Here's to Froggys!"

"¡Viva Los Schmids!" I toasted, raising my glass.

Now, it was their turn to entertain me. "You've been singing for us all day, buddy," Gary said. "Now you just sit back, relax, shut up and let us sing a few songs for you!"

Jason grabbed the guitar and away they went, with Gary and Kathie singing while Ken, Diane and the kids joined in, all singing along in a spontaneous "after-party" party. Soon, someone passed the guitar to Ken. I'd soon found out *he* was a guitar player too!

"Amie, whatcha gonna do?" he sang softly. *"I think I could stay with you…"*

As Ken played, I took another sip of my rum and coke, looked around and savored the moment. It truly had been quite a day.

Suddenly, Gary turned to Jason. "Ready?"

Jason nodded at his Dad, paused a moment, and began to sing. Within seconds, gorgeous, harmonies from Gary and Kathie instantly filled the evening air.

"There are stars in the southern sky.
Southward as you go."

I couldn't believe it. "My God, I can't believe they're playing *this* one!" I closed my eyes and smiled, instantly taken back in time to a chilly night in San Carlos, decorating our Christmas tree in our living room. As we hung the ornaments with little Marcos, Adela asked if she could turn off the James Taylor Christmas album we were listening to and put on an Eagles CD that contained her favorite song instead. One called "Seven Bridges Road."

She put the disc in the CD player, closed the lid and hit "play." *A cappella* harmonies filled our home as Adela smiled happily. "I don't know what they're saying in this song, but it sounds so beautiful," she remarked as the song ended. "Can I play it again?"

Little Marcos and I rolled our eyes jokingly as she played it over and over again. "Leave me alone, it's my favorite song in English!" she said playfully as she caught our reaction. "Just one more time, OK?"

"There is a taste of thyme sweetened honey
Down the Seven Bridges Road"

"Wow, guys, you'll never believe this. That's my wife's *favorite* song in English!" I exclaimed. "In all these years, I've never heard anyone play it live!"

"I didn't know that," answered Gary with a big smile. "Wow, that's really cool!"

What are the odds? I sat there, amazed that out of hundreds or even thousands of songs they could have chosen to play, they just happened to choose Adela's favorite to sing to me. I smiled and sipped my drink while Gary, Jason and Kathie prepared to play another song, when just then a telephone rang from off toward the house.

"I'll get it!" shouted Carly, racing toward the house, hopeful it might be a call from her husband Tim in Afghanistan.

"Great job, Jason," I said in the meantime. "Adela would have loved to hear you sing that last song. I only wish she had heard it."

Jason smiled, ready to break into another song. But before he could strum a single chord, we heard a voice. It was Carly, approaching from the house, cordless phone in her hand.

"Mark," she called out. "It's for you."

Chapter Six

"Mark! Mark, is that you?"

"Who is this?" I asked, puzzled by the distant, unfamiliar voice on the other end of the line.

"This is Kim McDonald, Mark."

Kim McDonald? From Mexico? I was completely bewildered. Although Kim had resided in San Carlos for even longer than I had, it's not like we were ever close friends or hung out together. How did she track me down at this number? And why would she be calling me?

"Listen to me. There's been an accident, Mark!"

An accident? I fumbled for words as my heart began to race.

"What? An accident? What are you talking about?"

"You've got to get home right away," Kim said, calmly as she could. "Your wife and kids are hurt. Don't worry, they're alive, but you've got to get home as fast as you can."

I stood there, holding the phone, shocked at what I was hearing. "What... what happened?" I stammered.

Kim, informing me that she was an official ward for the U.S. consulate in Sonora, hurriedly described the details. There had been a head on collision on Highway 15 leading from San Carlos to Guaymas earlier that night. There were serious injuries, but beyond that, facts were fuzzy. Kim assured me she would call me back as details continued to come in. "Come home as fast as you can, Mark," she instructed me just before I heard the phone hang up.

My entire world was suddenly was a blur.

****

Carly looked upset as she reappeared to her family, unaware of what was being said on the phone, but with a sinking feeling in her heart that something was not right. *Why would someone call Mark here, tonight?* she wondered.

Suddenly, she dropped to her knees. "Mark needs us right now, I can feel it! We need to pray!" she exclaimed, out of the blue. Within seconds, Carly was leading her shocked family in prayer, as they joined hands and surrounded her.

Meanwhile, far away in Guaymas, Doña Telma was patiently

waiting for her daughter to arrive when she, too, got a phone call. Not understanding what some stranger with a foreign accent was saying to her, she passed the phone to Adela's youngest sister Eva. Doña Telma's life would never be the same again.

****

Frank Ross was relaxing at home on a beautiful San Carlos Sunday afternoon, when he heard a knock on his door. It was a neighbor, coming to tell Frank there had been an accident. A bad one, involving his good friend Mark's wife and their two children. An oncoming northbound vehicle had crossed over a median, hitting them head on at high speed. The details weren't clear, but it didn't look good. Frank grabbed his phone, quickly making a few calls and trying to make sense of the details that were beginning to emerge. Moments later his phone rang.

"Frank! Tell me what's going on!"

"My God, Mark, I can't believe this. Listen, I don't know much about what's happened. But I've heard the kids are OK and at the hospital over in Guaymas," he reassured me.

"What about Adela?"

He paused. "I've heard her injuries are worse, Mark. It sounds like they couldn't treat her in the emergency room in Guaymas. They're taking her up to Hermosillo as fast as they can."

Hermosillo, that's more than an hour away! I thought.

"Find out what's going on, Frank, please!" I pleaded, desperate for answers.

The best way to for Frank to do that quickly would be to race over to a small medical facility known as *"Rescate,"* situated across the street from our San Carlos home. There, they could hopefully fill him in all the details about Adela and the kids, where they were, and how they were doing.

"Stay put, Mark. I'm going down to Rescate right now to find out what exactly is happening. I'll call you from there," he assured me.

Meanwhile, downstairs in the Schmid's basement, I remained glued to the phone, Gary and Ken by my side lending me moral support, while the rest of the family remained upstairs, waiting anxiously and praying for any kind of good news. We were swamped with calls, coming at us from every direction. There was an update from Kim. There was a call from Alex, the owner of Froggys, assuring me that he and his wife

Susan would find my boys and make sure they were taken care of, telling me not to worry. Soon there was another call, telling me Alex's truck had broken down and he couldn't get to them. No one seemed to know where Adela was. Stories began to conflict. At one point, amidst the utter chaos and confusion, it was unclear whether or not Marcos and Luis had survived. The emotional toll was becoming unbearable.

****

When Frank arrived at Rescate, my old friend Jim Huff was already there, a somber look on his face."We've heard Adela didn't make it, Frank," he said sadly. "But that the kids are both alive and in the hospital up in Hermosillo."

Frank couldn't believe his ears. Before he even had time to fully grasp what he was hearing, his cell phone rang. It was me, calling from Indiana, wanting to know if he had learned anything.

"Mark, I just got here." He paused, struggling for words as he told me that it appeared the boys were injured but going to survive.

"And Adela?"

Frank was shaking. "Mark," he began. There was another long pause. "Mark, I'm hearing she didn't make it."

Didn't make it? I stood there, stunned as Frank tried to continue. Angrily, I interrupted.

"Damn it, Frank, that's not true!" I insisted. "I just heard from someone moments ago who told me she's alive, seconds ago! Please, Frank, find someone who knows where she is!"

Frank had no idea what to do. "I'll call you right back, Mark. Just hang on!"

Maybe this *was* misinformation. After all, Frank too had been inundated with different stories from different people. It would be up to him to find out the truth. He turned to a *Rescate* volunteer.

"I need you to connect me to whoever drove that ambulance, right now!" he demanded. Within seconds, he was on the phone, speaking directly to the ambulance driver up in Hermosillo.

"Señor, ¿dónde están los niños?"

"I just took the boys to the children's hospital," the ambulance driver replied.

"And their mother?" Frank asked.

"I took her to the morgue."

Moments later, as Gary and Ken stood beside me, literally holding me up, I heard Frank's voice on the other end of the line.

"Mark... Mark, I do *not* want to be the person to have to tell you this."

My heart stopped.

"Adela has passed away."

Chapter Seven

"Lo siento, señor. We can't let you into see those boys if you're not a family member," the receptionist replied firmly.

"I'm their uncle," Frank blurted out. After flooring it all the way up the highway from San Carlos to Hermosillo, he wasn't about to be denied access to Marcos and Luis, even if he had to lie to get in. Besides, it was exactly what I had instructed him to do just over an hour before, knowing otherwise my boys might find themselves alone at such an incredibly traumatic moment.

"Right this way, señor."

There they were, lying next to each other in adjoining beds. Little Luis appeared to be unconscious, his internal brain swelling as a result of the massive hit he had taken to the head following the impact of the collision.

Next to a lifeless Luis lay his big brother Marcos, expressionless and in shock, both legs broken, his femurs shattered.

"How are you doing buddy?" Frank gingerly asked.

"My mama's dead," Marcos answered stoically.

****

Carly Schmid was angry. "This can't be happening!" she stammered. "What about the white dove? Things *have* to turn out OK!"

Tears streaming down her face, she started to say something about the power of the Holy Spirit being upon us, but I was already on emotional autopilot, no longer able to process anything going on around me. After calling shocked family members in Arizona to break the news, I was simply numb to all that was happening.

Before Gary and Ken could hustle me out the door to drive me to the airport in Cincinnati, the phone rang one last time. It was Frank.

"Mark, I'm sitting here with Marcos. He's awake and wants to talk with you."

"Does he know about his mom?" I asked. Suddenly I heard Marcos's voice on the other end of the line.

"Papá?"

It was a welcome relief, just hearing his voice. "Marcos, are you OK buddy?"

"Mama's dead."

"I know she is, Marcos," I said, fighting back sudden tears. "I love you and I'm coming home to be with you and Luis right now. How's your brother?"

Before he could answer, Frank was back on the line. "Luis is here, but in shock. He's dazed and out of it, just laying there. I think his leg is broken too. Mark, we've got to get your kids out of this hospital and over to CIMA, fast!" he said, referring to a private hospital located across town in Hermosillo. "This place doesn't even have the painkillers their own doctor prescribes. They don't even have a neck brace for Luis! They've got nothing we need. I had to run out to a pharmacy down the street and pick up everything myself!"

Frank was right. There was no way the government-run hospital would be able to care for my boys, not with the shape they were in and the lack of resources the facility had to deal with. We had to get my kids over to CIMA as quickly as possible, so they could get the immediate attention they needed. Marcos would require immediate surgery on both legs, and with all the unknowns regarding Luis's head injury and brain swelling, time was of the essence. Luckily, Adela and I had just bought a catastrophic health insurance policy only months before. I gave Frank what information I could and asked him to make some calls. Next thing I knew, we were pulling out of the Schmids' driveway and headed for the airport in Cincinnati.

Kenny had gone on-line and booked two airline tickets, one for me and one for Gary. We'd fly to Houston together. From there, Gary would return and I would fly on to Hermosillo, arriving sometime in the morning. After making hasty travel arrangements, family members from Phoenix would already be there by then, ready to pick me up at the airport.

While I was on the plane, Frank would speak with a highly recommended orthopedic surgeon at CIMA, who told him to call as soon as my plane touched down in Hermosillo. Doctors at CIMA would be ready to take in my boys as soon as I could finalize paperwork on an ambulance transfer from the children's hospital.

Still in shock himself, Gary barely said a word as he sat next to me on the flight. Instead, whenever he saw teardrops welling up or felt like I needed his support, he would simply grab my arm. Other than that, he sat silently and prayed. As confused and alone as I felt, it was reassuring to have my friend alongside me, at least for that first leg of the flight.

By the time we got to George Bush International Airport, it seemed like the afternoon concert at the Schmid farm had ended days or even weeks before. So much had happened in the span of just a few hours. Hugging me and saying goodbye, Gary got back on a plane heading straight back to Cincinnati, leaving me at the gate to catch a connecting flight to Hermosillo a couple hours later. Those hours lasted an eternity.

****

"Doña Telma," I cried, any intention of being strong for her evaporating as I held the phone to my lips.

"Marcos, Marcos!" she sobbed, crying so hard I could barely make out her words. "I've lost my daughter! You've lost your wife!"

"I'm so sorry, Doña Telma," I repeated over and over, tears streaming down my face as I stood there at the payphone. "Your daughter loved you so much. She would have done anything in this world to make you happy."

I pressed the receiver harder against my ear, trying to understand what Doña Telma was struggling to say. Finally, she paused, then sighed.

"Mi hijo..." Doña Telma simply couldn't speak any more. Exhausted, she hung up the phone.

Chapter Eight

Outside San Francisco de Asís Catholic Church, just up the street from Adela's childhood home, cars were pouring into Guaymas's Fátima neighborhood. Inside the church, it was already standing room only. Pews were packed with friends, family, and mourners from Guaymas, San Carlos, and as far south as Mexico's Michoacán state, fanning themselves in the baking Sonora summer heat.

It seemed like the whole town was packed into the church that Wednesday afternoon. Everybody was there, that is, except my boys. Marcos and Luis lay injured in a hospital room over an hour away, cared for in Hermosillo by a couple family members so I could attend the funeral in Guaymas.

But aside from my children, there was another notable face missing in the crowd: Doña Telma. Her seat next to mine in the front pew remained empty as the funeral was about to begin. Adela's brother and sisters were there, and we had already waited a few extra minutes to begin the ceremony. But there was still no sight of her mother anywhere. *Where was Doña Telma?* And how could she possibly be late for her own daughter's funeral?

Before I had time to think about it more, the Mass had begun. It was time to say goodbye to Adela Ruiz Fuentes, dead at only 30 years of age.

****

"I have the most beautiful mother in the world," Adela confided to me one sunny day in 1996. It was our first conversation ever, yet within minutes, it seemed as if I had known her my entire life.

Come to think of it, it *wasn't* our first conversation. It was actually our second. Sometime the year before, at the technical school in Guaymas where I privately tutored a few members of the office staff with their English, Adela had approached me, asking if she could possibly join our study group even though she was a student, not an employee.

My heart raced the first moment I met her. She was absolutely stunning, with gorgeous brown eyes, beautiful dark hair and a million dollar smile that melted me from the start.

There was only one slight problem. I had a fiancée up in Nogales, four and a half hours to the north along the Arizona-Mexico border. With so much distance between us and the fact that we only saw each other every other weekend, the last thing I needed was temptation. And judging from the way my heart was racing, Adela was definitely the kind of temptation that would be hard to resist were I ever to let her join our group.

"Sorry, I wish I could have you join us, but the office staffers hired me out of their own money and want to keep the class private for just them," was my admittedly reluctant response.

"That's too bad," Adela answered, still smiling. "If that ever changes let me know, OK?"

As she walked away, my mental reassurances that I had done the morally correct thing were completely drowned out by a competing thought: *WHAT WERE YOU THINKING, YOU IDIOT?*

Little did I know that by September of that same year, my fiancée would make a key decision in her life. In other words, she would dump me. Apparently, during our time apart, she had gotten involved with someone else, fallen in love, and soon it was *adiós, Marcos.*

So when I next saw Adela in late spring of '96, waving to me from across the dilapidated old *mercado municipal* (our downtown public marketplace), options were very different than when we had first met.

I waved back. She smiled and waved again. And without as much as a thank you, "excuse me" or "gotta go," I completely blew off the shoe saleswoman I was dealing with, shamelessly walking away at mid-sentence and finding myself face to face with Adela.

"*¡Hola!*" I said nervously. "*¿Te acuerdas de mi?*"

"Of course I remember you," she answered. "*¿Cómo estás?*"

Surrounded by a busy marketplace full of butcher shops, produce stands, trinket salesmen and beggars, we reintroduced ourselves. It didn't take long for us to find ourselves completely immersed in conversation, talking about our lives, our families, and how a gringo ended up in Guaymas teaching English, as flies buzzed and crowds of bargain-seeking shoppers pushed their way around us.

The more we talked, the more I knew, I didn't want our conversation to end. Could we possibly continue getting to know each other in a slightly more intimate place, perhaps one where pork legs weren't hanging from ceilings?

But this wasn't the United States of America, where a guy could just offhandedly ask a girl out without a second thought. Down here, even in the mid-nineties, there still were a few unwritten "rules" that had to be observed. Put simply, if a guy was mildly interested in pursuing a girl, he'd have to go through hell.

One of the unspoken assumptions was that any girl with a sense of decency would automatically say "no" to the first invitation. Within days, a second request would likely be greeted with either another "get lost," "sorry," "I have plans," or with any luck, an "I'll think about it." Finally, if a guy were the persistent type, desperate as hell, or simply got off on being rejected, he would ask again. If the girl were interested, and some other dude hadn't moved in and stolen her by now, the third time would be the charm and she'd say *"sí."* Settling the Israeli-Palestinian conflict involves less work.

But you weren't off to the races yet. You might still have to put up with being "chaperoned" for that first date or two. That unfortunately meant you'd be forking out additional pesos on movie tickets for an accompanying aunt, watchful older sister, or if you were really lucky, a girlfriend of hers who could be paid off with a box of popcorn to leave you two alone on your date.

It wouldn't be a wise idea to try any funny stuff on that first date, not until you've officially asked her to be your *"novia,"* or girlfriend. My gringo friend Michael's face is still smarting years later from the slap he got, trying to kiss a girl after a couple dates without having asked the big question first. But I digress.

Being an American and adopting "cultural differences" as my excuse, I had pretty successfully avoided the routine (and the face-slaps) up to that point, but didn't want to blow my only chance at getting to know Adela more by appearing too forward, even by simply asking her to cross the street and grab an ice cream cone with me. A fellow had to think fast, especially when he'd soon be heading out of town for the summer and had little time to make an impression.

"Adela, can we pretend that I asked you to join me for an ice cream across the street, but you said no?"

Adela appeared confused. "Why would we pretend something like that?"

Admittedly, it sounded a bit ridiculous, especially as I continued. "Hold on a second. Can we also pretend I came back a week later and asked you again, but you rejected me again?

She stared blankly at me. OK, maybe I'm overly paranoid, obsessing over "rules" that had quite possibly been taught to me merely as a practical joke on some clueless, unsuspecting gringo. But I was in too far to back out now.

"Now let's fast forward, and say I'm back for a third time. OK, here I am. Want to join me for some ice cream across the street?"

She paused.

Uh-oh! She thinks I'm a raging psycho! Surely I had blown my one chance at conversation with a girl who was way out of my league to start with. Undoubtedly she thought I was nuts. *She'll never...*

"OK."

Yes! I had bought myself some more time to get to know Adela Ruiz. Without a clue as to where it would one day lead, away we went, crossing Guaymas's busy *Calle 20* to *La Flor de Michoacán* ice cream shop. From there, we walked together over to the boardwalk that lined Guaymas harbor, sitting alongside the bay, laughing and talking and getting to know each other more. She was ten years younger than me, and surprised that at thirty years old I had never been married.

I was struck by how much she talked about her family. Though she didn't say much about her father, she told me all about her brother Jorge and her three sisters, Katy, Eva, and Crisanta. But the one she went on and on about was her mother, telling me what a good person she was, how hard she worked at raising her family, and how pretty she was. Looking at Adela that day, I knew her mother surely had to be beautiful.

Before we knew it, more than an hour had passed. Adela had to get home. After the conversation we had just experienced, I couldn't let her get on a local city bus. Buses are bad enough. But Guaymas buses? Crowded, filthy, graffiti covered death traps adorned with shrines to the Virgin of Guadalupe, driven by sixteen year olds? Hey, at least it made for a good excuse to spend more time with Adela.

"Can I give you a ride home?"

Admittedly, a slightly forward question to ask a Guaymas girl who had just met me. And one far more motivated by self-interest rather than public transportation safety issues. But a few minutes later, there we were, pulling up to her house in Fatima in my old Isuzu pickup truck. She turned to me, smiled and thanked me for a wonderful time.

"Adiós Marcos, mucho gusto." she said, reaching for the door handle.

If the ice cream invitation and offer of a ride home within ninety minutes of meeting her were somewhat brazen by Guaymas standards, asking her out on an actual date this soon would be really pushing it. But figuring I had a halfway decent chance of getting around "the rules" by once again pleading cultural ignorance or just good old fashioned stupidity, I gathered up my nerve and went for it.

"Adela, would you like to go out with me this Friday?"

"Gracias, Marcos, no puedo," she replied, informing me she couldn't because she already had plans.

OK, time to quickly assess things. Had I violated "the rules"? Should I grovel? Was this some customary "no" on the first invitation, one that would eventually lead to a "yes" after days, weeks, or months of persistence? Or had I misread things? Was she simply not interested? Either way, shocking as it may sound, I had my pride.

"OK Adela, mucho gusto."

She opened the door, but just before she got out of the car, she turned to me and gave me a kiss on the cheek. "Ask me again sometime, OK?"

With that, the passenger door closed, and Adela disappeared up the steps that led to her front door. My life had changed forever.

****

Where was Doña Telma? The funeral was already beginning, and soon my oldest brother John would be delivering the eulogy.

Just down the street from the church, my buddy John Hibbert and his Guaymas-born wife, Fabiola were still sitting in the Ruiz home. Growing up, Fabiola had been friends with one of Adela's sisters, and she wanted to visit the family to grieve with them in the hours before the funeral. They had come all the way down the coast from Puerto Peñasco, or "Rocky Point," as it was known to Americans.

Before the service started, Adela's brother and sisters had already walked up the street to the church, but inside their mother's home, Doña Telma just sat there, unmoving, refusing to budge. Exhausted and overwhelmed with grief, she simply couldn't summon the strength to attend her daughter's funeral.

"I can't do it," she sighed, too worn out to speak. "I just can't!"

"You have to go now, Doña Telma," Fabiola urged. "The funeral is about to start!"

"I can't go. It's too much!" Adela's mother cried. "Please, just leave me here. I can't watch them bury my daughter!"

"*Señora*," John insisted. "You *have* to be there! If you don't go right now to that church, you'll regret it for the rest of your life."

Doña Telma continued to resist, unable to muster the strength to walk on her own, until finally, Fabiola gently took her arm, helped her to her feet, and led her outside where to John's waiting SUV.

"Let's go, I'll take you," he urged her, helping her up into the passenger seat. "You can do this." He continued to reassure her as he drove her up the road to the church and helped her out of the car.

Moments later, there she was, sitting beside me in the front pew as John delivered a heartfelt eulogy. It was an emotional tribute, delivered in both Spanish and English for the mixed crowd of Mexicans and Americans hanging on to his every word. Doña Telma wiped away tears and nodded as John delivered his final words and took his seat.

Throughout the ceremony, I couldn't help but glance again and again at that coffin, just sitting there in front of the altar. Did it really contain that beautiful woman in the framed picture displayed before a packed church, full of mourners? Were we really talking about Adela in the past tense? Would I wake up to find the last four days had been nothing but a bad dream?

Looking at her face in the framed picture, I couldn't help but wonder what her final moments were like. Did she pass away peacefully? Or, as much as I dreaded to think about it, had she suffered?

I had spent ten years with Adela. We knew each other inside out. Now I didn't even know what her last words were.

I couldn't stop thinking about our young boys, destined to grow up without a mother. As close as they were to their mom, how *would* they? Marcos, having to undergo surgery to repair his shattered femurs, unable to walk? One and a half year old Luis, with his head injury and brain swelling, much less a broken leg and ankle? Doctors had already warned me that his brain might *never* fully recover from the severe trauma he had undergone. He hadn't reacted to me once since the accident. *My God, what if Luis never responded to me again?*

Couldn't I have prevented Adela's death if I had only left her our sturdy Nissan X-Trail SUV instead of the compact Volkswagen Derby she died in? After all, the entire reason we had bought the Nissan in the first place was because of its safety records on the highway, how well it would handle a rollover, etc. Why? Why didn't I leave her that car and take the Derby instead?

As I looked at that framed picture on the altar, it slowly hit me that I would never see Adela's beautiful smile again, never again kiss those lips, never hear her voice again. I'd never have a chance to say "I'm sorry" to her for all the things I had ever said to her in anger. Or raise my children with her. We wouldn't grow old together. We would never even say goodbye to each other. Adela was gone.

The door of the hearse closed.

****

On the outskirts of town, a huge crowd was gathered around a freshly dug grave at the north end of *Héroes Civiles de Guaymas* cemetery. A musician played a somber song while mourners fanned themselves in the scorching July heat, waiting for the priest to arrive so the burial could begin. Tears were flowing and random voices shouted out from the crowd surrounding the grave.

"*Dios, ¿por qué?*" implored a sobbing relative.

"*Descanse en paz Adela,*" a friend cried, tears streaming down her face.

The voice of mourner after mourner rang out through the grief-stricken crowd as we waited impatiently for the priest to arrive. Where was he? We couldn't begin without him. But it was getting late.

"*¿Dónde está el sacerdote?*" people began to ask, wondering where the priest was and what had delayed his arrival. Finally, word came into the cemetery. The news wasn't good. The priest had run over someone's leg with his front tire while pulling out of the church, on his way to the cemetery. Apparently he had taken that person to the hospital, and was delayed to the point he would not be able to make it to the cemetery at all.

So there we were, a huge crowd gathered around an open grave, no priest or deacon, the clock ticking, and no idea what to do.

Doña Telma cleared her throat. Two hours before, she had been too wiped out to even consider attending her own daughter's funeral. But now she stood at the edge of a grave where her daughter would be buried, summoning every ounce of strength she had to address the crowd.

"*Gracias a Dios.*" Her trembling voice grew stronger as she spoke. "Thank you Lord for my beautiful daughter. Thank you for lending me Adela for her time on this earth."

The crowd was hushed as she continued.

"Our lives don't belong to us. They never have. They belong to you, Lord. Now take my daughter back, she's yours again. Bless her and welcome her into Heaven."

"Amen," responded the crowd. Doña Telma, turned to me and took my hand. "Speak," she gently said.

I hadn't expected to address the crowd that day, and don't remember what I said except for asking people to pray for Adela's soul. Whatever I did say, it could never come close to exhibiting the wisdom of Etelvina *"Doña Telma"* Ruiz, a poor uneducated woman who never attended grade school, unable to read nor write, grieving yet unshaken in her faith. If only I could say the same about me.

Chapter Nine

Just give me a sign.

I stared into an open Frigidaire and talked to God. I hear he's everywhere. Surely he hangs out in refrigerators too?

I need some light at the end of the tunnel, Lord. Marcos can't walk. Luis won't respond to me. Adela is gone forever. I have no clue what to do or how to do it. I'm terrified and alone, Lord, and I need your help. Please, Jesus, just give me some kind of sign that everything is gonna be OK. I ask this in your name."

You'd assume I'd have been praying non-stop since Adela died, but I was so occupied constantly that prayer seemed to be the *last* thing on my mind. After the funeral, there were hospitals and doctors to deal with, medical insurance issues, auto insurance hassles, trips back and forth to Hermosillo, constant emails and phone calls from grieving relatives and friends, and a house full of family members visiting from the States. It was like a constant whirlwind, swirling around me.

By the time my head actually hit a pillow at night, I just wanted to forget it all, close my eyes, and sleep. But that morning, after putting prayer last on my list of priorities during those chaotic first days, I finally broke down. Staring blankly into my refrigerator, forgetting why I even opened it up, I prayed.

"Just a sign, Jesus. A sign that's it's all going to be OK. It's all I ask of you."

****

Luis Antonio Mulligan got off to a rough start in life. Born prematurely, mistakenly delivered by C-section well before what should have been his correct delivery date, his lungs weren't ready for this world.

"Run!" the doctor yelled, as he and his team raced from the delivery room down the corridor toward the incubators. I tried to follow them into the room where they would lay my tiny newborn son, but the doctors quickly shut the door and closed the curtain. Seconds later, I found myself locked outside, confused and panicking.

Is he OK? Is he gonna make it? Terrified, I paced back and forth, occasionally peering through a crack between the closed curtains.

About ten minutes later the door flew open.

"I need the truth, and I need it now!" the doctor demanded. "Did your wife do drugs before or during her pregnancy?"

I was shocked by the question. "Of course not!"

"Marijuana, cocaine…?" he continued, speaking in an accusatory tone, looking me straight in the eyes as I answered.

"Nothing!" I insisted. "Adela doesn't do drugs, and I don't either. I swear! What's going on? Why are you asking me this?"

Ignoring me, he continued. "Did your wife consume alcohol during the pregnancy?"

The interrogation continued, with the end result being a pediatrician telling me Luis had very serious problems with his lungs, and aside from that, warning me he may even suffer from long term physical deformities. Only time would tell.

Meanwhile, just down the hall, Adela was in a medicated daze, experiencing an immediate bout of depression like none I had ever witnessed from her before. I couldn't understand it, since no one had yet fully shared with her the baby's condition, given the physical state she was in. As far as she knew, we had a healthy baby. Why would she be depressed? Why would she choose this moment to repeat over and over that she had wanted a girl and not a second boy? Not knowing a thing about giving birth or depression that might be somehow related, I scolded her gently.

"Come on Adela, our baby didn't ask to be born a boy! OK, sure, a girl would have been nice. But he's our son! And he needs us right now!"

That night, as Luis lay in his incubator, I stood there alone and watched as his tiny chest pumped up and down like a jackhammer, breathing harder than I thought a newborn was capable of doing. I remained by his bedside all through the night and the next, catching catnaps whenever I could. Having originally planned to be at the hospital for one night only and not realizing we'd be delayed, at one point, I actually had to leave the hospital to go play a gig somewhere. Entertaining a crowd while my son was in the hospital was the last thing I wanted to do, but without insurance to cover Luis's additional medical bills, what could I do? We needed every dollar we could get our hands on, especially now that Luis was going to remain hospitalized days longer than expected. I raced to the show, sang, and got back to the hospital just as fast as I could.

Soon after I returned, one of the nuns who managed the hospital came in, informing me that if Luis's belabored breathing didn't improve that night, there would be no choice but take him by ambulance to Hermosillo the following morning. Not only did the local hospital we were in lack a ventilator, but there were none anywhere in the entire city of Guaymas.

"I don't mean to scare you, but he could die if he stays here," the nun said grimly. My heart sank. As she closed the door behind her, I closed my eyes and prayed for my son.

That ambulance never did have to take him to Hermosillo. In fact, less than twenty-four hours after the warning, Luis had improved so much that the hospital sent him home, with doctor's instructions to keep a close eye on his breathing and bring him back to the hospital if we noticed any difficulty whatsoever.

He's gonna be one stubborn kid, I thought to myself. I turned out to be right.

****

I closed the refrigerator door and walked into Luis's bedroom, where he quietly lay in a crib, staring blankly at the ceiling.

"*Hola* Luis," I whispered, bending down and putting my face close to his. "Hi buddy. Can you hear me?"

For a moment his listless eyes opened a bit wider. But then suddenly, just like he had done each time I tried to get close to him after the accident, he scowled and angrily turned his head away, inserting two fingers into his mouth and staring at the wall. Luis wanted nothing to do with me. Zero.

I shouldn't have taken it personally. After all, he wasn't warming up to anyone like he had before the wreck. In fact, the only time I had seen Luis react happily to anything at all was when Eva walked into his bedroom one morning, calling out *"hola bebé"* in the same cheerful, sing-song voice his mother used to greet him with every morning. For a split second Luis's eyes lit up, and he squirmed excitedly, only to realize moments later that it wasn't his mother after all. And he went listless.

****

"No way around it, your little boy is going to need surgery," the pediatrician informed us back in spring 2005. "At a couple months old, a hernia can be a very serious thing."

"Doctor," I asked hesitantly. "Is this something that can wait a couple weeks?"

"If it were my child, I wouldn't let it wait at all," he replied. "Look, although the likelihood of a problem isn't great, there could be serious consequences to putting this off if something happens to go wrong. Why take that chance?"

Holding Luis in her lap, Adela looked at me. "Don't cancel the trip," she said. "Like the doctor said, this will be a routine thing and the baby will be fine. One of my sisters can go with me to the hospital so I won't be alone. Go to Nashville. You've got to. You invested a ton of our money into this album, canceled work to go there, and we can't walk away from all that, especially now. Like it or not, we'll need *that* to pay for all of this," she added.

The doctor smiled and looked across his desk. "She's right. Go, we've got a great team here and your baby will be fine. And your wife will be right there with him. He'll be safe, I assure you."

A few days later, I boarded a plane bound for Nashville to record tracks for the upcoming *Journey Around The Sun* album. Meanwhile, Adela sat nervously in a hospital waiting room, until finally she was whisked through a door to see her little boy. The first sight of her just-operated on son, his body totally lifeless, shocked her momentarily.

Oh, my God! she panicked, momentarily frightened that something had gone terribly wrong. A second later she realized her baby was fine, just heavily sedated from the surgery.

But that millisecond of fear changed everything. No more second thoughts, wondering what if she'd have had a girl. From that moment on, you couldn't pull that kid out of her arms. She would never let little Luis out of her sight again, watching over him and caring for him like nobody else could. The two were inseparable.

****

"Mark, I've watched how Luis is with you every time you touch him," my sister in law Michelle confided in me. "I know it must hurt."

Married to my younger brother Paul, they had gotten word of the accident at their home in Maryland and immediately reached for their suitcases. As Michelle packed, she grabbed something she knew she'd need on the trip. It was a small, silver crucifix. This wasn't just any old cross. This was one Michelle had blessed by none other than Pope John Paul II at World Youth Day in Canada, six years before. Ardent Catholics, even naming their son after the Pope, this little 1 ¾ by 3 inch crucifix had big meaning in Paul and Michelle' lives.

"To be honest with you it bums me out, Michelle," I answered, shaking my head in frustration."I have no idea why Luis rejects me like he does. He just doesn't want me near him at all. Maybe this is just the way it's gonna be from now on."

As we continued to talk about the boys and all they were going through, Michelle fidgeted with that crucifix in her pocket. *Is this the time?* she wondered

****

OK, I admit, I never was a big fan of Saint Peter. Yes, I learned about him in grade school religion classes, and how when his best friend Jesus needed him most, Peter denied even knowing him. Not just once, but *three* times.

You can almost picture the guy calling a press conference, wagging his finger and stating, "I did *not* have a friendship with that man!"

What a chicken, I thought.

Pete definitely didn't sound like the kind of friend I'd want to hang out with at recess. When I got paddled by Sister Koszak for talking in class, my buddy Richard Holzer willingly took the same punishment right alongside me. And unlike Saint Peter, when Mrs. Buskirk busted me for throwing paper airplanes during class, Richard pled guilty too, getting detention right alongside me. Now *that* was a friend, not this Peter wimp who would have probably pointed the finger at me and walked away scot-free.

How could a guy witness the miracles Peter saw first-hand, yet still bail on Jesus? After all, with his own eyes he had seen Jesus cure the sick, give sight to the blind, heal the lame, raise the dead, cast demons out of possessed people, walk on water, and calm angry seas with his voice.

It's not even like he had to rely on some far-fetched story passed down from generation to generation, or base his beliefs on the writings of some book he read two thousand years after the fact. He was right there for it all, seeing it with his own eyes. You'd think after all that, he'd have no doubt that his friend really *was* who he said he was, and that he'd stick with Jesus through thick and thin. After all, we're talking about the boss… *"el jefe"*… the head honcho here! But when push came to shove, even that fact didn't matter. He was weak. He turned his back on Jesus. Can you say *loser?*

What kind of miracle would it take for this dude to believe? Christ on the mound, leading the Cubs to a World Series victory? A Republican winning in California? Come on, what would it take for this guy to have a little faith?

Yeah, sure, tell everyone he's your pal when he's changing water into wine. Then, run like hell when the party ends and your buddy's about to get his butt kicked. Nope, I never was a big fan of Saint Peter.

Had I been there back then, I wouldn't have turned my back on Jesus, I insisted to myself as a child.

Turns out ol' Pete and I had a thing or two in common.

****

"Mark, do you have faith?"

Michelle stood there in my kitchen, a silver crucifix in her hand. During our conversation about Adela, the kids, and everything that was going on, she had been wondering to herself if I'd be open to receiving it from her. Or if I had become angry or doubtful of God and would somehow reject it.

"Honestly, Michelle, I don't know if I have all that much faith any more," I stammered, surprised by the direct question she had put forth. "I don't know what I believe anymore. So much has happened."

"I understand. But do you *want* to have faith?" she persisted.

No doubt, my sister in law wasn't about to let me off with easy answers. *Meet The Press* could use an interviewer like her.

"I do. I really want to have faith in God again," I answered. That was apparently good enough for Michelle.

"This little crucifix is really special to me," she said, holding it out for me to see. "Would you let me hang it in Luis's room, in his crib where he can see it?" she asked.

Sounded kind of strange to me. The kid was a year and a half old. But Michelle continued.

"I know you think I'm crazy," she laughed. "But amazing things happen when you have faith."

For a moment I envied her. How could she be so confident in what she was saying when I was faltering at the first real challenge I ever faced? But faith was what Michelle was all about. She and Paul had even named their oldest daughter "Faith."

"You wanted to go to the cemetery today," she continued. "Marcos is resting right now. So go, do what you have to do, and give me a little time to spend with Luis, OK?"

Before I knew it, she had disappeared into Luis's room, silver crucifix in hand.

Chapter Ten

"Are you guys ready to go?"

Nearly an hour had passed since Michelle had offered to be with Luis, and I didn't want to waste any more precious time. After all, I might not get another opportunity to visit the cemetery with members of the American side of my family again, once they'd head home. Before heading out the door, I checked on Marcos to make sure he was sleeping, then finally opened up Luis's bedroom door to let Michelle know we were finally going to leave.

There she sat, eyes closed, deep in prayer, reciting the rosary and rocking Luis gently in her arms. He was awake, but as usual, didn't respond at all to the sound of his father's voice.

"Sorry!" I whispered, embarrassed to have barged in without knocking. "Just wanted to let you know we're leaving!" Luis continued to ignore me as I backed into the kitchen and closed the door so they could be alone, just Michelle, my boy and a small silver crucifix.

****

Thomas F. Mulligan wasn't exactly the kind of guy to get emotional on you. Unless, that is, you happened to be discussing liberals, lawyers, the Internal Revenue Service, racial quotas, federal judges, the estate tax, or striking professional athletes. Then, he could *definitely* get emotional on you, the specific emotion emitted defined as "rage." Tick my dad off and he'd make a Bobby Knight look like a pansy.

Needless to say, Dad was definitely not a guy who would cry at the drop of a hat. And true to form, standing there at the edge of his daughter-in-law's grave, he held it together in genuine Tom Mulligan fashion. Even as the family members gathered there with him began to began to pray aloud, each taking a turn, he was hanging tough.

But then, after a lengthy silence, came his turn to speak. Before he could open his mouth, tears welled up in Dad's eyes, and he choked up to the point he could barely speak at all. He struggled to say a few words, fighting back emotions as he wiped away a tear. Turning to me, he simply said, "I'm so sorry."

If my Dad was a wreck, I could only imagine what my mom was going through. Unlike Dad, Mom was as sentimental as they come.

Where my dad could nearly always hold it in when something happened to a loved one, Mom could cry when something bad would happen to a stranger. This was no stranger lying in the grave in front of her. Adela had become her daughter. But it wasn't always that way.

Going back to when Adela and I first started dating, my mom had been somewhat wary of the ten year age difference between us. It probably didn't help that Mom, like much of my family, adored the girl I had been engaged to in Nogales before that relationship ended so unexpectedly. Frankly, her personality and Adela's were complete opposites. A decent shrink would have probably hit the nail on the head had he said I sought that dynamic out intentionally, following the breakup with my fiancée.

Mom could deal with the fact that the two women were very different from each other. And she gradually came to accept the age difference between us. But it definitely didn't help Adela's case when Mom would somehow overhear my end of countless long distance calls to her from the States. Mom often noticed as I happily dialed the phone, only to eventually hang up half an hour later, exhausted and depressed after some unexpectedly out of the blue argument.

"Why do you always have to answer so many questions?" Mom would ask me. "Come on, she doesn't really think you've got somebody on the side, does she? " No, Mom didn't appreciate one bit the constant, non-stop grilling I got.

And one morning, while overhearing me yet again haplessly defending myself against a flurry of unfounded suspicions, Mom had had enough. "Give me the phone!" she demanded.

I had never seen my mom like this. She was mad as hell. And soon Adela would find out.

The two went at it over the phone, Adela fiercely defending herself, while my mom insisted she lay off the suspicions. Back and forth they went.

"I know he's your husband but he's also my son! What has he ever done to make you so suspicious of everything he does?" Mom finally asked, exasperated.

"Men can't be trusted. They're unfaithful, and that's just the way it is," Adela coldly replied. "You have five other sons. They're probably that way too!"

My mom didn't take kindly to that.

"For your information, my sons were *not* raised to be that way!" Mom answered firmly. "What you think about all men being unfaithful to their wives is just plain ridiculous!"

I stood a few feet away, listening to conversation as it grew more heated by the second. *It's over,* I thought to myself. *Any chance Mom and Adela had at a relationship is over.*

"Your mother is a good Christian lady. Why don't you talk to her about this?" Mom persisted, unaware that Doña Telma was probably not an ideal one to reference in vouching for a husband's faithfulness.

"Don't *ever* talk to my Mom about this!" Adela shot back. "She doesn't need to know anything about my marriage! It would only upset her!"

Mom knew she had struck a nerve. But as anyone who's ever met my mom will tell you, there's only so long she can stay angry at anyone.

"Adela, you need help," Mom said, breaking down into tears as she spoke. "I say that out of love. You're making Mark suffer, but the person suffering the most is *you*! It's not healthy. It's sick! And it's making me sick to watch! You're my daughter and I want you to be happy. Don't you want to be happy, Adela?"

There was a long silence on the other end of the line.

I don't know how it happened. But thanks to Mom, the conversation that could have destroyed their relationship for good suddenly took a turn. Several minutes later, Adela had calmed down, quietly explaining her side of the story, then listening to my mother's response. They talked and talked, and by the time Mom hung up, Adela thanked her for caring about our relationship so much that she'd intervene. The advice Mom offered her had surprisingly been taken to heart. I don't know how my mother did it, but in a way, a knock-down fight that would put a Jerry Springer guest to shame actually led to the start of a brand new, real mother-daughter relationship.

I wonder if that phone conversation went through Mom's head as she prayed at the cemetery that day. I know it went through mine, watching as she tried to keep herself together, praying tearfully over the grave of a daughter she never got to say goodbye to.

****

"Adela, I'll make you a deal," Michelle said softly, rocking Luis gently in her arms. "I promise to hold and kiss your little boy for you. Would you do the same for my little Peter in Heaven?"

He would have been her second son. Losing him during her pregnancy had been a traumatic loss for Michelle. It had happened just months earlier. As she thought about the son she would have given birth to, she continued to pray and rock Luis, who had fallen asleep over the past hour.

She reflected on her faith, thinking for a moment about her own belief that Jesus frequently used physical "things" in performing his miracles. Like the loaves of bread and fish he somehow multiplied to alleviate a huge crowd's hunger, or the water he miraculously changed to wine. Like the spit he put on a blind man's eyes to give him sight, rather than simply saying "be healed." Looking at it that way, it wasn't hard for her to understand that a blessing attached to an item could be used to bring healing and holiness. And sometimes, even miracles.

She got up and laid Luis down in his crib. Then, using a piece of ribbon she had found earlier in the day, she took the crucifix and tied it to one of the bedposts on the side of his crib. Suddenly, Luis woke up, opening his eyes widely. Very calmly, he began to stare at the shiny silver object that was now catching his eye. As Michelle readjusted it to give him a better view, Luis continued to focus, unblinking, on the tiny crucifix placed in front of him.

The bedroom door opened. "We're back from the cemetery Michelle." I whispered softly, amazed that she was still in Luis's room with him, nearly two hours after we had left them together there.

She quietly motioned for me to come in. When I did, I looked down into the crib and saw Luis, his eyes wide open and fixated on the shiny crucifix hanging in front of him.

"Wow, look!" I remarked, intrigued by his intense focus. "He can't take his eyes off it!"

If only he would react to my voice the way he reacted to that crucifix. But he wouldn't. Several minutes went by, and straight ahead he stared, fascinated by the glittering cross. As usual, he paid me no attention, as if I wasn't even there. Sadly, I left the room, leaving Michelle and my young son behind.

By now, the entire family had gathered in the living room. In spite of the tragic reason behind our get together, it was great to see everyone. Getting Dad, Mom and all eight kids plus their spouses together was not an easy task these days, given everyone's busy lives.

Seems everybody wanted to do something, anything at all they could, to help out. Like sitting bedside with the kids, as my brothers and sisters took turns volunteering to do. Like cooking or going to the store for us. Like John, who quietly covered the entire deductible on both boys' hospital bills, freeing up money I would badly need in the coming months since I'd have to take several months off of work. That's the kind of family I have, close-knit and there for each other. It's the way I wanted to raise my own kids. What would become of them now?

Marcos had some serious challenges to face, wrapped up in a lower body cast from the waist down. At least with his positive attitude, I was confident he would learn to walk again, no matter how much effort it would take.

It was Luis I was more worried about. It felt strange to be out in the living room, sharing a laugh with my brothers and sisters, silently wondering inside if my youngest boy would ever be the same happy little kid he used to be ever again. He was only on the other side of the bedroom door. But he felt so far away.

Light at the end of the tunnel. I needed a burst of it, and fast. *Just a sign that things are going to be OK.*

While my brothers and sisters socialized, I suddenly felt an urge to see Luis. Walking back to his bedroom and quietly opening the door, I peered in, only to see he wasn't in his crib after all. The silver crucifix remained hanging on the post, but Luis wasn't there. Instead, he was once again in Michelle's arms, his back to me as she sat, patting him gently. It looked like she was trying to put him back to sleep. And here I was interrupting again.

"Sorry!" I exclaimed, backing up toward the doorway so I could leave them alone. But before I could turn to close the door and leave, something happened.

Little Luis Antonio lifted his head from Michelle's shoulder and turned around. He had heard his father's voice.

For the first time since before the awful accident that took his mama's life, Luis looked right at me, directly in the eyes. Shocked that he had reacted to the sound of my voice, I froze, standing motionless in the middle of the room. Then, before I could say a word, his lips curled into a small smile as he stretched out his arms, reaching for his daddy.

I rushed to Luis and took him in my arms, hugging him tightly, as a relieved Michelle watched and smiled. We stood there in the middle of the room for a moment, just my little boy and me. As I gently patted him on the back, he whimpered softly, holding me tightly and not letting go.

Moments later, the entire living room erupted in cheers as I walked out of the bedroom with Luis in my arms, Michelle following close behind.

"It's a miracle!" Mom exclaimed over the loud celebration.

"Lou Boy is back!" someone shouted happily as everyone crowded around to see little Luis. Family members were celebrating and thanking an exhausted Michelle, as she shared what had just happened moments before. Finally Mom couldn't take it anymore. She grabbed Luis from me, kissed him, sat him down on her lap, and began to feed him his favorite candy, M&Ms.

He was reacting happily to everyone, seemingly enjoying the rousing reception and especially the candy. As I watched him put another M&M into his mouth, one of my brothers quickly pulled me aside. "Wow, bro, pretty amazing. This whole thing, do you think it's a miracle?"

"Who knows? Maybe it was just time," I replied, looking across the room at Luis. "I'm really happy he reacted to me, but maybe he would have come to anybody."

At that very second, as if to underscore just how ridiculously cynical my answer was, far across the room on my mother's lap, tiny Luis quietly pulled a candy out of the bag. Holding it precariously between his fingers, he slowly began looking around the room, intently studying the many Mulligan faces gathered around him. Apparently, for some reason, there was one in particular he was looking for.

From across the room, his eyes finally caught mine. Before I knew it, he smiled and stretched out his hand, offering his brightly colored M&M to me. In a flash I crossed the room, taking Luis from my Mom and sitting him on my lap, where he proceeded to spend the next several minutes feeding candy after candy to me, placing each gently in my mouth. It was best candy I ever ate!

The celebration continued, until several minutes later, when Luis's eyes began to grow a bit listless. Seconds later, he suddenly put two fingers in his mouth and gazed at the wall again.

"Oh darn, he's doing that again!" Mom noticed worriedly. "He was doing so great just a second ago!"

As I watched Luis begin to fade, my prayer came back to me from that earlier that morning. *Please, Jesus, give me a sign.* I hadn't asked the Lord for a cure, but instead for a sign that would give me hope. *Light at the end of the tunnel.* I remembered how intensely I had prayed, asking God to grant me this favor. And I remembered Michelle's words from earlier. How amazing things can happen with faith.

God had responded, with a small miracle. It might not be the Cubs winning the World Series, but it was indeed, doubtless to anyone but the most cynical among us, a small miracle. I looked around the room at the joy on everyone's faces, as we were now filled with hope rather than wallowing in depression for the first time since the accident.

"It's OK!" I reassured my mom. "He's going to be fine, I'm sure of it. I never told you, but just this morning I really needed hope that things would improve. I prayed to God asking for a sign. We just got *exactly* what I asked for. Luis is back! He may have a long way to go, but now I know he's in there. And he's going to be OK!"

We were all going to be OK. Even Marcos, suffering in his lower body cast and unable to walk. But Marcos is another story.

Chapter Eleven

"He's got your chin," the stranger commented, watching me peer through the glass window at my newborn son, lying in his incubator.

"You think so?" I asked, smiling proudly.

I was a father! A whole new chapter of life had begun for Adela and me, as baby Marcos would quickly grow into a cheerful, handsome little boy.

"I think I'm going to be a very young grandma," Adela would joke, watching as young girls constantly surrounded Marcos squealing, "Play with me! Play with me!"

And you just couldn't keep a soccer ball away from the boy. At five years old, he was already kicking one around everywhere he went. One day, he told me, he would play for Mexico City's *Club America*, his favorite team. Constantly running and jumping, nothing could slow Marcos down.

Until July 16th, 2006.

****

"Marcos! Marcos, are you alright?"

"*¡Mamá!*" he shouted in the darkness. "*¡Mamá!* It hurts!"

It was happening again.

"What hurts, Marcos? Tell me!"

"My legs! My legs!" he cried, his eyes closed and body shaking uncontrollably.

It was the third episode since he had fallen asleep six hours before, lying next to me in my bed in his body cast. The doctors had warned me after the accident he could suffer from post-traumatic stress. Little did I know it would be like this.

"*¡Mamá!*" he screamed, his voice piercing the darkness. I tried to restrain his arms as he began pounding himself in the face.

"It's OK, Marcos, I'm here," I whispered into his ear, trying my best not to wake him as I held his arms back behind his head. His whole body was trembling and his head shook side to side.

"Wake up, *Mamá*," he pleaded. "Wake up!"

How Marcos could go through this several times per night and wake up with no memory of it the next day was beyond me. Each episode would last only a few minutes. But they were exhausting, seemingly endless minutes, for both of us.

The first occurrence shocked me, leaving me as terrified as he was in the nightmare he was experiencing. But gradually, as they occurred more and more, I learned that depending on how emotional he was, I could actually converse with him through it all. He could somehow hear me speaking as if I were sitting next to him in the back seat of that car. He would relate to me, in detail, what was happening in the chaos that ensued following the bloody wreck.

"What's Mama doing?" I asked him, restraining his arms so he wouldn't hurt himself.

"She's in the front seat and the car's all smashed against her," he answered, shaking as he spoke.

"Is she moving?" I asked.

"No. Her head is down. There's blood!" Marcos shouted, fighting to free his arms from my restraint.

"Is mama talking Marcos? Is she crying, or saying anything to you or your brother?" I pressed him.

"No, but now there's a man talking to her," he answered, his head thrashing side to side.

"Who's the man?" I asked, holding his arms back tighter as he fought back.

"I don't know!"

"Is she talking to him?" I continued.

"I don't know! I can't see! *¡Ayúdanos!*" he cried, begging for help.

"What else, Marcos?"

"Luis is crying! His voice suddenly changed tone. "It's OK, Luis" he said soothingly. "It's gonna be OK. The man says he's going to get you out."

Who was this man Marcos referred to? An EMT? A cop? A motorist who stopped to help? Whoever he was, he just might have some answers to questions lingering in my mind.

****

"Can I help you?"

"Yes," I replied. "My name's Mark Mulligan. I'm the husband of Adela Ruiz Fuentes, the woman killed in the auto accident on Highway 15 the evening of July 16th."

Wow, did I just say that? Just uttering those words, *"the woman who was killed,"* felt surreal.

"I've come here to see if anybody, perhaps a police officer who was at the scene, might be able to answer a couple personal questions I have about that night?"

An attendant at the *Rescate* clinic had already done his best to answer them the day before, indicating that Adela was unconscious by the time the ambulance and EMT arrived at the scene. As for information about anything prior to that, all he could do was send me to the police department. So here I was.

Unfortunately, information doesn't ever seem to come easily in Guaymas. While the rest of the world had entered the digital age by 2006, Guaymas was still largely a word of mouth town where a secretary would type a report by hand, assuming it wasn't simply scribbled with a pen or pencil and shoved off into a file somewhere. Unfortunately, that often meant you couldn't just pull up any information you wanted with the click of a button or a simple google search.

My own past experience in dealing with local immigration officials had made that fact painfully clear. Record keeping in Guaymas was shoddy by even Mexican standards. Details that would be permanently stored on a hard drive in the United States would frequently get discarded or misplaced amidst hordes of paper files, if ever properly recorded at all. Not to say that stonewalling didn't occur, but more often than not, the person attending to you simply didn't have the information in hand.

Nonetheless, as I explained to the secretary, it wasn't the recorded facts outlined in the police report that I came for. I already had a clear picture of the trajectory of the oncoming vehicle, the estimated speed of both vehicles at the moment of impact, the time of the incident, etc. Those items were matters of record. So was the report's indication of alcohol as a suspected factor, with the finger pointed at the driver of the oncoming car for allegedly driving under the influence, even though no toxicology results had been produced.

I just wanted to know something else, something that would put any lingering doubt to rest. Marcos had relived that accident in detail with me night after night, never once telling me of Adela speaking or ever calling out in pain, only seeing her lifeless body from behind in the back seat. But he *had* mentioned a man talking to her. Could it be that she was still conscious, even if barely? Could she have possibly whispered anything to him?

How could I have spent ten years with her, yet live the rest of my life not knowing what she was thinking, if anything, during her final moments? *Did* she have any last words? Did she possibly mention my name?

Did she suffer, God forbid? Or did she die painlessly, numb to the entire ordeal?

However important those questions were to me, there didn't seem to be anyone there who could provide me with any answers beyond those contained in the police report, and those facts I already knew. One particular officer might have been able to help me, given the fact he had responded to the scene before the ambulance arrived. But as luck would have it, he had just left Guaymas days before, apparently on some kind of long term hiatus for reasons unknown. No one knew where he was or when he would return, if at all.

I walked away empty handed from the police department that day, with no more information than when I walked in. All they could do was refer me to another department, the *Ministerio Público*, a government agency whose local branch was located in downtown Guaymas. Any information I would obtain would have to come from there.

Repeated visits to the office of the *Ministerio Público* proved equally frustrating. As we all know, bureaucracy is never fun to deal with. Just as in the United States, government employees in Mexico treat you as if you work for them, instead of the other way around. It's like the entire system is intentionally designed not to work, and to frustrate you to the point where you eventually lose hope and simply give up. While dealing with chaos at home, a mounting list of obligations, and limited time to pursue things, I was left sitting for hours at a time in waiting rooms, appointments constantly postponed or outright canceled.

When I finally did get my first face to face meeting with the head of the office, I was rushed in and out in a matter of minutes. After all, the *Ministerio Público* had an extremely busy schedule, I was told. And as you might suspect, getting anything beyond the facts included in the initial police report was impossible. Sure, I was provided information about the accident, but no answers that could put my other doubts to rest. Even among the reported "facts" of the accident itself, there were blanks.

If the driver of the oncoming car was indeed driving under the influence, as the police report had suggested in referencing a couple crushed beer cans found at the scene, then why hadn't any kind of toxicology report been produced? If, on the other hand, by some chance he actually wasn't under the influence, why on earth would he be driving that fast, eventually veering out of control and crossing the median at ninety miles an hour? Was it possible that instead of driving under the influence, he had instead suffered a heart attack, as rumors floating around town had suggested?

"He was drunk," the *Ministerio Público* declared, flatly dismissing any doubts as hogwash.

"But how do you know that for sure?" I pressed.

"Look at the police report," he retorted. "They found beer cans in the oncoming car."

"But even if they did, that doesn't necessarily mean he was legally drunk," I insisted. "It's his blood alcohol level I'm curious about, not whether he had beer cans in his car. Look, finding those at the scene, I too would venture to say he was drunk. He very likely was! But before we just state that definitively as 'fact', don't we have any results from a toxicology report to back that up?"

Apparently the beer cans referenced in the police report were enough to convince the authorities. End of story.

A definitive toxicology report wasn't the only thing missing. There was yet another blank. Supposedly there was a witness who had seen the entire thing, from the moment of impact. Before that witness departed from the scene, without ever speaking to police, someone overheard him say something peculiar. Apparently he claimed he had seen a police car on the other side of the highway, speeding northbound just moments after the wreck occurred, never turning around or stopping to assist victims at the scene. Had any other witnesses reported the same thing? Or had that anonymous witness simply confused a civilian vehicle with a squad car in the chaotic seconds following the accident, as the *Ministerio Público* had theorized?

Return visits to the police department and the *Ministerio Público* got me nowhere, leaving me forced to rely on newspaper articles, rumors, and images from my oldest boy's nightmares to formulate what picture I had of the moments immediately following the crash.

Over time I'd simply be left to slowly, and sometimes accidentally, glean bits of information from random acquaintances, even strangers who I'd suddenly discover had some connection to the wreck or its aftermath. A handful of people would appear in the days, weeks, months and even years to come with previously unknown facts and details. Though they didn't immediately complete the puzzle, they at least helped to put a few missing pieces together. But finding answers to the other questions that persisted in my mind, that was another story.

"Are you Mark Mulligan?"

Pushing my shopping cart down the crowded aisle, I stopped and turned to see a face I didn't quite recognize. Whoever it was, he was a stranger to me, but apparently he knew who I was.

"I've seen you sing at Froggys before," he said, introducing himself. "I even met your wife once, at the gym. I'm so sorry about what happened."

"*Gracias*," I replied politely, not quite catching his name as he continued on, quickly sharing with me how he had come upon the accident on his way back from San Carlos that fateful day.

"Is it OK to talk about this?" he gingerly asked, catching himself before he might unintentionally upset me by even briefly discussing something so personal.

"Please, do," I encouraged him.

"I've only got a second anyway," he assured me. "I'm running to get to work."

He had arrived at the accident scene after Adela had already been removed from the car and placed on a stretcher. "I watched them put her into the ambulance. I didn't know it was your wife, until I read it in the newspaper the next day."

"She wasn't in pain, I guarantee you that," he quickly added as if he were reading my mind. "She was at peace, like she was asleep through it all. I just wanted you to know that."

Asleep through it all. At peace. They were reassuring words that brought comfort to Adela's family and me. Just knowing that no one had seen her screaming in agony or suffering endlessly would help us deal with our own pain in the weeks, months and years ahead. At least we all had that, though I still would have given anything to talk to the very first person who found her. Whoever it was that Marcos saw in those dreams, night after night.

****

"Professor Marcos!"

It's how my ex-students referred to me. Yes, only in a city like Guaymas could a guy with such limited brain capacity as me be known as *"Professor."*

He was a doctor who had studied English with me back when I first came to town. He had been returning from the beach in San Carlos the evening of the accident, coming upon the scene by chance soon after Adela had been already taken by ambulance to Guaymas's emergency room. He had managed to speak with a couple witnesses, though he never realized it was my wife and children who had been involved until he read it in the papers the next day. He shared with me what witnesses had described.

As he spoke, I pictured her being put into an ambulance and driven away. "I can't help but wonder, if only they had taken Adela straight to Hermosillo, she might still be here," I remarked sadly, thinking about that precious time wasted in vain, since Guaymas's emergency room wasn't equipped to deal with injuries as severe as hers.

"I still don't believe she would have survived," he replied, shaking his head. "Not with the injuries she had."

"I guess we'll never know," I sighed. "Man, I just wish I could go back in time and be there with her while this was all happening. We never did get to say goodbye to each other."

I remembered a frantic call from the Schmid's basement to someone, possibly Frank, begging them to find Adela and put her on the phone with me. How I wanted her to hear my voice and know that I was with her from far away. That I loved her.

I wiped a tear from my eye. "And even though my kid was right there and has never mentioned her being awake or suffering, I just can't help but wonder if..."

He nodded his head. "Mark, I've seen similar injuries from accidents like this more times than you can guess. Seconds after it all happened, I very strongly doubt she ever felt a thing. I hate to say it, but with the kind of high speed impact she underwent, she was probably knocked out right from the start. She likely never even knew what hit her."

"I know you're probably right. And it's not like I don't believe my son," I began. "But they *are* dreams..."

"I wouldn't tell you something if I didn't believe it myself," he interrupted. "And I think what your boy is describing in his recollections is probably accurate, more so than anything else.

"You know Mark," he added, "there's going to come a time when you have to let this go. Focusing on the details of the wreck, guilt about not being there, wanting to change things that can't be changed… sooner or later you'll have to let that stuff go and focus on the good things. That's what your wife would want, wouldn't she? To remember her for the person she was, and let all this go."

God, I'm tired, I thought. *Tired of running in circles, tired of talking about death, tired of questioning the answers I've already got.*

He was right. It made sense what he was telling me, confirming all my boy had shared without even realizing it.

Just let it go…

> *A sunset can be a beautiful thing*
> *When you can let go and learn to let it be*

Chapter Twelve

"Uncle David is gonna live with us!"

The news thrilled young Marcos. And it was a welcome relief to his dad.

The eighth child in the Mulligan family, born seven years after number seven, David obviously wasn't the product of meticulous family planning on my folks' part. Yes, welcome to that wacky little world known as "*Catholicism.*"

Anyway, in spite of our thirteen year age difference, Dave and I had always had a lot in common. Though we grew up in seemingly different generations, we shared many of the same musical tastes, me introducing him to everything from Jim Croce, James Taylor and Merle Haggard to relatively obscure "americana" bands. Both of us were extremely outgoing and pretty much free spirits, managing somehow to experience quite a bit of this world on shoestring budgets, usually from behind the wheels of vehicles with far more miles registered on the odometer than remaining on the engine.

In a family with a successful orthodontist as a father and a loving mother who raised eight kids, each of our siblings had also found success in their own right. One was an anesthesiologist. Another a pharmaceutical rep. There was a police officer. A teacher. A Naval Academy grad. A bilingual church choir director and dedicated volunteer worker..

David himself was on the way to a successful career, having just gotten his masters degree in special education. Given our many similarities and my musical influences, I'm sure my parents breathed a sigh of relief the day he graduated, knowing that degree would provide him with gainful employment as a productive, tax-paying citizen just as soon as he got back from one last vacation, a trip to Yosemite for the High Sierra Singer-Songwriter Workshop.

David had really looked forward to this experience, one where he'd get a unique, once in a lifetime chance to backpack for four days among a small group, led by two of his favorite artists and songwriters. The first was Steve Poltz, Jewel's ex-boyfriend and co-writer of her big hit, "You Were Meant For Me," the longest running song on the Billboard Charts Top 100. The second was Tim Bluhm, guitarist and vocalist of *The Mother Hips*, David's favorite band from the Bay area. A huge fan, Dave caught every live *Mother Hips* shows he possibly could, somehow ending up backstage with the band after a concert one night. Now, on the

High Sierra trip, he'd have the opportunity to not only spend time with Tim, but get songwriting advice too. Sure, music was a hobby to Dave, but he was passionate about it, counting down the days until the trip.

Then, a couple weeks before he was supposed to leave, the phone rang. Suddenly Dave found himself in Mexico, watching me grieve as Adela's casket was somberly loaded into a hearse. Standing there, he felt completely helpless. Summoning up all the wisdom he could, he said it better than any of his older siblings ever could have.

"Sometimes the best thing you can do for your brother is just stand there and feel shitty with him."

Dave stood there, and in his own words, "felt shitty" with his grieving brother. But watching that hearse pull away and head off toward the cemetery, he wanted to do more than that.

****

"I'm coming down, bro. I'm gonna help you out around here."

I couldn't believe it. Come down and live with me in Mexico? It was a pretty darn generous offer from Dave. But I couldn't accept it. No way. After all, the guy had a job waiting for him at the end of the summer.

And this was an actual job. Not like the one where he hoarded gasoline in Yuma, Arizona, transporting it in five gallon containers to Phoenix to resell out of the back of his used Chevy Blazer during a local fuel shortage. Or his short-lived career arranging for bulk purchases of cigarettes and redistributing them at incredibly inflated prices to fellow students in his college dormitory.

No, this was the beginning of an actual job. You know, one where you do something productive and they pay you. I've heard about those.

Dave was insistent. "That's it bro, I'm coming down. I can worry about that other crap later."

Back and forth we went, as I tried to talk him out of his own proposal. You'd think he would have realized that whenever I'm the fellow in the conversation making logical sense, we're all in big trouble. But he persisted. Finally, I gave in. Well, sort of.

"OK, Dave, you can come down, but only on one condition. You go to that songwriter's workshop in Yosemite first. Then you come down."

"Forget the trip…" he began.

"Here's the deal. If you don't go on that expedition, you don't come down," I demanded.

A couple weeks later, David was off somewhere in California's Ansel Adams wilderness, his thoughts still on his brother and nephews far away in Mexico. But as urgently as he knew he needed to return to Mexico, it was a trip well worth the wait, especially when an impressed Tim Bluhm offered heartfelt encouragement after listening to Dave's songwriting.

"You should come by the studio in San Francisco and record with me."

Fact is, Dave had written some really good songs previous to the workshop, like "Don't Wake Up" and "Postcard." On the trip, he was inspired to write even more, collaborating with Poltz to write "Collapsible Plans." Suddenly Dave had more than a half dozen solid, original songs under his songwriting belt. And now Tim Bluhm was inviting him up to record them in his studio?

Dave thought long and hard. He had put a lot of time into getting that masters degree. A good job was waiting for him around the corner. One with decent pay, benefits, security and all the kind of stuff that convinces most people to perpetually put their dreams on hold.

Adela was only a few years older than I am, Dave thought to himself. *What did she dream of? What if she had known her life was going to end so suddenly? And so early?*

By the time Dave walked back through my front door, something had happened. He had made a decision. He wouldn't be teaching in the United States that upcoming semester. Nor the semester after that. He would be picking up a guitar and giving this music thing a shot. Who knows how long he would be with me in San Carlos. Maybe six months? Maybe longer? But he would use whatever time he wasn't helping me out with the kids to write songs and improve his playing. Where would it lead from there? He didn't have a clue.

****

For now, though, any hopes of triple encores, sold out stadiums and a world tour would have to wait. There was too just too much on the plate, from helping me to get things in order, to caring for Luis, to physical rehab for Marcos, who was in a wheelchair still unable to walk.

Marcos had boundless optimism, even though his lower body was constrained by that cast. Always smiling and excitedly talking about all he would do once he got out of that wheelchair, one couldn't help but admire the boy.

Marcos became somewhat of a local hero. Pushing my five year old down the sidewalk in his wheelchair along San Carlos's main boulevard, seems like every car would honk and wave, with Marcos smiling and waving back. Often people would pull over, rolling down their windows to offer him encouragement. Like my friend Tony, a local cab driver, who pulled his taxi off the road one afternoon to offer Marcos unforgettable advice, choosing to give it in the best English he could muster.

"Hey champion," Tony said, giving Marcos a friendly slap on the back. "Be hard! Never cry! *This* is the convenient for you."

No one could accuse Tony of resorting to psychobabble. OK so it wasn't exactly advice you would hear from Dr. Phil, but at least his heart was in the right place. Like so many others in San Carlos, Tony lived to see the day Marcos would get out of that chair and walk again.

That would take time. And it wouldn't be easy. All along, Marcos had convinced himself that when the lower-body cast came off, he'd instantly be capable of walking, running, and jumping again. For all he knew, he'd be doing bicycle-kicks on the soccer field or running marathons, once the cast was removed. Thinking he would simply pick up right where he left off, he soon would discover that wasn't the case.

The day the cast finally came off, Marcos learned that it would still require a lot more time and physical rehab for him to stand up on his legs again, much less walk. It was the first time I had seen him angry since the accident.

"I can't walk? *Still?* After all this time?" he cried. "That's it! I quit! I don't want to walk again! I give up!"

Given my oldest boy's always-positive attitude, his unexpected reaction startled me. Marcos sat there, glaring angrily as the doctor quietly offered his advice.

"Get him in a pool. Get him gradually moving those legs underwater. It's the best thing you can do for him. Eventually, he'll improve."

****

"I don't want to go in, Dad!"

"Marcos," I replied firmly. "You heard the doctor. We've got to get in that water. Come on, buddy, I'll help you out."

"*No!* I'm not going in!" Marcos shot back, gripping the arms of his wheelchair and holding on for dear life. "Please, Dad!"

This had been going on long enough. "Let's go, Marcos. Now!" Left with no other choice, I grabbed his hands and pried them off the wheelchair, yanking him out and dragging him toward the water.

"No, Dad! Please!" Marcos shouted. "I don't want to drown!" He tried to fight me off with his arms, but to no avail.

"Dad, I can't do this! I'm gonna drown!" he screamed, tears rolling down his face.

"I'm here Marcos, and I won't let you drown. Come on buddy, hold on to me and try to move those legs!"

A panicked Marcos was scared to death, begging to get out. "Please Dad, another time!" he pleaded. "Let me out! I don't want to drown!"

"Marcos, don't you want to walk again?" I insisted "Now *kick*, damn it!"

Thank God YouTube hadn't fully caught on yet, or my chance at Father of the Year award would have instantly gone up in flames. A half hour later, I finally gave up, hauling Marcos back into his chair, drying him off, and wheeling him home. I was disappointed in him for not wanting to try, but even more ashamed of how I had snapped at my injured son.

That evening, I tucked Marcos into bed. After saying our usual nightly prayers, I asked Marcos if he'd like to simply talk to God from the heart for a moment, as we often did together.

"*Si papá*," he answered, closing his eyes. "God, please take care of my mom. Tell her I miss her."

"And God," he added, pausing and furrowing his brow. "Send the man who killed her to hell!"

It was shocking to see that kind of anger in my five and a half year old son. Not having had the time to read any of the books given to me about how children deal with grief, I didn't know what to say.

"Marcos, I know you hate that guy and I get it. I'm angry with him too. I don't know why he was driving so fast and took your mama from us like he did," I tried to explain. "But remember how we just said The Our Father moments ago? Remember the part where it says '*as we forgive those who trespass against us?*' Jesus was talking about those people who do bad stuff to us. He told us we have to forgive them. I can't say I've done that either, but we're supposed to try."

"Was that man a good guy or a bad guy?" Marcos asked.

"I don't know, Marcos. Only God knows people's hearts," I explained. "Sometimes bad people do good things, and sometimes good people do bad things."

Marcos listened intently, his lower body propped up on a pillow as he lay there.

"And only God knows why those things happened that night," I continued. "It's hard to let Him judge and not do it ourselves. But if we call ourselves Christians, it's what we gotta do. Sometimes it's really hard to be a Christian, like right now." As I wondered whether any of this unexpected lesson actually sunk in, Marcos looked at me.

"I want to be a Christian, *papá*."

Bending down, I squeezed his hand. "You know what, Marcos? Right now, at this very minute, God and mama are both proud of you. And I am too. You're a good boy. We've got to hang together now, OK?" Kissing him on the forehead, I reached over to shut off the light.

"*Buenas noches*, Marcos." As I turned to leave the bedroom, I heard Marcos's voice call out softly in the darkness.

"Dad?"

"What is it, Marcos?

"Sorry I didn't kick my legs in the water today," he said, regret in his voice..

"Marcos, it's OK buddy," I answered, sitting back down on the edge of his bed. "I'm the one who's sorry. For snapping at you like I did. Sorry I was such a jerk."

"It's OK, Dad," he reassured me, reaching out and taking my hand. "We'll try again tomorrow."

Chapter Thirteen

It had been a long time since I had passed through that front door at Froggys. Those packed-house Tuesday nights, as well as my other local shows, seemed like such a distant memory. And although I was starting to give a little thought to showing up somewhere with a guitar in my hands, there was just too much going on at the moment.

So instead of singing "Saint Anywhere" or "Sara, Tara and Jenny Marie," Tuesdays found me down the road, at home with Dave and Adela's younger sister Eva. Both were doing their best to help raise my kids, stabilize things around the house, and get me back on some kind of firm footing. I certainly wasn't making it easy on them, however.

"Dude," Dave exclaimed, "you've *got* to read the recommended dosage on the bottle before you give Luis medicine! You're gonna turn my nephew into a drug addict!"

Apparently I had confused my son's medicinal needs with those of Guns N' Roses lead singer Axl Rose. No doubt about it, I was lousy at this. I'm sure one year old Luis was beginning to think the same thing. If only it had stopped there.

"Mark, I don't mean to nag, but don't you think he should eat a bit more balanced meal now and then?" David asked, staring at the plate of refried beans and tortillas I had heated up for tiny Luis. "How about a little fruit? Maybe some mashed vegetables?"

"He likes beans," I answered. Frankly, I was just proud of the fact that I had even opened the can for him.

It quickly became obvious to everyone just how much responsibility Adela had taken on in raising her two young boys. Where in the world had I been during all that? Thank God for Dave and Eva, or my kids would have spent those first few months of recovery eating Flaming Hot Cheetos and watching the Late Late Show.

Aside from my own obvious deficiencies in the art of parenting, there were still lingering insurance issues to deal with, frequent medical checkups, and lots of trips to Hermosillo. Although that "single father" routine wasn't exactly coming easily to me, at least Luis was making progress, slowly but surely. Like his brother, he still couldn't walk, but the important thing was that he hadn't experienced any lasting neurological damage. Dave was even teaching him a few words in sign language so we could better communicate with him. I'm guessing he had a particular hand gesture in mind when I served him his "meals."

As for his lack of verbal progress, some were a bit worried, suspecting it may have been related to the accident and the blow he took to the head. But for kids simultaneously absorbing two different languages at such a young age, that slow rate of progress is actually quite typical. They may not utter a syllable in either language for their first couple years, as they grasp two totally different grammar structures and process twice the vocabulary of other kids who merely have to master one language. But when they finally do speak, they converse in either language with a native's accent, switching back and forth between Spanish and English with relative ease. Once they speak, you can't shut 'em up! Consider older brother Marcos as Exhibit A for that theory. So even though Luis wasn't the most talkative fellow in our household, I wasn't worried.

Speaking of Marcos, his pool therapy had continued, and he was now able to move his legs freely underwater. Even though he was forced to skip the Fall semester at Guaymas's *Colegio Americano* while he was recovering, he was already chomping at the bit to get back. Yep, there were a whole lot of cute little first grade girls just waiting to push him down the hall in that wheelchair. With the progress he was making, I could tell it wouldn't be long.

****

"Send me a postcard from where you wind up when you're gone…" Listening to Dave strum his guitar in my living room, I began to wonder. Even after I returned to Froggys, how was I ever really going to be able to keep my musical career going after all that had happened? As the only parent my boys had left, could I really still do this full time?

What about my travels? I couldn't support a family by just playing local, nightly gigs in San Carlos. Those road trips were my bread and butter. I couldn't survive without them. But could I really leave my kids behind and continually take off like that, each time leaving them behind to be raised by paid help?

What about that day down the road, after Marcos returned to school, when Luis would go to kindergarten? Working nights in San Carlos meant that by the time they'd both get home, I'd be off setting up for a show at Froggys or any of the other bars I performed at. And by the time *I'd* get home, they'd be sound asleep. Along with private events, that could be four, sometimes five times per week. That would all be fine and dandy were their mother home to care for them during that time, but

- 74 -

what now? Should my kids really spend that many days per week not seeing an actual parent at all?

Even as I pondered picking up the guitar again, I couldn't help but think about these things. Changes would have to be made. After all, financial help from John wouldn't last forever. As for David, in time he'd head back to the States and get his own life going again. I couldn't continue to expect Eva to keep sharing the load with me. She had her own family to take care of. What would I do when she wasn't around to help anymore?

I hadn't counted on making major changes at this point in my life. Since before I was legal drinking age I had performed in bars, first hopping onstage with a fellow named Matt Theiss during college, playing Croce songs at Flagstaff Arizona's Alpine Spaghetti Station. Aside from a couple years spent hawking real estate and a part time, mostly volunteer job as an ESL teacher, music was it for me. Despite my business degree, I had never even interviewed for anything else, and wasn't sure I was qualified to be anything more than a trash collector or Seven Eleven cashier.

So as I grabbed the handles of Marcos's wheelchair and pushed him through Froggys' front door that afternoon, it wasn't to set up my speakers for another Tuesday night gig, or for a sound check, but to pick up a donation someone had generously left for my boys up at the bar. It was supposed to be a very quick stop, but of course, that never happens when you walk into Froggys. There were faces there that I hadn't seen since long before the accident, all wanting to catch up and learn how we were doing at home. People wanted to know about Luis, and how he was recovering from his injuries. Everybody, of course, wanted to say hello to Marcos and wish him well.

These were the same people that had shown up on my doorstep night after night since the wreck, bringing with them homemade dinners so I wouldn't have to cook for my family. People who had helped to house my family members when they came down for the funeral. People whose financial donations, many of them anonymous, helped us to make it through tough times. It's the kind of town San Carlos is. Like the song says, "my kind of people."

"Mark, how are you doing buddy?" Howard asked, greeting me with a big hug. Howard was the only one who had showed up at my doorstep without a home-cooked meal, instead bringing take-out pizza from his favorite restaurant out in Empalme. Oh, and a bottle of rum.

"Good to see you, Howard! Heard you've added on to your fleet!"

How the crusty, always-wheeling and dealing Howard convinced his lovely wife Jane to stay with him was beyond me, considering the fact the old sailor had basically become a one man boat dealership.

And it was good to see Alex again. "When are you coming back?" he asked, slapping me on the back and putting a cold *Pacifico* in my hand. "Everyone is asking!"

"Soon!" I promised. Then, turning to shake hands with another old friend, it suddenly happened.

"Dad!"

"*¿Qué pasó, Marcos?*" I asked, leaning down to whisper in his ear.

"I want to walk!" he answered, determination in his voice.

"I know, buddy," I said, patting him on the shoulder. "You will."

"No, I mean I want to walk. Now!"

I knelt down in front of the wheelchair, looked into Marcos' eyes and knew right then, he was serious. "Marcos, are you sure you're ready for this?"

"*Sí, papá.*"

"You don't have to…" I began. But it was too late. Before I could say another word, Marcos clasped the arms of the wheelchair that had constrained him for two months. Eyes fixed straight ahead and arms trembling under the strain, he began to lift himself up. Struggling against his own weight, he pushed harder, exerting all the force he could to lift himself up.

"Hey, everybody, look!" someone shouted. Instantly every soul in the bar turned to look at little Marcos, fighting to rise up out of the wheelchair. There was a collective gasp from the entire bar as every conversation came to an utter halt.

You could hear a pin drop as Marcos wrestled himself out of his wheelchair, lurching forward, nearly collapsing as his feet touched ground for the first time in months. He staggered a bit, then with eyes still focused straight ahead, fought to regain his balance. Just like that, Marcos was on his feet, standing there, upright in front of the hushed crowd.

With every bit of strength he could muster, he lifted his foot and took a small step forward. Froggys erupted! Marcos lifted his other foot and took a second step, inching forward across the barroom floor as the crowd went wild. Not satisfied, he thrust his foot forward and took a third, final step, before finally collapsing into his wheelchair, exhausted from what he had just accomplished. Sailors, old men, drunks, even tourists who had never met Marcos before, cheered in celebration, standing on their feet to give him an ovation, some wiping away tears and raising their glasses to toast one another.

"I did it, Dad!" Marcos shouted over the noisy celebration. "I walked!"

"You did it, buddy!" I exclaimed, kneeling in front of him and hugging him tightly. "You really did it!"

"Hey Dad," Marcos beamed. "Next time I'm gonna run!"

****

Marcos was right. Soon he *would* run. He'd even dance. Just ask the crowd that came to "Mulligan's IslandFest" a month later. Nobody remembers what song we were singing when someone helped Marcos onto a stage with Gary Seiler, Rob Mehl, Kelly McGuire, and me that night at Paradiso Resort. What they'll never forget is the sight of my son, hunchbacked but standing on his own two feet, dancing across the stage with a big grin on his face. It was as if he wanted to show San Carlos, and the world, that nothing was going to defeat him. Nothing would stop him. He was going to recover, fully and completely.

Little did anyone in the crowd know how long that would take for his dad.

Chapter Fourteen

"Hello?"

"Mark, is that you?"

I didn't recognize the voice on the other line, and honestly, was already regretting having picked up the phone in the first place. Seemed like for months every conversation I had with anyone, whether on that telephone or in person, would somehow wind up in a discussion about the same topic: Death. It was now the end of November. I just didn't want to talk about it anymore.

I was tired of repeating the same conversations over and over again. Exhausted with well-intentioned folks asking "how are you holding up?", saying "if there's anything I can do," or telling me, "I know how you must feel." Sick of people who knew just as little as I did about God, explaining to me why he "called Adela home." Tired of strangers informing me that she was now an "angel" looking after us from Heaven. I began to wonder, do people only say these things because they don't know what else to say?

I didn't want any more advice. I didn't want to be asked how I was doing. I didn't want to again hear, *"I'll pray for you."* I just wanted to hide from the world and be left alone. The best way to do that, aside from not going out in public, was to not pick up the telephone. To unplug it. Or to just let it ring.

"I'm gonna get rid of that damn thing," I had insisted to Dave.

"Don't you think that's just a bit extreme, bro?" By now, my younger brother was quite used to crazy things coming out of my mouth, but this, along with my plan to permanently close my email account, struck him as meriting a logical response. "Come on, what if there's a family emergency up north?"

"Adela and I lived on a beach with no phone for a long time," I replied. "We got by just fine. If there's an emergency, they'll find me."

"And if at some point in your life you actually feel like making… a phone call?" David asked, puzzled.

"I'll use a payphone."

Luckily, David had prevailed in that conversation.

****

"Who is this?" I asked.

"It's Bradley. Bradley Craig."

Bradley Craig. I had performed at his annual "Cartridge in a Bear Tree" Christmas event up in Phoenix several years in a row. At one of those parties, a close friend of his had told me about Bradley's traumatic, near death experience a couple years before. Though I'm not exactly sure what illness it was that put Bradley's life in such grave danger, the entire experience changed his life dramatically. Up until that point, apparently, Bradley hadn't exactly been the world's most fervent believer in God, but when doctors ultimately gave him almost no chance to survive, he resorted to the power of prayer. After begging all his worried friends, some of them non-believers, to join him in praying on his behalf, he stunned doctors with a miraculous recovery. From that point on, he would never be the same Bradley Craig again.

"Mark, I'm hosting my party again in just a couple weeks. I know it's real short notice, but would you come up to Phoenix and sing at it?"

"Bradley," I sighed. "I don't know if you heard about what happened..."

"I did, Mark. I can't believe it," he interrupted. "And I can't tell you how sorry I am to hear about your wife," he interrupted. "But still, I do hope you come up for this. You've *got* to be here for the event. Would you come?"

"I wish I could, Bradley, but I just can't," I replied. "In fact, I've canceled just about everything on my calendar. I just don't think I'm capable of putting on a very entertaining show right now."

"I understand," Bradley said. "But still, I really wish you'd make this one."

"Problem is, it's a party Bradley," I responded. "And I just can't be the life of the party right now. I can't get up, act all happy, and entertain other people when I feel the way I do."

"You don't have to," Bradley promised. "You can do whatever you want. Mellow stuff, background stuff, whatever works for you to make it through the night. Just strum your guitar if that's all you want to do. But you've got to be here, Mark."

I thought about that for a moment. "I don't know, Bradley. People have expectations of a certain kind of show I do. It's upbeat, it's happy..."

"Mark, most of these people who are coming to my party won't know who you even are," Bradley interrupted. "You really can do whatever you want. Just be here, OK?"

I thought about it more as Bradley continued to urge me. Maybe I could do this. If I didn't have to energize a crowd singing "Drinking Mexico Dry" or "Brown Eyed Girl," and could just kind of hang in the background while people mingled, then maybe it was possible after all.

"Bradley, I'll be there."

****

"¿*Mayonesa con limón?*" Dave examined the label on the jar he pulled out of the refrigerator. "Come on, is there *anything* in this country that doesn't have lime in it? Really, *mayonnaise?*" The disgusted look on his face said it all.

"Hey, at least it doesn't have chili powder in it," I replied, for some reason feeling the obligation to defend of the taste buds of two hundred million Mexican citizens.

"Yeah, but that lollipop Luis is eating is covered with it! Chili powder on a sucker? Who thought of *that?*"

It was obvious. My brother needed a break. From Mexico, from us being recognized everywhere we went, from *sombreros* and accordions and *norteña music*, and from being away from his friends and his life in the States.

He needed a break from Marcos and Luis, who due to my own lack of progress in the single-fathering thing, had turned Dave into the lead character from *Mr. Mom* instead of a free- wheeling, songwriting, guitar-toting babe magnet.

Most of all, he needed a break from me. It was time for him to get back up to the States for a few weeks, see some friends, eat something that didn't have lime or chili pepper on it, and get into the recording studio with Tim Bluhm in San Francisco to start work on a few things. The timing was right, as I could take him across the border with me on my way to the Christmas event in Phoenix, leaving him in Tucson where he could fly out the next day.

As I dropped Dave off in Tucson that December night, I thought about the help he had been to me throughout the past five months. Being that aforementioned eighth child in our family, I was already out of the house for much of the time David spent growing up. All these years later, this unexpected time together had been good for us, even with the constant ups and downs I was putting him through.

Dave had "stood there and felt shitty with me" after the funeral when I was overwhelmed by grief. He was there to witness intense joy following "the miracle" with Luis, only to watch the resulting joy slowly dissipate as the impact of the moment became lost among everyday hassles. He saw his older brother, confused and increasingly bitter, slowly begin to "circle the drain." More and more he heard him saying incredibly stupid things, consuming ridiculous amounts of alcohol, dwelling in self-pity, turning his back on God, and rushing to satisfy his needs for affection again, all in a span of mere months following Adela's death. And he only saw some of it, not the parts I managed to keep hidden. Had he seen it all, he would have given up on me and moved in with someone more stable, say, Charlie Sheen.

Dave himself was hurting, remembering Adela fondly as he helped to raise her children. Sure, he had heard about her ongoing jealousy issues, but in spite of that, loved her for so many other wonderful qualities she exhibited. He recalled playing guitar for her when he was still learning, sitting alone on a porch in Kino Bay while she listened.

"David, you're really good!" Adela told him that day, impressed with how quickly my brother had learned to play the guitar. "What song is that?"

"*Crash*," David answered, smiling as Adela applauded. "By the Dave Matthew Band."

From that moment, before the rest of our family ever realized it, Adela knew that Dave had the kind of talent that could lead to a future in music. If she had only lived long enough, she would have heard him eventually release his own CD, *The Late Great Southwest*, followed by a later EP, *Runaway Blues*. She would have been in the front row, cheering Dave on as he worked his way up through thirty dollar a night bar gigs, eventually achieving his dreams joining the band Nicki Bluhm and the Gramblers. She would have been thrilled to watch him perform with the band on the *Conan O'Brien Show*, as well as the *CBS News This Morning* program, among others. In a span of just a few years, he would accomplish more than I had in a lifetime of effort, as the band would open for major acts, release new albums, headline the Fillmore in San Francisco, and perform everywhere from New York City and Los Angeles to Costa Rica and Canada.

Neither of us yet knew any of that as Dave hopped out of my car that December night. We also had no idea what would become of his relationship with a girl I had introduced him to soon after his arrival to San Carlos. A girl named Elsa.

****

"See you in a few weeks bro. Hope your gig in Phoenix rocks tomorrow!" Dave picked up his guitar, waving as I turned the car around and headed back toward the interstate. The relaxed smile on his face told me he was glad to be north of the border again, at least for a while.

A few minutes later I was back on I-10, heading toward Phoenix. It was already dark and I was getting tired, having been on the road most of the day after leaving San Carlos early that afternoon. But in less than two hours, I'd finally be at my folks' place. Sipping my Circle K Thirstbuster, I focused on the road in front of me.

As the miles flew by and the lights of Tucson disappeared in my rear view mirror, I noticed something over the hum of my motor. It was quiet. Very quiet.

Nobody was talking to me. Nobody was knocking on my door. No phones were ringing. Luis wasn't crying. Eva wasn't instructing me on how much medicine to administer to Marcos. Jimmy Buffett and Johnny Duncan songs weren't blaring from my boombox. David wasn't laughing while kicking my butt in foosball for the thirty-seventh straight time.

There was simply silence. Peace and quiet. I had slowly forgotten what those words meant. What silence actually sounded like.

Ever since Adela died, constant chaos had surrounded me. It had simply become a way of life. Whether real or existing only in my mind, it seems there was always something happening to keep me from being at peace.

But tonight, all I had to do was drive. For the next two hours, until I got to my parents' condo in central Phoenix, I didn't have to do anything but that. Just drive.

Chapter Fifteen

"OK, I've described my ideal girl for you," I answered, looking at Adela as she sat across the table from me, sipping her drink. "Now it's your turn. What kind of guy are *you* looking for, if you could have your pick of anyone in the whole world to be with?"

Adela laughed, tossing her head to one side and smiling. She paused, then looked me right in the eyes. "Somebody exactly like you."

For a couple weeks, ever since meeting Adela, under the shameless guise of helping her with her English, we had been building a friendship. But that night, when we hopped in my truck and headed for the dilapidated old movie theatre in downtown Guaymas, I finally got the nerve to reach for Adela's hand. She took mine.

****

Snapping to my senses, I flicked on my high beams. *Phoenix 89* announced big white letters on a green reflective sign.

All alone and surrounded by silence, memories of Adela had somehow taken over my mind, consuming my every thought since Tucson had disappeared in my rear view mirror. Memories of happy times. Memories of sad times. Even memories I thought had disappeared altogether, until they unexpectedly rushed back to me, one after another, flooding my mind as I flew down the interstate. I gripped the wheel and concentrated on the road ahead.

****

"Come on, Adela, just get out of the car. The wind's not *that* bad!" Flying sand from Cochorit Beach pelted the windshield as I spoke.

"There's a sandstorm going on, Mark!" Adela exclaimed. "Why do you insist on us walking down the beach right now?"

If only Adela knew why we were here. If she had only heard my conversation with a buddy the night before, when I secretly confided in him that I had finally bought a ring and was going to pop the question. On Cochorit Beach, a place that was very special to me.

I lived there when Adela and I first met. She was shocked when she found out that the tiny, run-down shack I was renting for fifty bucks a month had no electricity, and that I actually had to run an extension cord from the landlord's house next door. That I had no running water, but instead paid ten pesos per week for a truck to fill an empty garbage can so I could shower outside on a small concrete pad. That my "refrigerator" was an ice chest. That my "kitchen" consisted of a Coleman camp stove on the front porch. That my bed was a sleeping bag spread out on a dirt floor.

But what a beach! Unknown to most gringos forty-five minutes away in San Carlos, I basically had it all to myself. Except for a few Mexican fishermen, occasional lost tourists, truckers scoring with hookers and weekend visitors from the town of Empalme, it was just me, my guitar, my windsurf board and my old Laser sailboat.

Ever since we met, Adela had seemed a bit embarrassed to show me her family's home. Although Doña Telma kept it clean, the Ruiz residence was certainly not the Taj Mahal. Adela was nervous, not knowing how comfortable this newcomer in her life would be in her humble surroundings. She wondered, would I look down on her and her family as being "poor"? Her pride would never allow that.

Truth is, I knew exactly how she felt. I had no idea if the moment Adela saw my home, she'd think less of me. After all, most Americans in the area lived in beautiful homes along the beaches of San Carlos, not in rickety old dumps like mine on Playa Cochorit. Being a gringo, what her expectations were of me? Would money, or lack of it, affect whether she wanted to get involved with an American? We'd been dating for nearly two weeks. It'd probably be nice to know sooner rather than later, I figured.

"Why don't you come see where I live?" I asked her one day, inviting her to come out to my place on Playa Cochorit. Any doubts I had of Adela's intentions were quickly put to rest when she walked through my door.

"You live here?" Her eyes grew wide.

"*Sí, Adela.*" I studied her reaction as I spoke. "Since my first couple years here were as a volunteer over at the Casa Franciscana, I didn't have much money when I finally moved out. I'll eventually move into something else closer into town, but it'll probably have to be pretty simple too. But hey, at least living here for a while will give me a chance to save a little money."

Adela smiled. "What a great beach you've got, all to yourself! Let's go sit on it for a while, OK?"

So here we were again, two and a half years later, with gale-force winds suddenly screwing up my meticulously prepared plans for a romantic, sunset wedding proposal. On top of it, I was scheduled to leave Mexico the next day, and wouldn't return for over a month. Call me impatient, but I didn't want to wait that long.

"No! Like I've told you over and over, I'm not getting out!" Adela answered firmly.

I guess I'd have to wait that long.

"Fine, have it your way!" Exasperated, I popped the key into the ignition.

"Where are we going now?" she asked.

"Home," I muttered. "I've got a long trip tomorrow anyway." I fired up the engine and hit the gas. It was a long, silent drive back to Guaymas.

"Are you mad?" she finally asked, as we pulled to within a few miles of town.

"To be honest, yeah, kind of," I responded. "All I asked you to do was take a walk with me. Come on, so we had a little wind…"

"A *little* wind? Come on! Really, you're mad 'cause we didn't do things *your* way," she interjected. "Fine, if you want to take me home, take me home. Be that way! I don't really feel like hanging out with you either."

How did this all happen? Weren't we supposed to be, at this very moment, happily celebrating our wedding engagement? What was this, the pilot episode to some future reality show about failed expat wedding proposals?

This was dumb. Both of us knew it.

"You're right. The walking on the beach idea was kind of stupid," I finally admitted. "Sorry for being a jerk about it. I just had hoped we were going to have a really nice time on my last night before I go. *Perdóname*, OK?"

"It's OK," she answered. "Forget it."

"Hey, I know it's lousy weather outside, so do you want to go see a movie or something?" I asked. "We can get something to eat afterward, anywhere you want. What do you say?"

"*OK, Marcos*," Adela replied, taking my hand. A little while later, we pulled up to the movie theatre in Guaymas to catch whatever flick was playing that night. With only one movie playing at a time, it wasn't like we expected a lot of choices. As it turns out, we wouldn't even have one choice.

"*Lo siento señor*. The movie has been delayed."

Delayed?

"Please understand. The tape is on a bus coming up from Ciudad Obregón," the uniformed manager of the movie theatre informed me. "But the bus broke down on the way up, in the town of Vícam. I just got a call from the bus driver that everything's almost fixed. He'll be back on the road real soon and be on his way. Come back in an hour, maybe an hour and a half, and we should be ready!"

Only in Guaymas.

"You've *got* to be kidding!" Annoyed but undeterred, I turned to Adela. "How about we grab a couple beers and head for Las Playitas? We can drink 'em in the car and come back after that if we want to."

The "beach" at Guaymas's Las Playitas wasn't much, but at least it was only minutes away from downtown. Sure, the bare patch of hard-packed dirt that lined the polluted municipal bay was nothing like the beautiful sandy shores of San Carlos or even Playa Cochorit. But at least the darkness of the night would hide the plastic bags, beer cans and broken Bud Light bottles strewn all over the place. And the reflection of the city lights on the water wasn't bad. Besides, options were limited.

Minutes later, we rolled up to the water's edge and I cracked open a couple cold *cervezas* I picked up on the way, handing one to Adela and taking a swig of mine as we gazed out the windshield, over the bay.

"*Que bonito,*" Adela exclaimed, pointing to the yellow moon rising into the sky.

"Yeah, it is pretty," I said. Noticing how the fierce winds had calmed since leaving Cochorit at sunset, I chuckled to myself. *Just my luck, NOW the wind dies!*

"What's so funny?" she asked, noticing the slight grin on my face.

"*Nada,*" I replied, taking another sip of beer and squeezing her hand.

The whole thing was kind of funny, come to think of it. Yeah, so much for my plans of getting down on one knee at sunset in the perfect spot. Only to wind up here. Oh well, at least I hadn't lost the ring. Now *that* would be my luck. Paranoid about misplacing that shiny piece of jewelry, whose value exceeded that of twice the rest of my assets combined, I had been subtly checking every five minutes or so since picking Adela up earlier that night, periodically fumbling around in my pocket to make sure the ring was still there.

I checked again, just to be sure it hadn't fallen out at the movie theatre. Still there. *Whew.* I'd need that sucker for round two sometime next month. That is, assuming no sand storms, crashing asteroids or tsunamis would unexpectedly hit town and mess up my plans.

Finishing my beer, I crumpled the can, tossed it on the floorboard and pulled Adela closer. Then, completely out of the blue… it hit me.

You idiot! How could you forget?

How *could* I forget? Two and a half years earlier, on that very first unexpected "date" when Adela took my hand for the first time at the movie theatre, I had asked her to come here afterward. *Here!* Not only to Las Playitas, but to this very exact spot my truck was now parked on. Obviously not the romantic that listeners of my songs may picture me as, I had completely forgotten. This spot we were sitting on was the first place I had ever kissed Adela. It's where our relationship first went beyond friendship, and where our *noviazgo* began when I asked her to be my girlfriend.

"Adela, you do know exactly where we are, right?"

She leaned against my shoulder and smiled. "*Sí.*"

Change of game plan. We never went to the movies that night. And when I finally took Adela home, she wore a ring on her finger.

****

The sound of crackling static cut through the silence. Reaching to turn it off, I wondered just how long I had been oblivious to the sound.

Phoenix, 73.

****

"How many times have we been over this? *Please!* Can we cut to the chase?" Our marriage counselor seemed taken aback by my momentary outburst.

"Let's all face it. Adela wants me to quit singing," I continued. "She's jealous of any attention I might receive from a female, OK? She wants me to do something else. But she doesn't realize that if I do something else, it won't take care of the problem. She doesn't trust me. If I worked in an office, she'd think I was having an affair with the secretary. If I were a doctor, she'd think I'm getting too much attention from nurses. It doesn't matter what I'd do, she wouldn't want me to do it. I've got to make a living. Music is what I do. And excuse me doctor, but *no,* I won't 'scale it back' like you're suggesting. It's my job, for God's sake!"

Before our therapist could interject, I turned to a tearful, exhausted

Adela sitting beside me.

"Adela, don't you realize that I love you? That in spite of all the problems we've had, that I'm still *in* love with you?"

The time had come. It was down to this. Do or die. Now or never. A Doug Flutie "Hail Mary" pass into the end zone.

"Look, I realize I'm an imperfect guy. I've made plenty of mistakes in the past and have a *lot* of things I can work on now. If you want me to quit drinking, I'll quit drinking. Want me to quit swearing? I'll quit swearing. Want me to do just about anything, just name it and I'll do it. Whatever it takes for us to stay together. I love you, Adela, and always will."

She nodded, wiping a tear from her eyes as I continued.

"But ask me to quit singing my songs? Ask me to quit being the person I am? To stop being the man I was when you met me? Sorry, *not* gonna happen. Not now, not ever. My music was there before you ever were. And when I'm eighty years old, I'm still going to have a guitar in my hands, even if nobody's listening. I'm gonna keep singing 'til they bury me. Everything else is negotiable, but not that. Because it's not just something I do. It's who I am."

I took a deep breath, realizing the risk of what I was about to say.

"And Adela, if you just can't accept that, there's the door. Walk out of it, right now. I'll understand. I won't hate you. Just go. Now." I pointed toward the door.

Nodding her head, she reached for a tissue and dried the tears that were rolling down her face.

"But Adela, before you do walk out that door," I added, "if you could just accept once and for all that I love you and only want to be with you, we really could leave all this crap behind us. I just know it. We could make this thing better than it's ever been. You truly accept me for who I am, and I promise, I will never, ever leave you, no matter what. The choice is yours, Adela. It's up to you."

Before I could say another word, she reached over and took my hand...

Phoenix 51

****

"I have an emergency. Can we pull over at the store just for a second?" Adela pointed toward the Ley shopping mall.

My friend Jim Bomberg and I looked at each other in the rear view mirror, rolling our eyes, knowing full well that "just for a second" means something entirely different to someone born south of that fence extending from California to Texas.

"Adela, we're already going to be late getting to Alamos. Is it really that important?" I didn't want to get into details, given the fact that being a female, it might be something embarrassing that she didn't want to share in front of Jim and her mother, both sitting in the back seat.

"Like I said, it's an emergency!" Adela answered, urgency in her voice. I knew that look in her eye. This was obviously important.

"OK, whatever, but can you make it as quick as possible?" By the time the words came out of my mouth, she was already out the car door and bolting toward the mall.

"What's this all about?" Jim asked, puzzled.

"I don't know, but she says it's important. And that it will be quick."

Jim decided to kill time by practicing his Spanish "skills" on Doña Telma. To put it lightly, it was painful to listen to. Especially given the fact the lines he just happened to be "practicing" were the most flirtatious ones he could come up with.

Is that SOB trying to pick up on my mother-in-law? I wondered, looking into the rear view mirror. Good thing Dona Telma had absolutely no clue as to what Jim was saying in the first place. She just laughed. Which is probably what she would have done anyway, had she understood what he was actually trying to say.

Five minutes went by, then another ten.

"Where the hell is your wife?" Jim asked impatiently, looking at his watch.

"Like I told you, she said it was an emergency," I answered. "Whatever it is, we'll all enjoy the trip a lot more if we let her take care of it now."

"Well, I wish she'd hurry," he retorted. "We're going to lose our whole day down in Alamos if we don't get a move on!"

Personally, I was just relieved he was speaking English again. But Jim was right. We had to get on the road. I momentarily thought about going into the mall to look for her, but then realized that would entail leaving Jim Bomberg alone in a car with my mother-in-law. I quickly vetoed that thought.

Jim looked at his watch again. "Mark, it's been a half hour now. That's it! I'm going in!" You'd think Jim was Navy Seal on a military raid instead of some hapless, mildly perverted senior citizen, the way he charged out of the car.

"Check the pharmacy first!" I yelled as he disappeared across the parking lot, heading off on his reconnaissance mission.

Ten minutes later, Jim finally reappeared, Adela in tow. "Guess where I found her? In the shoe store!" he exclaimed, exasperated, slamming the door as he got back in the car.

I turned to her, eyebrows raised.

"It *was* an emergency," Adela insisted. "My shoes didn't match my outfit!"

****

Welcome To Phoenix.

I turned the key and walked through my parents' front door, quietly closing it so I wouldn't wake them up. The last thing I wanted was for them to see me in the condition I was in, after the exhausting emotional rollercoaster I been on for the past couple hours. Heading straight for David's old bedroom, I set my guitar down, kicked my shoes off, turned off the light and got into bed. Completely drained, all I wanted to do was sleep.

****

Buy diapers. Water the plants. Clean the refrigerator.

Nobody wakes up thinking they're going to die that very day. Adela certainly didn't. Not with all she planned to do that day.

Her list of things to do lay on the kitchen table as I turned the key and walked into the house. It was the first time I had been there since the accident days before. The lights were still on. A ceiling fan whirred in our living room.

I picked up that list, scribbled on a sheet of scrap paper. *Defrost chicken. Wash clothes. Return video.*

Did Adela ever get those things done? And how many things on a far bigger list of "things to do," the ones she wanted to accomplish over her lifetime, never got done? How many dreams went unfulfilled? In a life that ended way too soon, just how much remained "undone"? If she had known she was going to die young, what would she have done differently?

No, nobody wakes up thinking they're going to die. But *"like a thief in the night"*…

****

"*¿Por qué, Eva?* Why have *you* gotten messages from Adela, but I haven't?" Eva could sense the frustration in my voice.

"Mark, you know as sisters, Adela and I always had a special bond," she replied.

"But didn't I have one as her husband?" I asked, frustrated. "I would think that if you get messages from her, that by now, I would have gotten one too."

"Pray and ask God. Give it time, she'll come to you," Eva answered calmly.

"But I already did that right after the accident, Eva," I insisted. "And all I've had are dreams about the past, nothing about where she is now. But you, you've actually heard her voice in dreams telling you she's OK, giving you advice about the kids, whatever. It's not that I don't believe you, Eva, it's just that for once, I want more than just a dream about the past."

The frustration had been building for a long time. "I want to hear from her now, Eva, like you. Is that too much to ask? She obviously cares enough to come to you. Did she forget about me? Did God forget about me?"

"He hasn't," Eva reassured me. "Keep asking Him. Just like He did with Luis, God will answer your prayer, but in His time and in His own way. I don't know how or when, but He will."

"Maybe it's not about that," I said, beginning to have my doubts about that whole crazy episode. "Maybe that whole thing I thought was a 'miracle' with Luis was just coincidence, and not the answer to some prayer after all. Maybe it had nothing to do with God. Maybe it was just me wanting to think He was there, and that He actually cared."

Eva shook her head and smiled. Don't give up, Mark." I admired her faith. Wonder if she noticed how quickly I was losing mine.

****

The clock ticked. 2 a.m. 3 a.m.

"Lord?" My pillow soaked with tears, I finally broke down. It had been months now since my prayer into that open refrigerator, asking God to give me light at the end of the tunnel and provide me with hope. Months since that unforgettable moment just hours later, when Luis came to me for the first time.

I had prayed after that. OK, maybe not as often as I could have, and true, maybe my prayers were a little rushed, but hey, I prayed. Starting with when I gave God thanks for bringing my son back. I did that many times, as a matter of fact. I owed that to God, right?

But then, as time went on, admittedly I moved on with life. Little by little, everyday worries, like how I was going to pay my bills, consumed my mind and occupied my thoughts, replacing the impact of what had been an incredible moment. Prayers still came from my head, but they competed with so many other thoughts that they didn't come so much from my heart any more. Besides, it's not like I couldn't do whatever I needed to get done on my own, now that Luis was OK. So sure, I checked the "said my prayers" box nightly when I tucked the boys into bed. But there's only so much a guy has time for. I had to get on with life.

A life in which God seemed to grow more distant by the day. A stressed, frazzled, often reckless, increasingly selfish life in which I played the main character. It was all about me.

That life was less and less about Adela. If people only knew how I had tried to cast her memory aside in hopes of "moving on," and the lack of respect I had shown, they would take every Mark Mulligan CD they owned and throw it in the trash.

It was no longer about her family, who silently grieved their own loss while focusing on helping me to recover from mine. It wasn't even about my boys, who deserved far better care from their actual father instead of having to rely on Uncle Dave to play that role.

It was all about me. A relationship with anyone, God included, would be on my terms. It would happen, if and when I needed it.

And I actually had the nerve to turn to Him now? To ask Him a favor? Are you kidding?

"Are you listening, Lord?" I prayed, staring up at the ceiling in the darkness. *"I can't blame you if you're not."* I closed my eyes.

"I've done everything possible to disappoint you. I let down Adela so many times in our marriage and even after she died. I'm sorry, Lord. I've somehow forgotten all you've done for me. I don't deserve another

chance. But here I am, coming to you again, asking for another favor."

I continued, praying with all my might. *"God, let me hear her voice. I want more than just a dream. I want to know that Adela's OK, and that she's in your hands. Tell her that I'm sorry for being the jerk I've been. Let me know she still loves me. Please, just once, send me a message from her. Let me know that she hasn't forgotten me. I'm begging you, in the name of Jesus."*

Chapter Sixteen

"Good morning, Mark! Are you awake yet?" Lifting my head off the pillow, I glanced at the clock. 10 a.m!

"Hi, Mom. I'll be right out, OK?"

Who knows what time I had finally fallen asleep? Last I remembered seeing the clock, it was almost four in the morning. Rubbing the sleep out of my eyes, I quickly recalled the sudden flood of memories that had washed over me on the trip up, and how hard I had prayed before finally falling asleep. Hadn't Eva insisted God would answer me if I prayed as hard as I could? I had. In fact, I couldn't pray any harder if I tried.

And he hadn't answered me. Glumly, I got out of bed.

****

"Merry Christmas, Mark!"

Whatever illness had nearly led to his death at one point, Bradley certainly had recovered from it, smiling and looking healthy as ever. "Go ahead and get your stuff set up, OK?" he said. "And God bless you. So glad you decided to come."

Lugging my speakers through Bradley's backyard gate, I thought about that decision.

This'll be easy. I can do this. After all, not only had I performed at IslandFest back in October, but just nights before coming up to Phoenix, I had joined David and a few other local San Carlos artists for a Castaway Kids fundraising event in the Froggys parking lot. True, at tonight's event, I'd be on my own, without relying on support from any other musicians to entertain the crowd, but Bradley did promise me I could keep it mellow. That aside from a few Christmas songs, I could stay in the background with quieter cover tunes, rather than hitting his guests with a livelier "party" show or having to play festive beach songs. Tonight, it's not like anyone would be expecting me to be a screaming Sammy Hagar or pull a Pete Townshend, smashing my guitar to bits on stage as a final encore.

Most importantly, being in the background, I could avoid answering exactly the kind of questions I didn't want to answer, like the ones I'd surely have to address at home or other public events where people knew me. Like Bradley had already assured me, most of his guests had never heard of me. It was nice to know, death would not be a topic of discussion tonight.

****

"So I'll have to say I love you in a song."

As I hit the final A major 7, there was no applause, just the sound of guests mingling among themselves in Bradley's backyard. Normally, that lack of attention would have annoyed me to no end. Tonight, it was perfectly fine with me.

In fact, the only thing that wasn't working for me was my wardrobe. *Shoes? Socks?* Yep, I'd be forced to wear 'em. After all, even though it's a desert, Phoenix gets cold in December. And tonight was chilly! Not only was I was wearing long pants, but even a long sleeved shirt. Very seldom did I ever slap on one of those suckers, since I rarely sang in places where temperatures dipped low enough to require anything more than short sleeves. When I did venture outside Mexico or similar warm-weather climates, however, I always brought along one long sleeve tropical shirt, hand-made by my sister in law Crisanta, just to be safe. Besides, in my rush to leave San Carlos, it was the only shirt I had that was neatly folded so I wouldn't have to iron! Case closed.

"When you comin' home son, I don't know when but we'll get together then, Dad. You know we'll have a good time then." As I finger-picked the final notes of a Harry Chapin song, Bradley motioned to me from the side of the stage.

"Great set, Mark! Hey, go ahead and take a break while I make some announcements. Can I use your microphone?"

"Sure, go right ahead Bradley," I offered, unwinding the cable from the microphone stand and handing it to him. Carefully setting my guitar onto its stand, I hopped out onto a patio full of Brad's invited guests, wanting to remain nearby in case he had any feedback problems while talking on the mic.

"Can I have your attention please?" Bradley called out. "Please, everybody, can I have your attention?"

It took a few moments, but slowly the crowd halted their conversations and turned their attention toward their host.

"Merry Christmas, everybody!" he exclaimed. "I want to thank you all for coming to my annual party. It's good to see you all again!" As the crowd cheered, Bradley continued, informing everyone about the charitable cause the party was benefiting, before finally acknowledging friends and faces in the crowd.

"There's one more person I want to mention," he added, looking in my direction. "Our entertainer tonight, Mark Mulligan." The crowd politely applauded as Bradley continued. "There's something I want to say about Mark."

I waited for him to say something about having traveled up from Mexico, or maybe mention that I have CDs available for sale. I hadn't prepared myself, though, for what Bradley was actually going to say. "Mark wasn't supposed to be joining us for the party this year. Back in July, his wife was in an auto accident..."

I couldn't believe my ears. Hadn't Bradley understood that I *didn't* want this mentioned? That I trying my very best to avoid this topic, running from it every chance I could? That the only reason I was doing his event in the first place was because nobody there knew anything about me? That the last thing I wanted was to discuss death with strangers? Reopen wounds? Be pitied?

"Mark's two young boys survived, but Adela unfortunately did not," Bradley continued. The crowd was hushed, turning to look at me as he spoke.

Man, this was *not* supposed to happen. Not tonight. Last night's flood of dreams had already wiped me out. Praying myself to sleep had completely, emotionally drained me. Now this? Embarrassed and not knowing how to react to the crowd's attention, I just closed my eyes and stood there, Bradley's words fading into the background as my mind instantaneously raced off to a million places.

"Adela"... "accident"... "death"... For some reason, those words swirled around inside my head as Bradley spoke, leaving me momentarily oblivious to all that was happening. Until from somewhere behind me, somebody placed a reassuring hand on my shoulder. Head bowed and eyes still closed, I reached up, squeezed it firmly, and let it go.

Then, it happened.

For some reason, while bringing my own hand back down from my shoulder, I inadvertently brushed it against my shirt pocket, my finger catching on something sticking out of it.

Bradley's voice echoed in the background as thoughts continued to race through my head. As he finished his comments, I was still nervously fidgeting with whatever was in my shirt pocket.

"Our thoughts and prayers are with you Mark," Bradley concluded, finally setting the microphone down and exiting the stage. The whole thing, however long it had lasted, had been a blur. My mind was still a mess as I awoke from my momentary daze, only to find the crowd giving me a supportive round of applause. And a tiny, folded white slip of paper I had pulled out of my shirt pocket resting in my hand.

It was just a small scrap of paper. But looking closer at it, I noticed familiar handwriting. I quickly turned around to see who had been behind me, but he had since disappeared into the crowd.

The handwriting was in Spanish. This is what it said.

Never forget me, because I never could forget you. I love you so much. Your wife.

Chapter Seventeen

He's back! Mark Mulligan Tuesday!

As I stood there in the jam packed parking lot and looked up at the sign, I could feel excitement in the air. A standing room only crowd waited for me inside the bar, an hour before showtime, ready to get the party started.

"It's been too long, Mark. Welcome back!" Alex greeted me, grinning broadly.

"*Gracias*, Alex. Here's to a lot more great Tuesday nights at Froggys!"

No doubt about it, it was going to be a good year. One where I could put the nightmare of 2006 behind me and start over again. Marcos was back in school. The new CD, *A Bar Down in Mexico,* was finally out. Luis was smiling. Dave was back. Little by little, things were coming together.

I was already looking ahead to the future, as I began laying the groundwork for another IslandFest event. Paradiso Resort was back on board, and with Kelly, Gary and Rob all willing to come back down to perform, plus plenty of time to put an event together and advertise it, I knew this had the potential to be our biggest and best 'fest yet!

Finally, with Adela's sisters still helping out and Dave helping me out for another four or five months, I'd be able to book all the gigs I needed through the end of tourist season. At that point, in June, if Marcos and Luis kept improving, we could head up to the States for the summer and they could join me while I played road dates up there. Yep, the game plan was finally coming together, at least for the short run.

Most of all, I felt renewed. Finding that message from Adela in my shirt pocket, had done wonders for me, providing exactly the spark I needed to keep moving forward. Even after learning "the facts" and finally piecing together how that event mysteriously unfolded at that precise moment, I was riding a spiritual high. That faith that had begun to fade following Luis's recovery was now recharged.

As for my younger brother, he was spending more and more time with Elsa, who would drop by the house after work as often as she could. But even with the direction they appeared to be going, Dave was still helpful as ever with the boys, freeing me up to get back in touch with the world I had isolated myself from since July.

"I feel like I'm past all that," I told my brother John, using the new

Magic Jack phone gadget my brother had bought me. "Like the worst part is over. I think I've finally turned a corner."

"That's funny, 'cause last month you told me the same thing," he replied.

Was that a good thing or a bad thing?

****

What in the world...?

I stood there in shock, my head spinning as I stared at the handwritten note in my hand. Before I knew it, I was wandering down some side street blocks from Bradley Craig's home, sobbing and alone, the sounds of the Christmas celebration slowly fading into the night. I walked. And walked...

****

"Your father-in-law always hides love notes for me around the house whenever he travels," Mom had confided to Adela one day. "Just little messages that say he loves me and misses me, wherever he may be."

"Really?" Adela was incredulous. "*Your* husband does that?"

"Yes, he does! Tom will leave love notes for me everywhere. Beneath the pillow, under the telephone, even in my shoe!" Mom answered. "And later on, if he calls and I haven't mentioned finding one, he'll get a little annoyed and even ask me, 'didn't you find my note?'"

Adela couldn't believe it. My Dad didn't exactly strike her, or anyone for that matter, as the romantic type. Now she finds out her father-in-law was more Michael Bolton than Archie Bunker.

"Now Adela," Mom warned. "He doesn't want the kids to know. He's worried they'll think he's a softie."

Adela laughed. "I won't tell," she promised.

****

"This song off the new CD goes out for you, San Carlos."

Slapping my capo on the second fret of my guitar, I finger-picked the intro as the overflow crowd spilled onto the Froggys dance floor.

"My kind of people, in my kind of place…"

Luckily, packed as it was, it was a slow song, or a "butt-squeezer" as I would call it. With a crowd that large, very little space, and no actual stage to sing on, things could get a bit crazy on the fast songs. More than once, my mouth had been bloodied by a microphone that someone's errant dance move had sent smashing into my face.

And those speakers, perched precariously on stands beside me? My friend Tom had learned the hard way about keeping your distance from them while dancing, when a heavy 15 inch JBL came crashing down onto him after tripping on the base of the stand with his foot. Two seconds later, Tom's head resembled that of beaten truck driver Reginald Denny during the Rodney King riots. Anyway, by the time they finally mopped the blood off the floor, both parties had reached a legal settlement. No multi-million peso lawsuit, but the next *cerveza* was on me. If only the U.S. legal system was as just and efficient as ours.

"…my kind of moments, my kind of days."

****

Adela packed my suitcase while I checked last minute emails. Finally, she zipped it up and gave it a slap. "Finished," she said. "You're set to go."

"Hold on, I've got to pack my toothbrush," I began.

"Already did," she replied.

"But I left some extra guitar strings in my drawer!"

"They're in there, don't worry!" Adela knew how paranoid I'd be before trips about forgetting something I'd need. Though we both knew she was the better one at packing, she'd still have to put up with endless, annoying questions from yours truly.

"Oh, I almost forgot," I said, reaching over to the bed to unzip the suitcase. "I'll need to throw in a long-sleeve shirt for the Seattle show, just in case." Hey, it might be July, but it's the Pacific Northwest. You know me, if the temperature drops below ninety, I'm freezing.

Before I could re-open the bag, she stopped me and put her hand on top of it. "It's in there," she reassured me. "There's one all folded and ready in case you need it. You shouldn't have to even iron it. Now get on the road for Phoenix, OK? You've got a flight to Nashville to catch tomorrow morning."

Hadn't we just unpacked these bags from our Kino trip? Standing there in the bedroom with her one last time wasn't making it any easier to leave, especially since this time I'd be heading off alone. I lifted the suitcase off the bed, picked up my guitar with my other hand and looked at her one last time, standing in the bedroom.

"*Gracias, Adela, te amo.* And I'll be back before you know it."

The sound of my idling engine grew louder as she opened the door and headed out with me to the driveway.

I never did make Seattle. And I never did wear that shirt.

****

"Thank you Froggys, and thank you San Carlos! See you next Tuesday!"

What a night it had been. And according to my tip jar, a profitable one, with enough pesos stuffed in there to score at least a box or two of Huggies Supremes. Speaking of diapers, I glanced at my watch. 8 p.m. Pretty soon, I'd have to break down the sound system, pack it all up, and get back to my house so Cristina, the kids' babysitter, could head home.

That can wait for a little while, I thought as I waded through the crowd, shaking hands and greeting everyone I could before the place began to finally empty out.

Eventually, my voice sore from all the talking, I made it up to the bar. "You know what I'll have," I said, easing onto a bar stool.

The bartender smiled at me. "How does it feel to be back here singing again?" she asked, flashing a pretty smile as she handed me a Captain Morgan and diet Coke.

"Good," I answered, taking a sip and grinning back at her. "Really good."

****

That folded long sleeve shirt sat in the bottom of my suitcase, hidden by shorts, underwear, guitar strings, CDs, a toiletry bag, an iron, and a pile of other short sleeve tropical shirts that made the trip to Nashville one summer day.

From there it traveled on to Indiana, where it again spent a night unseen, covered by a now messy pile of clothes that needed to be washed.

And from there, it made a hurried, unexpected trip back to Mexico, where in a hasty unpacking job, it was never taken out along with the dirty clothes to wash. Instead, it sat there in the bottom of a suitcase, still neatly folded, in a closet sitting high on up a shelf.

It sat there, hidden and unnoticed, for five months. Until one day, I opened that suitcase up to pack for a Christmas party I hadn't ever planned to sing at.

Cool, there's one less shirt I'll have to fold or iron, I thought, leaving it where it exactly where it was and throwing the rest of my stuff into the suitcase on top of it.

On to Phoenix that shirt went.

"You might want to wear a jacket, Mark," Mom advised as I dressed before the party. "It's supposed to get pretty cold tonight."

"I hate wearing jackets when I'm singing, Mom," I answered. "They always bug me when I try to strum my guitar. I've got an undershirt, and somewhere in this bag I've got a long sleeve shirt. I'll be fine."

Looking at the clock, I knew I had to run if I was going to going to get my gear set up before guests started to arrive. After digging around and finding it, hurriedly I threw my shirt on, still buttoning it as I raced out the door.

****

"Do you think it was a miracle?" a friend asked, after hearing the story.

I paused, aware of how crazy what I was about to say would sound to any rational person.

"Adela had never, ever written me a note like that before, not once." I began. "Why now? Think of something else for a second. Had she randomly chosen to put it in any of my other shirt pockets, in my shorts, or any other place in my luggage, I would have gotten her message in Nashville, perhaps Indiana, maybe even Phoenix, or who knows, Seattle if I had ever made it there. I would have read it, thought 'that's sweet', called her and thanked her on the phone, and soon forgotten all about it. But she didn't put it in any other pocket. She put it specifically into a pocket that would somehow turn out to *not* be opened."

I continued. "On that tiny slip of paper, she had written words that didn't need to be heard back then like I needed them now. That little message from Adela came months later, just when I needed one so badly that I prayed to God, begging for one."

"You can call it what you want to," I concluded. "But do I think it's 'a miracle?' Absolutely."

And the second one, I thought to myself.

They say the third time's a charm.

Chapter Eighteen

"Run, Marcos, run!"

Who would have guessed this was the same Marcos that, not long ago, was confined to a wheelchair and wrapped up in a lower body cast? Nothing could hold him back him now. And nothing could erase that big grin from his face as he raced around that track, beaming the entire time as the crowd cheered.

"*¡Ándale Marcos! ¡Corre! ¡Corre!*"

Crossing the finish line, Marcos threw his hands into the air triumphantly, mobbed by his friends.

No one remembers who won the race that day. And no one cares. They only remember that Marcos ran.

****

"I love you me too bye bye."

"*¿Qué?*" Eva had no idea what little Luis had just said, a rapid fire succession of English words flowing out of his mouth as he played with his toy car. "What does all that mean?"

I chuckled a bit. *I love you me too bye bye.* That was Luis's unique way of saying *"Adiós, I want to be left alone."* Nope, no commas in there, and yes, it definitely got the point across. "I love you me too bye bye."

No doubt this kid was going to have quite the personality. Especially now that he had discovered a form of communication beyond the sign language David had taught him in those his first few months of living with us. Seemed like he was learning new words and short sentences every day. The more he gradually spoke, the clearer it became we were going to have our hands full with this kid.

"I wouldn't pick on him," I warned Marcos, watching Luis defend himself from having his Legos snatched by his older brother. "I guarantee you, this dude may be easy for you now, but the day's gonna come when you mess with him and he takes you down."

"I know Dad," Marcos sheepishly admitted. "That's why I'm picking on him now!"

****

"I've got a big surprise for you."

Luis's ears perked. After all, he had just heard one of his favorite words. As for Marcos, he couldn't take the suspense any longer. "What, *papá?*"

"You guys..." I began, pausing for dramatic effect, "are coming with me for a weekend... to the United States of America!"

Marcos couldn't believe his ears. "Do we get to see my cousins?"

"You bet, buddy!" I answered. "You guys get to play with them in Phoenix while I sing!"

Marcos jumped up and down gleefully. "We're going to Phoenix!" Luis was a bit more reserved, quite possibly because my two year old had no idea what the United States were, where they were located or what the English word "cousins" even meant. But after providing him with a quick Spanish translation, he was game.

Luis was fairly easy to travel with. Strap him into a car seat, hit the gas, and he'd be asleep in minutes. And no matter how long you were on the road, he wouldn't wake until you arrived to your desired destination, whether you were driving to the corner grocery store or to the border of Honduras. No speed bump or pothole could wake him. "Lazy Luis," we called him, partially due to his remarkable ability to doze off within seconds at any given time or place, on the spot. He could sleep through a Van Halen soundcheck, Lloyd from *Dumb and Dumber*'s "most annoying noise in the world," or quite possibly, Roseanne Barr belting out the national anthem.

No, Mexico doesn't often win medals of any kind, but if they ever do categorize "solo sleeping" as an official Olympic sport, Luis will proudly take a gold home for his country.

Marcos, however, was another story. You couldn't get him to doze off if you shoved a half-kilo of Lindsay Lohan's sleeping pills down his throat. Why? Because he didn't ever want to miss one single moment of whatever adventure he was on at the moment. He enthusiastically wanted to see it all. And know it all.

There's a reason he won the *Most Inquisitive Student* award at school. Heck, I never even knew the award actually existed until he brought it home. (I have suspicions his teacher awarded it to him merely to stop him from asking even more questions about why he *didn't* win it.) Needless to say, while Luis slept the whole way up to the border, I spent the entire duration behind the wheel being bombarded with question after question from Marcos. It was the type of persistent interrogation that would drive your average Guantanamo Bay suspect to a full confession, even after he had survived three sessions of waterboarding. Yes, you definitely had to be on your "A-Game" whenever Marcos began a line of questioning. Especially since he recognized when you were feeding him a line of B.S. or, worse yet, evading the question.

Not only did Marcos fire off endless question after question, but he assaulted you with them in two languages. As he customarily did back home, half the time he'd start a question using English only to end it in Spanish, unwittingly blending the two languages together in his own unique way. Given the way he seamlessly combined the two, he could foreseeably make a fortune, were he ever to copyright a first-ever edition of *Spanglish For Dummies*.

Eventually, after four and a half hours of enduring questions such as "why is salt white?" and "who created God?" I found myself in the city of Nogales, waiting in a long northbound line at the border. In case you're unfamiliar with the term, in post-Reagan American society, "border" refers to some fictional barrier secured by a non-existent fence guarded by Border Patrol agents who aren't there. This particular "border" was apparently so effective at deterring illegal entry that seventeen million "undocumented immigrants" are currently demanding voting rights, driver's licenses and free breakfasts in American public schools. I could have gotten my kids across in a mere matter of seconds had I simply paid ten lousy bucks for an immigrant-smuggling *"coyote"* to shove them through the nearest gaping hole in the fence, rather than patiently waiting my turn.

Looking at the long line in front of me, my mind immediately went back in time a couple years, to the first time I took Marcos across the border as a tiny tot.

"What's that, *papá?*" he had asked back then, pointing toward the official U.S. port of entry in front of us.

"That's the border, Marcos." I should have anticipated what question was coming next.

"What's a border?"

I hesitated. Given my politically incorrect views on virtually any given subject, the thought crossed my mind that perhaps I wasn't the person best equipped to fully answer this question for a child his age.

"It's the division between two countries, Marcos," I informed him. "See, on this side, we're in Mexico. And on that side is the United States."

"What's different about the United States?" he asked, curiously.

"Well, lots of things Marcos. Like the food, for example. And the music. Oh, and the languages people speak. See, here in Mexico, people speak Spanish. In the United States, people speak English." (Note to reader: The previous statement no longer applies to states such as Arizona, California, Texas, nor New Mexico.)

"They speak English? Really?"

"Yes, theoretically," I responded, thinking perhaps it was best we changed the subject. After all, there's only so much intellectual dishonesty I can engage in with my own son. But Marcos was just beginning.

"What does my grandma in Phoenix speak?" he asked.

"English," I replied.

"And my *abuelita* in Guaymas?"

Oh no, here we go. "Spanish."

His lips curled into a devilish smile. "And my Uncle Tom?"

"English," I answered.

"And *Tío Jorge?*"

"Spanish."

Suddenly, with no explanation, Marcos fell silent, a look of confusion on his face.

"Daddy?" he asked, completely baffled. "What do I speak?"

****

Not surprisingly, Luis was still sound asleep, head tilted to one side, strapped into his car seat. But Marcos was getting restless. "Daddy, are we almost there yet?"

"Marcos, you've been asking me that every two miles since we crossed the border!" I sighed. "Just hang on, we're almost to Phoenix, and you'll get to stay with your cousins. We'll be there in just about half an hour."

He looked at me impatiently. "I know, *papá*, but remember? You promised me and Luis that we would have a hotel party with you in the United States. We're in the United States! Can't we pull over and have one? *¿Por favor?*"

Hotel party. With Marcos, you could turn anything into a party. Just take any random event and add the word "party" to it. For example, Monopoly "party." Puzzle "party." Bubble blowing "party." With possibly the exception of "cleaning your room party," it successfully worked. The boy definitely liked parties.

Especially "hotel parties." Forget about what Jimmy Page or Mick

Jagger did at theirs, ours were the best. Because instead of boring things like drugs, alcohol and women, we got to really *par-tay!* Yep, at a hotel party we'd watch things on TV that Eva would never let us back home, like World Wide Wrestling matches, reruns of Sponge Bob, "*America's Funniest Train Accidents,*" you name it. And at hours that no responsible parent would allow the family pet to stay awake until. Midnight, 1 a.m., 2 a.m., whatever! Hotel parties always meant eating the least healthy foods possible, such as Jack in the Box tacos, Circle K hot dogs, Carl's Jr. Double Western Bacon Burgers, Flaming Hot Cheetos, etc, washed down with Slurpees or soda. Best of all, it meant jumping on the bed. All of us, Dad included. Luckily I pay for my motel rooms with cash and don't leave a credit card at the desk.

"Marcos, we're so close to Phoenix. Even a crappy motel is gonna cost me at least thirty-five or forty bucks. I know I promised you, but how 'bout we just keep going and..."

He hung his head sadly, not saying a word. It was almost like Old Yeller had just died. I sighed.

"Room 115," the clerk said. "Here's your remote. Sure you don't need the wi-fi code?"

"Nope," I replied, grinning at Marcos and Luis. "We won't be needing internet tonight."

****

"How was the trip?" Eva asked, welcoming Marcos and Luis back with hugs.

"It was *awesome!*" Marcos shouted. "Luis and my Dad and I ate Cheetos and stayed up until..."

"Marcos!" I interjected quickly. It was too late. Eva looked at me sternly.

I know, I know. Nobody needed to tell me. I had to get a backbone and toughen up with these kids, once and for all. But maybe that could wait just a little bit longer, right?

Chapter Nineteen

"Come on, Dave, let's go get haircuts!"

"Again?" Dave laughed. "You just got one last week!" My younger brother had apparently figured it out. When loneliness got to me, nothing was more relaxing than the feel of a woman's fingers running through my hair.

"Ah, yes!" I'd say, flashing a grin over to my patiently waiting brother as I'd sit back, close my eyes, and enjoy a rare gentle touch. And you wondered why I wear my hair so short! Problem was, there's only so much hair on a fellow's head. Sooner or later, there just wouldn't be anything left to cut, unless I bought a wig.

Apparently, weekly haircuts weren't going to be a permanent solution for my loneliness. More and more, I sought alternative remedies.

****

"You get off work at six? I'll pick you up then!" As I hung up the phone, I could hardly believe it. I'd be going out on a date, up the road in Hermosillo. Did she really say yes? Or was she confused, thinking she was talking to someone else?

Although the fact that she agreed to go out with me made me seriously question her judgment, I was excited. Sure, ninety-nine percent of the interest expressed between us had come from my end, but hey, that still left one per cent coming from her. Admittedly, the odds might be millions to one that she actually liked me too. But like Jim Carrey famously declared in the previously mentioned *Dumb and Dumber* film classic, "So you're telling me there's a chance... yeah!"

Just getting the time of day from a halfway decent looking female was nice. In this case, a very decent looking female. I had missed the feel of a woman casually touching my hand when she talked to me, or listening to me talk about anything other than death, or laughing at my stupid jokes, whatever.

She certainly had a lot of guys that liked her. Would she like me? At least, I wouldn't be finding out the answer to that question closer to home in San Carlos, where I knew everyone, and everyone knew me. A first date with anyone there would be virtually impossible. Aside from likely interruptions every five minutes, the reality is people would talk.

Who knows what they'd say?

People in San Carlos truly wanted me to be happy again. Most didn't want me to be alone for the rest of my life. They hoped my boys would one day have a mother again. But they also wanted it to be the right girl. One who was more than just a pretty face, who would love not only me but my kids equally.

Was it too soon for me to be out there in the dating world again? Some people said yes, it was way too early, that I needed to give things more time. Others said no, that I should move on from past tragedy, get back out there and live life again.

It would come down to doing what I wanted to do. If stupid decisions were going to be made, by God, I was the one who was going to make 'em.

"See you tonight!" I said, hanging up the phone.

****

"Daddy, why are you getting dressed? Are you going somewhere?"

I hesitated. "Out with a friend, Marcos."

"Jim Scheidler?" Marcos asked curiously.

"No, a different friend," I replied.

"Jim Bomberg?"

"No, not Jim Bomberg either," I responded.

"Then who is he?" Marcos persisted.

"Another friend," I replied.

"Oh. But why are you wearing pants?" he pressed. "And shoes? You look funny!"

"Do I really?" I momentarily panicked, rushing over to the mirror to see for myself. *My God, am I really taking a six year old's fashion critiques seriously?* I wondered, quickly straightening my collar. Heck, if Luis could properly formulate a sentence, he'd probably tell me I looked ridiculous too.

"Marcos, just be a good boy and behave for Cristina tonight. She's in charge, so do whatever she says. And help her take care of your brother, OK?" After kissing him on the forehead and giving Luis a quick hug, I turned to Cristina.

"Thanks for babysitting. Just make sure they're in bed on time, OK? And no Cheetos for Marcos, he already had plenty this afternoon."

I turned around and headed out the door, ninety minutes later finding myself in Hermosillo, sitting across the table from a beautiful girl over dinner. Nervous as I was, it was nice to be back out again. Even if she did, for some reason, glance at text messages on her phone a little too often.

Chapter Twenty

"I don't like her," Eva said firmly, her back to me and rinsing dishes as she spoke. "She's not at all right for you or the boys. And I still think this is all happening way too soon."

Eva was certainly a girl who had her opinions. And she wasn't afraid to share them.

"Going out on a date is one thing. But you've been seeing her for a while now. And you blow off your own kids every time the phone rings. They're supposed to come first right now, not some woman who I seriously doubt even feels the same way about you."

That stung a bit. "Why don't you like her, Eva? She's nice to you," I insisted. "And I think she's good with the kids, she's just busy and doesn't have much time to spend with them. Really, what do you have against her?"

"You don't see what other people do, Mark. You're blind and you're rushing things," Eva retorted, her voice rising. "I don't get it. Her smile is nothing like Adela's. What exactly is it you even see? Adela was sweeter and kinder and prettier than she'll ever be!"

"But Eva," I tried to interject. "She may not be the same person as Adela, but she's wonderful too…"

Hearing her sister's name mentioned in the same sentence as a newcomer she didn't trust was all Eva could take. Putting the sponge down, she turned to me and glared.

"She could never compare to Adela. And don't you dare ever try!"

****

I've heard it said a million times. "If I lost my spouse, I'd never be with anyone again." Don't we all naturally feel that way prior to the death of a husband or wife? After all, you married your spouse for a reason. Unless you're from some offshoot sect of polygamous Mormons, served as President of the United States from 1993-2001 or play in the National Basketball Association, you likely married the person you did because you wanted to spend your life with that person, and that person only.

After losing a spouse, there are many who prefer to remain alone, never seeking companionship from another again. This is especially true among elderly widows, or people who were unwittingly married to freshly executed mass murderers. But losing your partner in life at a younger age carries its own unique set of challenges.

A friend of mine once told me just months after losing his wife to a long bout with cancer, "Mark, I miss my wife so much, but lately every single woman who pays me any attention at all just seems so beautiful. I can't help it. I'm tempted to be with them."

I know exactly how he felt. It's quite an adjustment after years of marriage to suddenly go from happily spending night after night with the person you love to constantly being sad and alone. Sometimes one misses even the simplest of things: Hugs, kisses, affection, a gentle touch, someone to laugh with. Someone to talk to, to hold your hand, to laugh when you tell a joke, to take your mind off things, to make you smile when you're down. Someone to love.

Those might sound like lyrics lifted from a cheesy Air Supply song, but they're often true. Of course, people who miss all those things but respect their lost loved one are capable being strong. Some honor that departed soul mate by waiting years until they get involved with someone on any level again, whether physical or emotional. They don't just jump at the chance to fill voids first chance they get.

Me, however? I turned out to be the exact opposite of how I or anyone else had pictured I'd ever be. I found out how weak and pathetic I actually am. As evidenced by the fact that yes, I am an Air Supply fan.

Aside from questionable musical tastes, I also found out how recklessly stupid I can be. Here I was, so soon after the death of my wife, diving headfirst into a turbulent "relationship" with a woman who had plenty of her own issues to deal with. I let my desire for her affection consume me. One minute, I'd be high as a kite. The next, down in the dumps. The immediate satisfaction that came with filling the sudden emptiness in my life definitely came with a price tag attached.

****

The conversation had been growing more heated by the second. We had already moved from the kitchen into my room, so Marcos and Luis couldn't hear us argue.

"Why rush things? You're this involved, this soon?" Eva persisted. "You're making a fool out of yourself, focusing all your time on her and not on your own boys. Get your head together and be a father to your kids! How much time are you spending away from them these days? Adela was such a good mother and you're letting her down, messing around with someone so soon!"

That was it. My breaking point had been reached. I was suddenly sick of unsolicited critiques. Sick of being told how I should act. Sick of it all. I lost it.

"You get to go home at night to someone you love! I don't!" I shouted angrily. "Everybody I know goes home to someone. Your brother and sisters do, too. Even Dave's got Elsa to spend time with. I don't have anybody! So get off my back, damn it! If I want to have people in my life just like the rest of the world does, why shouldn't I?"

"You've let my sister down!" Eva insisted.

"You don't know half of what I did to keep me and your sister together, Eva! She had her faults too! But all everyone points out are mine. I'm tired of it! Tired of you, tired of everything and everybody!'

Not backing down an inch, Eva excoriated me. "You think only of yourself! You're selfish! You're not the only one who lost somebody. We lost our sister too!"

"Your kids… my sister's kids… come before other women who just want to use you anyway!" she added angrily. "Be a father!" She stormed out, slamming the door behind her and leaving me standing there alone, bitter and feeling sorry for myself.

And utterly oblivious to the fact that she was one hundred percent right.

****

Have you ever woken up and suddenly realized that everything you thought you were, you aren't? That your face in the mirror hides a person you wouldn't want the world to see?

Admittedly, I was never admired for my academic prowess. From an early age, it was a safe bet that I wasn't going to be an MIT grad or Rhodes scholar. Even the Phoenix School of Welding might be a challenge.

That being said, I figured I did have a couple of attributes that might look okay on a resume. Like being able to fly by the seat of my pants. Wing it in any situation. Remain optimistic when things looked doubtful. Make good decisions on the spot. Be strong. Have faith. Use common sense.

And when all else fails, sing.

That was me, right? Come on, humor me. Must be true, right? Consider how many people came to *me* for advice.

"Look on the bright side," I'd say to those who experienced misfortune.

"Get over her," I'd tell friends sulking about relationships that had ended.

"Give it some time before you move on," I'd suggest to those who had lost loved ones.

"Have faith!" I'd instruct those with doubts.

Who the hell was I to instruct people how to confront a challenge? Let's face it, my life had been pretty damn cushy for most of the ride. Forty years had been good to me, with no major financial, emotional, or health challenges. From the time I was born things had been easy.

It wasn't like I *had* to work to put myself through Brophy College Prep. Dad made a good living, and we kids grew up with plenty of food on the table in a comfortable, upper-middle class Phoenix home. Sure, I had a job, but who didn't when they were in high school? Besides, the hours spent washing dishes and bussing tables at Feeney's Restaurant was mostly for extra cash and not necessities.

After graduating from Brophy with a three point something cumulative grade point average, I pretty much blew through college as a business major at Northern Arizona University, usually memorizing just enough to score well on my exams and then promptly forgetting everything I learned. This wasn't exactly a Harvard Law degree we were talking about. Even with the unfathomable amount of brain cells killed while chugging beers on a fake ID, successfully graduating was a relatively easy task to conquer.

After scoring that diploma and proudly slapping on a gold Century 21 jacket, I quickly became "top rookie" in my real estate office, before moving on to similar success at Coldwell Banker. Even after taking my grandfather's advice and ditching that real estate career to chase other dreams, I found myself working in occupations that came fairly naturally to me, like teaching English as a Second Language. Given the fact that my mother is from Venezuela, we kids grew up with a decent enough handle on Spanish that teaching English was, pretty much like everything else before, cake.

Music? Being able to bang out a tune came naturally to me too. My piano teacher noticed it early on, when at age five I could already play with two hands. Later, as a young teen, when my brother John put his guitar in my hands and taught me how to strum "Horse With No Name," playing that instrument came easily too. Strumming along to Jim Croce records, I'd pick the songs up by ear, never using sheet music or even learning the names of the chords I was playing. I quickly became good enough to realize that if I had heard it before, chances are I could play it, or at least fake it. That made it simple to play requests that were shouted out in years to come.

So while others may have slaved their lives away in cubicles or turning screws in a factory, I got to play a guitar for a living. OK, is this the part where you feel sorry for me? I don't think so.

As I grew older and watched friends lose parents and loved ones, nearly everyone I had ever been close to was still alive and healthy. While folks I sang to night after night underwent chemotherapy, organ transplants and suffered through all kinds of health challenges, I hop-scotched through life with a clean bill of health, casually checking off boxes as I went. Moved to Mexico. Dated cute girls. Married a cute girl. Bought a nice little house with a cute girl. Had kids with a cute girl. Healthy, cute kids, of course.

Yep, life was pretty darn easy for this boy. Need some advice on how to live? Step right up! 'Cause I had this baby wired. Even my bad days were good, you might say. Hell, I could handle anything. A challenge? Bring it on!

****

"Mark just doesn't seem like himself tonight," someone said, accidentally speaking loud enough for me to hear as I tuned my guitar between songs.

2007 wasn't even halfway over yet, and it seemed like the positive shine I kicked off the year with had already completely faded away. The joy from those amazing events that had earlier recharged me had slowly been forgotten, gradually replaced by demons from my recurring past. The booze? The stupidity? The recklessness? The rush to find affection? The self pity? The selfishness? "We're back!" they seemed to shout out to me. Not only were they back, but on display at my local gigs for all of San Carlos to see. Some may have been unaware that I was slowly unraveling right before their eyes, but many of those who knew me best were disappointed in what they saw.

****

"Come on, Mark, you've *got* to get this stuff down!" David was starting to get worried. "Not just stuff like cooking and getting kids ready in the morning, but all of it. I'm gonna be out of here one day soon. And yeah, you've improved on a few things, but there are a lot others I'm kind of concerned about."

"Don't worry, Dave, I'm gonna be fine when you're gone," I replied, nonchalantly. Maybe it was partially due to the stiff rum and coke in my hand as the afternoon sun shone through my window, but apparently my words weren't very reassuring.

"I'm not so sure," Dave answered. "Come on, bro, you've got to buckle down and really get this right before I go. On helping them with their homework, on dedicating the time both boys need from you, on big stuff like that. Without Adela around and now with me leaving, that's all going to fall on you, and you've got to be prepared for it. I'll feel a lot better up in the States knowing that you've got your own crap together and can take care of my nephews."

Ever been scolded by your little brother?

****

"What the...?" Startled, I jumped to my feet and raced out to the living room to see what the noise was. There it lay, in a broken frame, amidst shards of shattered glass. Our wedding picture, with the note I had found in my pocket still taped to the bottom of the frame.

"Oh my God!" I shouted, as Cristina came running from the kitchen. Picking it up sadly, I held it up for her to see. "It just fell off the wall. I have no idea why."

Cristina looked at me sternly. "Maybe Adela is sending you a message. Maybe she's not happy with how you've acted. Good for her." With that, she turned and left.

****

Who are you? I stood there, staring into the bathroom mirror. *Who ARE you?*

Suddenly, I couldn't stop myself. "I hate you!" I muttered out loud, unable to stop the words coming out of my own mouth. "You worthless son of a bitch, I hate you." I stood there, staring in anger at my reflection miserably looking back at me.

"Daddy, are you talking to somebody?" called a voice from outside the bathroom door.

"No Marcos, it's just me," I answered, embarrassed that he had heard me. "Everything's OK."

"Will you come play a game with us?"

"Be right there, Marcos" I called back, drying my tears and reaching for the doorknob.

"Are you OK, *papá?*" he asked as the door opened, frightened as he looked at my face.

"I don't know buddy. Let's just go play a game together."

Chapter Twenty One

The sign says welcome to Phoenix, Arizona
Population more than I can take

"Sure is great to see my fifth kid again, Mark!" Mom exclaimed from across the table at Rosita's Place, our favorite Phoenix Mexican food restaurant. "Are you gonna see all the other kids while you're up here visiting?"

"I hope so, Mom," I answered. "Already saw John and Steve, and will talk to Paul and Tom later. Hoping to catch Mary and Patty too if I can get a chance."

"Hey, speaking of Patty, it's her last day of classes," Mom said. "She's got a meeting with the school principal, and then she's done for the year. Maybe you can buzz by Saint Thomas and catch her before she leaves there for summer vacation."

Saint Thomas The Apostle. Patty had been a teacher there for several years now. People would auction off their own body parts just to get their kids wearing that STA uniform. One of the highest ranked Catholic grade schools in the state of Arizona, it had everything you'd want for your child. Quality education, limited class size, religious instruction from nuns, discipline, etc. It had everything, all right. Everything a parent like me could never afford.

"Wouldn't it be cool if Marcos and Luis could go to a school like that?" I remarked, wistfully. "If only we had something like that in Guaymas or San Carlos. Especially since Marcos is such a good student. He really loves school."

I took another bite of my chicken flauta as the waitress refilled our glasses of water.

"*Hey!* "Mom suddenly had a curiously strange look on her face "I know this sounds crazy, but I think Saint Thomas sometimes offers aid in certain situations. You know, Patty's already shared with the principal all about what happened to Adela and your kids. They talked about it right after the accident. I'll bet you could work something out where they could somehow get Marcos in there. Especially with Patty's help!"

Sounded great, but there was one slight problem with her idea. Specifically, the fact that my kids and I live in another country, known as "Mexico." That's quite a morning commute.

"Mom, we couldn't come up here even if we wanted to. It took forever to get that work permit in Mexico, and it requires me living there full time to keep it. It's the only one of its kind in the whole country for a foreigner. And I could lose it, if I left Mexico for anything more than a very short period."

"If you left there for a year, would the government there even know?" Mom asked.

Good question. Despite the existence of this crazy little thing Al Gore claimed to invent called the "internet," things were still frequently done with a typewriter over at Guaymas's *Instituto de Migración*. Would anyone there actually go on-line and track down where I was if I left for six months, or even for a year? As I pondered the unlikelihood of a lazy government bureaucrat actually doing his job, Mom continued chattering excitedly.

"Mark, Sister Patricia should still be there for another few minutes. I really think you ought to get over there and talk to her! It's worth a shot, don't you think?"

I thought about it for a second. This was crazy. Just pull Marcos out of school, quit my Mexico gigs, pack up and head north? To Phoenix? After all these years of being gone?

Most of my adult life had been spent in Mexico. It was home to me. But there was a part of me that felt the urge to leave it behind and disappear, running off somewhere I could escape ghosts of the past and take a break from the chaos I found myself immersed in. After all, I've always been a proponent of the idea that one way to solve problems is to simply outrun them.

As the waitress came by with the tab, Mom quickly glanced at her watch. "You've still got time before she leaves for the summer. Go!"

Seconds later, I threw a tip on the table and raced out the door.

****

"Daddy, why are we the only ones in our family without furniture?"

Funny, it had been days since we moved in, but until Marcos mentioned it, I hadn't really noticed. Looking around our sparse second floor apartment, I could see the kid had a point. A lamp sat on the floor, leaning against a wall in the corner. Our living room furnishings consisted of a chair. A mattress lay on each bedroom floor, duffel bags scattered about. The only thing that could pass for a decoration anywhere throughout the entire apartment was a *Mulligan's Island* refrigerator magnet. Hey, at least we had a table in the kitchen.

"And it's got four chairs," I pointed out to Marcos.

"Anyway, buddy" I continued. "It's not like we're going to be here forever. I only promised you one semester, remember?"

"Can't we stay longer Dad?" Marcos immediately shot back. "I like it here with my cousins. And Saint Thomas rocks!"

No doubt, Marcos loved his new school. Bound and determined to maximize every minute possible, he made friends, played tetherball at recess, and helped the teachers whenever they needed volunteers. Sometimes he went a bit overboard.

"Daddy, my Spanish teacher speaks really weird Spanish," he said after school one day. "The way she says stuff isn't at all how we say it in Mexico. So I'm teaching all the kids how we really say it."

"What does your teacher think about that?" I asked, a bit concerned about what her reaction to being publicly corrected by a six year old might be.

"I don't think she likes it very much," he conceded, shrugging his shoulders.

"Why do you think that, Marcos?"

"She told me she hates it!" he answered with a guilty grin.

Finally, Marcos agreed to sit there and let the teacher do her thing, without embarrassing her by pointing out her errors.

"I'll try Dad. But it's not gonna be easy!" he warned.

****

As much as I dreaded the word, we soon had developed an actual "routine." Funny, I'd never really had one since graduating from college. But little by little, it happened. We slapped a calendar on the side of the refrigerator, outlined a general schedule, and based our lives around it. There was Marcos' daily morning drop off at school, then grocery shopping, errands, or coming home to cook, clean, do laundry and take care of Luis. Later, I'd load him up in his car seat and head back to Saint Thomas to pick up Marcos after school. There was daily homework, actually quite a bit of it. When he'd finish that, we'd spend some time playing on the grass or splashing in the pool at our apartment complex. There were trips to the library once or twice a week, where the kids could read, do puzzles or play games. There were cousins to visit. There was Monday Night Football at my brother Steve's house, breakfast with my parents at The Good Egg and family get-togethers at Sweet Tomatoes or Rosita's Place. There were shows to sing and money to be made.

What happened to "Mexico Mark"? After a lifetime away from the States, I had basically become your average, everyday American again, the kind who lives a safe, structured, comfortable middle class life. Coming from a guy who once lived as the token white guy on a desolate beach surrounded by fishermen, sleeping on the floor and showering with a bucket, that's not exactly something I figured I'd experience again in my lifetime. But still, as normal of a lifestyle as it would be for anyone else to adjust back to, there were aspects of it that felt foreign to me.

There ain't no sun setting over the water
There ain't no soft warm sand beneath my feet
I heard I was doing well, they call this place big time
But can't you see, this ain't me
And this ain't the town that I remember in my dreams

When you return to "the first world" after being in Latin America for a long time, you notice a whole bunch of little things that other people seldom do. Many are good things, like how clean your neighborhood is, how wide the streets are, or the fact that lanes are actually marked and paved. Traffic signs in the United States were actually obeyed as instructions, rather than ignored as mere suggestions. Garbage was actually put into trash receptacles. Toilets flushed. Cars ran. Lights worked. People were punctual. Dogs were on leashes.

The kids were amazed at how you could actually drink water from a public fountain. To them, riding on elevators and escalators was like going to an amusement park. "Everything is so shiny here," Marcos noticed.

Then again, you also notice the things that aren't so good. Like the fact that incredible sunsets go unseen, obscured by an endless sea of buildings and phone poles. Like the fact that you easily spend half your life in a car, racing from stoplight to stoplight, waiting for some mechanically operated bulb to turn from red to green so you can get somewhere you don't even want to go, but faster. Like the fact that you don't even know the person who's lived next door for ten years, until you read his name in an obituary.

Things are different in the Land of the Free. People wear ties. They put on shoes and socks. Many work in cubicles. Their cars are painted inoffensively beige and their conversations are often boring. They talk about their 401Ks, what kind of fertilizer they put on their lawn, and who did what on their favorite reality shows.

And the kids here
They don't play outside
You walk through the neighborhood
And there's not a soul in sight

How strange, I thought. *Front yards, playgrounds and city parks are empty. Where are the kids?*

Found 'em! Inside, watching YouTube or playing video games. Seems a whole new on-line, digital era had been ushered into American culture during those fourteen years I was off living along the Sea of Cortez. Back when I left, no one I knew had a laptop, and very few had cell phones. But now, everybody from kindergartners to senior citizens were plugged-in and constantly connected, everywhere they went, in their homes and in their cars, typing on keyboards and texting each other instead of talking with one another. Connected, yet disconnected. Seems everyone was suddenly running a thousand miles a minute, constantly doing three things at once.

These people, they never slow down
You gotta drive about an hour just to get to the other side of town.
But why go there?
It all looks the same.
Strip malls and stucco walls and hamburger chains

If you actually kidnapped and blindfolded me, stuck me on the corner of any random Phoenix intersection, then removed my blindfold and asked me where I was, I couldn't tell you what part of town I was in. A convenience store on one corner, a Walgreens on another, some golden arches and a gas station on the other two... it all looked the same. One suburb may as well be another. Phoenix may as well be Tucson, which might as well be Yuma.

How strange, I thought, that of all people, it was Americans (and Westerners at that) who would embrace uniformity as Phoenix, Arizona had. Walled-in tract housing communities, where every home was required to be painted the same color and every rooftop looked the same, were the norm. Chain restaurants had completely replaced unique little independently-owned Mom and Pop joints that could no longer compete with a forty-nine cent cheeseburger. Strip malls were bland, rectangular and utterly forgettable in their architectural design, or lack of it. Although orderly, predictable, safe, and clean, there was something gnawing at my soul more and more as the days passed. Yes, it was wonderful to be near family again. But aside from that, something about life up here just didn't seem like "life" up here.

My body's here but my soul is somewhere
Beside the sea

To anyone who hadn't spent much time on Mexico's Sea of Cortez, they probably wouldn't get it. Come on, Mexico is a mess, right? It's chaotic, disorganized, and as my old friend Kyle put it, "needs to be swept and mopped." Things are frequently done in ways that make no sense. There's poverty that goes far beyond what most Americans can envision. Yes, the local cop who pulls you over for a traffic violation may ask you for twenty bucks, and yes, cartel leaders occasionally like to cut each other's heads off when they get annoyed with each other. All true.

You'll die if you go to Mexico, right? Hey, that's what the guy on CNN said.

Why in the world would I miss any of that?

****

"Bye, Marcos, have a good day at school!" I shouted over gaggles of shrieking schoolchildren as Marcos ran off toward his classroom. "Luis, wave bye bye to your brother!"

Marcos turned to wave back at his little brother one last time, then disappeared into his classroom as the bell rang. Seconds later, Sister Patricia's voice came over the school loudspeaker. It was time for prayer.

"Our Father, who art in Heaven," she began. Luis and I stood silently, waiting for Sister to finish her prayers with her trademark "Remember, today you may be the only face of Christ someone in this world sees," before walking over to the church adjacent to the school. It had become a frequent part of that morning routine. Say goodbye to Marcos, then stop by for a few minutes to pray, just the two of us. Luis loved the sound of the church bells ringing, and he'd sit there patiently drawing on the church bulletin with a crayon while I knelt.

What was I expecting? A sudden burst of faith to magically re-inspire me? Another "miracle", like Luis's sudden recovery? It had been half a year since the whole "note in my pocket" episode, but its effect had now completely given way to bitterness, resentment and cynicism. They were like an infection I couldn't rid myself of, no matter what setting I put myself into. Needless to say, that temporary spiritual high I was riding had long since faded.

All along I had thought that a semester of school in the States would not only benefit Marcos, but somehow get me into a better frame of mind. The change of scenery would do me good, I thought. I could get away from things that were messing up my head and start anew. If I got back on the right track, maybe I'd even stay, as a few family members were suggesting. But the "right track" seemed just as far away as ever. I might not be making the same mistakes and stupid decisions that I was back in Mexico, but likely that was only because I didn't have the same opportunities to. My time away wasn't bringing me any closer to God.

So maybe it was some kind of last-ditch effort, walking through that door of the church a few mornings per week, kneeling there and praying. After all, even I recognized how half-hearted the words were that were coming out of my own mouth. My prayers felt empty and meaningless, as if I were merely reciting words someone else scripted for me. But hey, I figured, saying them couldn't hurt. Maybe going through the motions like that meant I could check the box marked, "tried". And even if my own faith was basically empty and worthless, inside I knew it would be a good thing for my kids to be raised with church in their life. My folks had given me that foundation, and I at least owed the same to mine.

I glanced at my watch. "Amen. Let's go, Luis."

Chapter Twenty Two

"Great Christmas party, Beave!"

Yes, after all these years we still called my Phoenix police officer brother Steve by his childhood nickname, "Beaver." And wow, not only had he cooked a huge dinner for a houseful of guests, but also baked the desserts *and* brewed his own home-made beer for the occasion. My little brother, tough cop as he was, easily put Martha Stewart to shame.

"See Mark, Christmas *does* rock!" he answered with a high five, knowing how I've never been a big fan of the holiday season. "I only wish you and the boys were gonna hang around this town longer. Come on dude, stick around! I'll whip you up all the lemon bars and home brews you want!"

Before I could answer, Mom hugged me. "Be careful down there, Mark. If you get tired on the road, be safe and pull over to sleep in front of a police station." Mom apparently doesn't know much about "police" in Mexico, mistakenly assuming their mission to be something ridiculous like "to protect and to serve".

"And don't forget," she added before heading out the door with Dad, 'I'm praying to Adela and my old buddy Saint Anthony to find you a nice girl. A *nice* one," she emphasized. "One that will take care of all *three* of Adela's boys." Mom smiled. "And no offense against Adela, but one that isn't jealous!"

****

Five o'clock madness out on the freeway
Come Monday plays on my radio
Tonight I think I'll blow right past that exit
Aim for the distance and keep on going

"Come on Dad, can't we stay here?" Marcos pleaded as we loaded up the car. "I like my school. And I like the United States!"

"I do too Marcos," I reassured him. "Believe me, it's been great for all of us to be near family again. But it's time. I promised you one school semester. Now we've got to go home."

"*Pero, ¿por qué papá?*" Marcos begged. "Why?"

Explaining the legalities of foreign work permits to my heartbroken son was pointless. He didn't care about the career I had spent years building up, or the fact that my entire future was built around being "Mexico Mark." He didn't care that I didn't want to wind up being just another musician in just another bar, like I had been before moving to Mexico and establishing something better.

He had never spent his life longing for different things than most people do.

If only Marcos could understand.

I need a sun setting over some water
I need some warm sand beneath my feet
Gotta watch a wave breaking on the shoreline
Can't you see, that's more like me
Forget about this town
I'm headed back to the sea

****

"Welcome back to San Carlos Mark! Happy New Year!"

"Thanks Jim!" I answered, lifting one of three shots of tequila Scheidler had just poured for the trio sitting around the table. "Happy New Year to you guys too. Here's to a great 2008!"

I'm not a tequila guy, but hey, it was New Year's Eve. What more could I ask for? A good friend, a cute girl sitting by my side, tunes on the stereo, and a bottle of Don Julio.

Somewhere around 1 a.m., the bottle was empty and we were all feeling good. Jim was getting tired, but two of us weren't yet ready for the party to end.

"Hey, it's late," Scheidler said, glancing at his watch. "Three's a crowd. I'll get going. *Buenas noches...*"

****

In case you haven't figured it out in twenty-one previous chapters, let me spare you the mystery. I am an idiot. After all, having just returned from nearly six months away and the perfect opportunity to break old habits, what do I do? Pick up right where I left off.

A few folks close to me tried to gently warn me about the train wreck

I was headed for before I ever went to Phoenix, hoping that time away might clear my head.

"She just doesn't seem like a good fit for you, buddy" Jim advised me. "She doesn't seem like she knows what she wants in a relationship. As your friend, I just hate to watch it mess you up like it does."

Elsa had shared a similar opinion with me. "She's not good for you. You two just don't seem to belong together. She'd be happier with someone else, and I have no doubt *you'd* be happier with someone else too."

It was a sentiment my brother had long felt, early on when he sensed that the rushed feelings I was experiencing were somehow misplaced. Dave had actually taken it a step further than that, months before on his second visit from California after leaving San Carlos. His relationship with Elsa had gone as far as it possibly could, but they both realized he had musical dreams to chase and wouldn't be coming back. The end of whatever they had between them had come. It never even had to be said. He knew it, and she knew it.

"Mark, I love Elsa. She's by far one of the coolest girls I've ever gone out with," he shared with me. "But I'm not ever going to marry her."

"Why not, Dave?" Honestly, I was surprised that his return visit hadn't somehow rekindled their romance. "You guys really seem like you'd be great together. Come on, she's fun, she's really low maintenance, she's beautiful, she isn't jealous like basically every other woman in this messed up country, and I really do think she'd follow you wherever you go. She'd definitely support you in chasing your dreams. I just don't think you can find anyone better than that."

"Besides," I added, "she's got to be the only girl I know who actually likes the same music you do." No offense to Dave, but one listen to the haunting murder-suicide saga of "Collapsible Plans" would send most gals fleeing.

"I did have a great time with Elsa and still do. I'll always love her, and she'll always be my friend," he answered. "But there's some stuff that would keep me from ever marrying her."

"Like what, Dave?"

"Kids, for one," he continued. "Elsa would make a great mother. She'd definitely want to have a family after she gets married. Me? As much as I enjoy hanging out with the nieces and nephews, I'm not even close to a point when I even want to think about having kids, and honestly I don't think I'll be ready for something like that for a long time. Maybe never. Not with the way I want to travel and all the stuff I want to do with music."

"I get that, Dave. But, maybe that's something you guys could agree on. I mean, is that it? Is it just the kid thing?" I asked.

"If it were just that, it wouldn't be that a big of a deal," he replied. "But there are other things that you can't just cut a deal on. The biggest one for me, in our case, is religion. You know me, bro, I believe in God, but as you know, I'm not Catholic. Elsa goes to church and religion is important to her. Believe me, I don't want to change that about her. But I also don't want to change who I am. Sure, she says it's not a deal-breaker, and religion might not be when you're just dating. But like it or not, it's a huge factor when you actually get married, especially if you want to one day have kids. There's no way of getting around it. Christianity is a big part of her life, and I admire her for that, but I'm just not on the same page as her on stuff that I think will matter to her when she spends her life with someone."

So much for my legal career. It was tough to argue with him on that one. Case closed. Seems they really weren't meant to be together, not as anything more than good friends. We grabbed a couple more beers out of the refrigerator and talked for a long time about how he had come to realize that.

"It's funny," Dave finally remarked. "Sometimes when all three of us are sitting around and religion or God comes up, you guys are able to just take off on your own and talk to each other about stuff in a way that her and I just can't. I guess it's just because you guys are on the same page on so many more things than she and I ever have been. It's like you guys understand each other in a way that she and I don't."

He took a swig and paused for a moment. Suddenly, it hit Dave out of the blue. *Oh my God,* he thought. For the first time, he realized something he had never recognized before. He looked across the table at his older brother, who sat there oblivious to the "aha" moment unfolding right in front of his eyes.

"You two," Dave exclaimed. "You two would actually make a great couple!"

Chapter Twenty Three

"It's over."

"How are you doing with that, buddy?" Jim asked, doing his best to conceal his joy at what he was hearing.

"I'm bummed," I answered sadly. "I cared about her. I don't know, Scheidler, I guess I actually thought one day I might have a complete family again. Maybe even, crazy as it sounds, a mother for my kids. And happiness for me."

The good news is, she hadn't wasted much time in dumping my sorry ass. While just a month earlier she had sounded excited on the other end of the line, hearing I'd soon be returning from living in Phoenix, apparently I didn't pick up on the nervousness in her voice or I'm simply a heck of a lot more attractive over the phone. Or maybe that other guy had something to do with it.

"Sorry things didn't turn out like you wanted," Jim responded, cracking me open a beer. "But truth is, even if you don't see it now, this is for the best. If it was never going to work out, hey, better to find out now. Just do yourself a favor and stick to your guns, OK? Resist the temptation to go back again, even if you get lonely."

I took a sip and nodded, finally realizing he and everybody else had been right all along.

"And hey, if you think your life sucks, just look at mine and you'll feel better!" he added, chuckling.

Jim was right. No, not about his life sucking, but about this being for the best. All along, starting not even six months after Adela's death, I had been forcing things that should have never happened. Why had I been so weak? So selfish and blind? So afraid of being alone? So disrespectful of Adela's memory?

Couldn't I raise two boys on my own? It's not like I'd be the first father in the world who had to do that. Adela would have been able to do it, had the tables been turned. Couldn't I?

If the past year was any indicator, apparently not. How had this happened? Or better yet, how had I let it happen? Things had to change. It was time.

****

"Park Place for Vermont? No way Bomberg!"

"He's right, quit trying to screw the kid over," Scheidler interjected. "Give him the railroads too."

"All of them?" Bomberg asked, clutching the four deeds in his hand.

"All of them!" Scheidler insisted.

"*Ay ay ay,*" Bomberg sighed, handing over Reading, B&O, Short Line and Pennsylvania Railroads to a grinning second grader. Marcos counted, just to make sure he had been given all four properties.

"Nice doing business with you Jim Bomberg!" he exclaimed proudly.

Welcome to another wild night at Lot 30, Sector Crestón in San Carlos. Home to not only countless, hard-fought battles of *Monopoly*, but also games of *Clue, Life*, checkers, *Battleship*… you name it, we played it, night after night. Even little Luis got in on the action, routinely kicking our butts in his favorite game, *Candy Land*. Like his preferred card game, *War*, it wasn't exactly the world's most strategic game, but hey, somehow the kid had it nailed.

"OK guys, time to eat!" I announced from the kitchen.

"Are we having chicken with sauce?" Marcos asked. For some reason, ever since he was old enough to speak, Marcos had described his favorite food as "chicken with sauce." It didn't matter what kind of sauce. Just "sauce".

"Barbecue, buddy" I replied, pulling aluminum foil off a hot tray. "And barbecue means barbecue *sauce!*"

"*Yay!*" Marcos shouted, as he and Luis raced to the dining room table.

"Marcos, before you start eating, it's your turn to say grace, buddy."

Luis folded his hands as Marcos thanked God for the food on our plates and the roof over our heads. Scheidler, who wasn't religious, patiently waited until Bomberg, the kids and I were done saying grace before digging in.

It was a common scene. Maybe "the Jims", as we called them, were there as some kind of extended "intervention," a planned strategy to keep me from turning into a bitter alcoholic whose rash foolishness might lead him down yet another wrong path. Or, perhaps those two fellows really *did* enjoy being there with us, sharing in all the chaos and noise that defined life in the Mulligan household. Or maybe it was just cheaper than hanging out in a bar night after night.

Bomberg himself was a widower, having lost his beloved wife Karen before he ever moved to San Carlos. He too had been through some serious ups and downs in the aftermath of her death, but for the most part, the old guy was hanging on, serving as a Eucharistic Minister at San Carlos Borromeo Catholic Church and helping me sell my CDs at my gigs. Doing the latter was an opportunity for Jim to get a little attention in what might otherwise be a lonely life.

And he milked it for all he could.

"Ladies and gentlemen, may I present to you the sexy Jim Bomberg!" I'd call out from the microphone. "Guys, difficult as it may be, please restrain your wives from rushing the stage. Jim, give 'em a twirl and show 'em the merchandise!" Jim would jump on stage, turn his back and bust into a little dance, his butt wiggling as the crowd would hoot and holler.

Occasionally 'ol Bomberg even got a dance out of the deal. OK, it never led anywhere, but there were several times Jim almost had a heart attack while slow-dancing with a well-endowed female. Being my "merch guy" had its perks!

And who cares if it never went anywhere? We all knew Bomberg was hopelessly in love with his housekeeper, practically drooling all over himself as he uttered her name. Poor Jim would actually clean his house before she arrived, just to impress her. He did such a good job, I actually thought of hiring Bomberg as *my* maid.

And even though he not-so secretly fantasized about his housekeeper becoming the future Mrs. Bomberg, it hadn't stopped him from shamelessly flirting non-stop with Adela years before. She thought it was adorable when he'd show up each morning, knocking on our door with a handful of fresh fruit or vegetables for her. Unlike Adela, I didn't think it was quite so cute.

"I see right through you, you dirty old SOB," I warned him.

"Me?" a flustered Bomberg would reply.

"Leave him alone. It's cute!" Adela would admonish me, Bomberg flashing a sly grin. Within seconds he'd be in my kitchen, eating whatever she had prepared for me that day.

The merciless onslaught of flirtation continued all the way through that last road trip we ever took to Alamos. On the way home, Adela had insisted we pull over in Ciudad Obregón at a Chinese food restaurant. Jim was exhausted.

"Can't we just go home?" he moaned as the waitress approached us with menus. "It's late and we've been gone all day. I'm wiped out!"

Bomberg was as much fun as a tax audit when he'd get cranky. I knew it, and apparently Adela did too. She got up from her side of the table, walked over to Jim, put her face inches from his, leaned forward and gave him a peck on the lips. Bomberg was so flustered he almost fell off his chair. Red-faced and speechless, he sat there stunned momentarily, before his lips slowly curled into a grin. Quietly, he just sat there, beaming. He never complained again the rest of the night.

As for Scheidler, we had met up the coast, years before he ever came to San Carlos to take a job as a teacher at Marcos' grade school, Colegio Americano. It was back in 1999, when Adela and I were first married and living in Rocky Point, that he first sauntered into the bar I was singing at, Margaritavilla (note the "a" at the end of the name), and caught my act for the first time. Talk about a dive. Margaritavilla was the original town prison, later converted to becoming a brothel called The Crystal Palace, then finally renovated and converted to a seafood and Thai restaurant.

With the kind of ambience that only a former prison can provide, you can guess what kind of clientele we usually served, especially since the bar offered free tequila from both 11-12 a.m. and p.m., with no purchase necessary and no limit on the amount of shots one could consume. I've actually seen people get served while crawling to the bar.

Scheidler appeared to be different from the normal crowd of, how can I put this delicately... drunks. Somewhat well-dressed, groomed and shockingly sober, he was sitting with the owners of Margaritavilla, Rick and Barbie, well after the bar closed one night.

"So how long have you lived here?" he asked immediately after shaking hands and introducing ourselves.

"Oh, less than a year," I casually answered.

"And how many nights per week do you sing?"

"Just Thursday through Sunday, but I get up to the States too," I replied.

The questions continued, one after another, each getting more specific. "So how much do you make on your average gig?"

Hmm. That was somewhat of a personal question. My Dad taught me that you should never ask people about their income. That it was a private, personal matter. Future presidential spokesman Jay Carney would have been proud of how "less than candid" I was in my reply.

But Scheidler continued. "Do you pay U.S. taxes on what you make down here?"

I was starting to get uncomfortable. Who was this guy?

"So how much of that income do you *actually* report to the U.S. government?" he persisted.

That was it. I had figured out why this dude was here.

"I'll be right back," I interrupted, before he could continue his interrogation. "I have to go to the bathroom." Getting up from my bar stool, I brushed against Barbie and leaned close to her as I turned to walk away.

"Don't tell this bastard anything," I whispered into her ear. "He's with the IRS!"

****

"This is good chicken, Dad. I like the sauce!"

"Thanks Marcos!" I answered, somewhat proud of the fact I could now whip up something other than a bag of Cheetos for my kids. Until now, like any other heterosexual male on the planet, I could grill burgers, chicken, or fish, but beyond that, there wasn't a lot I could do exceptionally well in a kitchen. There was no reason to when Adela ran the show. Maybe she had learned it from Doña Telma while growing up, but just her cooking alone would have led me to propose marriage even if the rest of her hadn't.

Even the Jims were getting in on this cooking thing. We didn't expect too much out of Bomberg, since he had basically had his butt wiped by his wife throughout their entire marriage and never once had to cook for himself. I wasn't sure he knew how to brush his own teeth. But hey, at least he'd proudly show up with a bag of frozen corn. I'd mix it up with some red bell peppers, *chile serranos*, cilantro and cumin and we suddenly had a side dish that Rachel Ray would have been proud of.

Scheidler had been on his own long enough to fend for himself in a kitchen, and he'd crank out some really good stuff too. If that little waitress he liked over at Marina Cantina had tried his cooking, she just might have given the boy a shot. Unfortunately for him, she hadn't. So here he was, stuck with a grumpy old man, a widower, a seven year old smart aleck Monopoly addict and a three year old with limited English skills who'd freak out like Rain Man if the tag inside his T-shirt rubbed against his neck.

But all in all, looking around the table as the kids ate their last bites of dinner, it was a pretty nice thing we finally had going on. Maybe this "stability" thing wasn't all that bad, after all. Months into it, I was actually enjoying it, crock pot and all. And little by little, I felt like I was slowly getting a handle on this single dad thing.

Could it really be that long since I had stumbled out of a bar, screamed at Jesus or done something horrendously stupid? I wondered if my long gone brother Dave would be proud, or at least less terrified.

Even Elsa realized that things were turning around. "You look good!" she said, stopping by the house one day to say hello. "And the boys look happy."

"You do too, Elsa! How have you been?"

"Really good. You know, to be honest, I was sad for a while when your brother left. But it was the right thing for him to do," she answered. "I'm really happy for him. And I wish him the best with his music."

Elsa Maria Osuna Leyva. It had been nearly three years since we first became friends, back when she was working at MarinaTerra Hotel as an event planner. With Dave gone, me occupied with the kids, and her busy as ever at work, we didn't see each other as often as we used to. But she'd still drop by every couple weeks to have a beer with me and catch up. It was always good to see her. Seems she always had a smile on her face and some funny story to tell.

She'd be pretty embarrassed, though, if she knew what my brother Dave had told me that time he visited. And that's not all. Turns out it wasn't only Dave who thought Elsa and I would make a good couple. Unbeknownst to me, my brother John had reached that same conclusion, right after meeting Elsa at one of my events, way back when she first started dating Dave.

And just to make the story even more interesting, my Mom had also reached the same conclusion. *What's Elsa doing with David?* she wondered, as she and Dad joined him, Elsa and me for dinner on a trip they took to San Carlos. "She'd make a much better fit for Mark!"

Mom's are wise, aren't they?

Chapter Twenty Four

Turns out that business about Elsa and me potentially making a great couple wouldn't have mattered anyway. Out of the blue one March day, she showed up at my house, like many times before. "I've got something to tell you," she said, closing the kitchen door behind her.

The pause after open-ended statements like "I've got something to tell you" can be terrifying for the average guy, since they're often followed by anything from "you're fired" to "I'm pregnant." Although neither of those applied to the particular situation at hand, I was still somewhat concerned.

"What is it?"

"Remember that job application I asked you to sign last month?" she asked. "The one where I listed taking care of your kids as actual 'job experience?'"

"Ah, yes, the one where you asked me to lie for you," I answered with a chuckle. "I mean, bend the truth."

"Oh, whatever!" She rolled her eyes. "Well, guess what? I got the job!"

I couldn't believe it. "Wow, congratulations, Elsa! That's great!" I hugged her as she elaborated excitedly on the news.

"Well, it's not really a job. I got accepted as part of the *Au Pair* program. I'm going to be a nanny for a family, taking care of their two little kids. In New Jersey!"

New Jersey?

"Summit, New Jersey!" she continued. "It's a year-long program, but after that you can apply to extend it for another year, really easily!"

Wow! For at least a year, and likely two, Elsa would be leaving. But, as she proudly filled me in about her wonderful new opportunity, in the back of my mind I began to suspect something. She'd never come back.

There's a reason buses heading north toward the border are jam packed, while returning southbound ones are empty. As fast-paced and hectic as American life may be, its temptation of money, possessions and comfort are tough for most to resist, especially newcomers who have never experienced it. Like Marcos said, "everything in the United States is shiny." One outing to an American shopping mall usually seals the deal. Heck, even a trip to an American public bathroom, where you can actually flush paper down the toilet rather than put it in a trash can, does the trick for most.

My friend Elsa was really leaving. I remembered the day I met her, when she first got her job at MarinaTerra Hotel, working as an assistant to the event coordinator I was working with. How within minutes of talking with her, we were laughing like old friends.

I thought of that time when her boss inadvertently booked a noisy, chaotic childrens' party in the exact same pool area that 2005's IslandFest concert was scheduled to be held. How when the event coordinator realized her mistake and disappeared, leaving me completely on my own to deal with a hundred fifty potentially angry guests and a nightmarish situation, it was Elsa who came to the rescue, taking care of the situation even though she was "off the clock" by then. How she stayed there all the way through our concert just to make sure no more problems would arise, even helping to break down tables and fold up chairs when the event was over, all with a smile on her face.

I remembered all the times, sitting in her office, when we'd talk for what seemed like hours. How she didn't somehow get fired is a true testament to liberal Mexican labor laws and why the country's GNP is so shockingly low.

I recalled Valentine's Day, when she realized that I wouldn't be getting a gift from anyone, how she took time away planning a romantic date with Dave just to bring me something special: a giant, hand-made, decorated pyramid of ready-to-drink Tecate beers. To hell with Hallmark. No offense to Adela or any other girl I had ever loved from kindergarten on, but that was the best Valentine's Day gift I ever got. Heck, she even helped me drink 'em!

And now, she was leaving.

A month later, there was a knock on my door. There, outside, stood Elsa. "I just came by to say goodbye, Mark. My bags are packed, tomorrow I'm gone!"

I guess part of me thought she would have gone on-line at some point, googled "New Jersey," and immediately withdrawn from the program. New Jersey has that effect. But apparently she was busy googling other things. So one last time I'd say it.

"Come on in, Elsa!"

It turned out to be a much longer goodbye than expected. We talked and talked, seemingly about anything and everything, from the day I met her to the day she found out about Adela's death. About how I introduced her to David when he came down to help me out. About how I told him, "date anyone you meet down here, but if you take Elsa out, treat her right." About stupid mistakes we had each made over the past couple years. About the day my brother came back down from the States and told her his roads would be taking him elsewhere in life. About how even though both of us unexpectedly ended up alone, we were doing OK.

And then I told her something else. I hadn't expected to, ever. It's not even like we had been drinking leftovers from her Valentine's Day gift and I could blame my bringing up the topic on one too many beers. Somehow, innocently, it just came up.

"Funny as it sounds, there are people who think you and I would have made a much better couple than you and Dave."

Apparently not satisfied to leave a stunned Elsa with that bombshell, I dropped another whammy.

"Including Dave!"

I have no recollection of the rest of the conversation. Only the kiss that soon followed.

Chapter Twenty Five

"It's official, Scheidler! Brent Burns is coming down for IslandFest!"

Wasn't it only yesterday little Marcos was electrifying an Island Fest crowd with his dance moves? Here we were, already planning 2008's event.

"That's great news, man! It'll definitely sell some tickets! And that's the whole reason you invest in bringing these guys right? Speaking of which, are the other guys confirmed?" Jim asked.

"Rob Mehl and Kelly McGuire are definitely on board. Both have already committed and I'm already advertising them," I replied. "Rob's done a great job before, and Kelly's such a big name draw that certain people are coming just to see him! I just wish Seiler could make it. But with him getting married this year, he's got a lot on his plate."

Gary Seiler. I was gonna miss having that boy down to join us. It'd be our first IslandFest ever without him.

It had been nine years or so since we first met, at Juanito's Cantina in Baja California. Gary had built himself quite a reputation in the town of San Felipe, often coming down from San Diego to play Baja events while I sang my songs on the other side of the Sea of Cortez. With seventy five miles of Sea of Cortez waters between us, we had never met, until one night a group of us made the trip from Rocky Point around the gulf. My friend John Hibbert, who Juanito's Cantina was named after back when he previously ran it, had helped to line the whole deal up. Finally, I would finally meet this character I had heard about and join him onstage for the night.

I had heard Gary was one crazy dude. I mean, how does a guitar player get his hand caught in a *ceiling fan* while performing?

Gary didn't disappoint me or the big crowd that showed up that night. His show was just as I had heard it would be: Lively, energetic, hilarious, and downright exhausting to be a part of. Gary was a fireball, without a doubt. Just keeping up with him on stage wore me out, the Coronas going down like water as we cranked out Buffett tunes and beach songs in that raucous Baja bar.

Yes, he was every bit the partying wild man I had anticipated he would be. But by the time I loaded up my guitar and headed back to Rocky Point, I had noticed something in Gary. Underneath that façade of beer and tequila-induced craziness was a really good, solid guy. One that quickly would form a relationship with me that went beyond friendship.

It happened before we even knew it. We became brothers.

It was a brotherhood and friendship I wouldn't change for the world, even if like all siblings there were moments we wanted to duke it out in the backyard. Guess when you put two lead singers together that's bound to happen. Ever hear of Sammy Hagar and David Lee Roth? Or Don Henley and Glenn Frey? You get the picture. But through ups and downs, Gary always knew he could rely on me no matter what, just as I knew I could count on him for anything when the chips were down.

Like one July day in 2006.

****

"What do you want me to say to these people, Mark?" His voice trembled nervously on the other end of the line. "Everybody up here in Seattle wants to know the details about what happened. They're asking me all kinds of things about Adela and the accident. Honestly, I don't know what to say."

I felt bad for Gary. It wasn't supposed to be like this. After all, I was supposed to be there alongside him that night, singing our songs, having fun, and sharing "just one drink" after the show as we traditionally did. Instead, there he was, overwhelmed by a crowd of shocked onlookers who just one week before had gotten the tragic news. News Gary himself had received from a phone booth in Houston, in a distraught, barely intelligible message left on his answering machine.

Luckily, my friend Eric Stone was up in the area on his own Pacific Northwest tour. Having heard about the accident, he stepped in as a friend to cover me, offering to help Gary out with the show. It wasn't the likeliest fit, given Eric's wild reputation and the fact that Gary had mellowed considerably over the years. In fact, Seiler was on a path to getting baptized and would soon settle down for good, having gotten engaged to his soul mate, a wonderful Christian woman named Audrey. If not for her, Gary would probably still be stuck in some Mexican bar with a broken finger jammed in a ceiling fan.

For now, though, Gary had to figure out what to do, and quickly. It was almost time for the show to start, with a hundred twenty people there that night, each pulling him aside and asking him to retell the same emotional story again and again, it was overwhelming. Having been fond of Adela himself, it was especially difficult.

"I feel like I need to address this to the whole crowd at once, Mark," he said. "I need to handle it when the show starts, right off the bat. Talk, pray, I don't even know, I'm just gonna wing it. But I've *got* to address this. Is that okay with you buddy? And is there anything you want me to share with them?"

"Gary," I responded, "Just let them know how much I appreciate their support and their prayers. Especially from those who haven't prayed for a long time. It really means a lot to me that they'd do that for Adela and my family."

"You got it my brother," Gary answered. "And Mark, remember, God loves you! Don't give up, okay?"

As I hung up the phone in San Carlos and went back to attending to Marcos and Luis, Gary summoned up all the strength he could and approached the microphone. "Could I have your attention everybody, before we start the show?"

The next day my phone rang. It was Gary.

"Mark, it was incredible, absolutely awesome!" he told me excitedly. "I didn't even know what I was going to say when I started talking, but somehow it felt like God gave me the words. It was like the Holy Spirit was shaking my soul!"

"And the crowd was *amazing*," he continued. "You could have heard a pin drop. The whole thing gave me goosebumps. Wow!"

"Gary, I'm proud of you bud," I assured him, grateful for all he had done. "Proud of everything you've become. Man, I want to be more like you."

"Bro, before you get *too* proud of me, I gotta be honest," Gary interrupted. "This is Seattle, not the Midwest. Up here, folks probably think I'm insane for even mentioning the word 'Jesus.' Yeah, it looked to me like they all prayed along, but for all I know not a word of it really sunk in with anyone in the crowd."

Before I could answer, our conversation was interrupted by the sound of a call waiting signal.

"Give me a second, Gary, let me see who this is," I said, clicking the receiver button to see who was on the other line. "Hello?"

"Mark!" The voice had a distinct, southern accent. "Mark, this is Eric Stone."

"Eric!" I exclaimed. "Hey bud, thanks *so* much for doing that show last night. Gary told me it was great, and how you donated the proceeds. So cool of you, amigo."

"You got it, man. I'm so sorry about all that happened," he replied. "Listen, I just called to tell you something, really quickly."

"What, Eric?"

"That buddy of yours, Seiler…" He paused, unaware that Gary was on call waiting.

"Yeah?"

"Man, he said some stuff last night that touched my soul," Eric exclaimed.

Hold on a second. Was this the non-stop, hard-drinking, life of the party, wild man Eric Stone talking to me, or some crank caller? "Hold on a second, Eric!" I quickly interrupted, clicking back to Gary.

"You're not gonna believe this, bud," I said. "Let me call you right back!" Gary hung up and Eric came back on the line.

"Anyway, that prayer he said, and the stuff he said about God, I swear it was incredible." Eric continued. "You know, I've always had a connection with God, the Holy Spirit, the Almighty, but I guess I just got turned off by organized religion, especially with hypocrites and thieves who prey on God-fearing people and take their money. Listening to Gary talk from the heart, and everything he said, really meant a lot to me. It was truly awesome."

Ended up being the coolest conversation Eric and I ever had.

****

Little did I know that while Gary, Eric and I were talking, friends and fans in Arizona, California, Idaho and as far away as Florida were already at work organizing fundraisers for my family. Parrothead Clubs from all over the country had sprung into action after hearing the news of Adela's death on Radio Margaritaville, sending financial donations, emails and heartfelt letters. Artists like Gary and Eric, Jim Morris, Brent Burns, Sunny Jim, KD Moore and countless others were jumping in to lend a hand however they could. Even my producer Kenny Royster got in on the action, quietly mixing and mastering *A Bar Down in Mexico* for free so I could get the album out once the dust had settled.

Yep, it's a pretty good bunch, these folks I sing for and play with. Sure, my "trop-rocker" friends I join onstage aren't knocking any pubescent pop stars or angry hip-hoppers off the Billboard charts. They're not dodging paparazzi or gracing the covers of Rolling Stone. They're not doing lines of coke and trashing hotel rooms after their shows. In fact most of the motel rooms they can afford to stay in have unfortunately already been trashed by someone else.

And no, our so-called "fans" aren't obsessed with image nor awash in the latest fashion trends. In fact, most of them think nothing about showing up to a show in a bright orange tropical shirt with palm trees and parrots splattered all over the fabric. Besides, if they were truly worried about what people thought of them, they probably wouldn't be hanging out at our gigs. For that matter, neither would the guys on stage! But in the "trop-rock" world, there's a mutual love, friendship and respect you won't often find in other genres anymore. Not even country.

When it comes down to it, us guys with guitars in our hands and microphones in front of our faces really don't look at folks in the front row as "fans" anyway. They are friends. If that wasn't certain before, July 2006 proved it beyond a shadow of a doubt.

Who could ask for anything more
Than when you're singing for my kind of people

Chapter Twenty Six

"OK guys!" Kenny called out, quieting the chatter in the studio as Pat McGrath handed the band copies of their song charts. "We've got one more to go on this project. Let's take a listen to what Mark's got and nail this thing!" he said confidently, forwarding my advance-prepared demo CD to the last track and hitting the "play" button.

"Hey Pat," I whispered quietly as the guitar intro of the acoustically performed demo intro filled the room. "I'm not sure if I can pull off singing even the scratch vocal on this one more than once. I haven't sung it since I wrote it. You'll see why when the lyrics play."

He looked at the title scrawled on the top of his chord sheet, "When Adela Smiled."

"Don't worry," he reassured me, "We'll get this one down right off the bat."

As my demo vocal track rang through the monitors and the band members silently scribbled notes, I sat back and closed my eyes. Just one more song to go. Saved for last, the most important song of the whole CD. An album that two years earlier, I never dreamed I'd be recording. For a long time, I hadn't planned to jump behind a microphone in Kenny Royster's studio ever again. Or anywhere else, for that matter. In the midst of the chaos I suddenly called my life, I went a full year and nine months without writing a single note or lyric.

Until it hit me.

****

"This album is driving you crazy, isn't it?" my friend Nikki laughed, watching as her boys Kody and Cooper splashed in the pool with Marcos and Luis.

"Nikki, I have no idea how I'm gonna get all these songs done in the next three weeks!" I replied, putting my pen down momentarily. "Sorry to be doing all this writing while you and your husband are down here with us on vacation, but I'm running out of time. This whole thing was all so last minute."

"Mark, you just do your thing," Nikki said cheerfully. "If you want to go inside and write by yourself, Rodd and I are fine watching the boys and hanging out with your brother and his wife."

Frankly, I think she secretly preferred to watch me agonize in public. Nikki Landon was always known for having an evil sense of humor. No doubt she enjoyed watching me as I'd scribble madly away in my notebook, only to rip the page out in frustration, crumple it up and start over again.

"How's that song coming?" she'd ask with a big grin. Luckily Nikki was pretty. Otherwise, she'd have far fewer friends.

Even when I wasn't sitting by the pool with a pen and paper in my hand, I was likely a pathetic sight that entire trip, periodically jumping out of the water with a blank look on my face or simply abandoning Rodd, Nikki, Steve and Yvette at mid-conversation to race inside with some fresh lyric that had just come to mind. No, it's not exactly how the Nashville song factory cranks out hit songs. And it certainly wasn't how I spent most vacations at my family's condo in Kino Bay, just up the coast from San Carlos.

But that's how it goes when, for some crazy reason, you pick up a phone and reserve a flight to Nashville, telling your producer to book a band and reserve the studio for an entire week before you ever have a single song written.

"What's the name of the project?" Kenny had asked me that day, two and a half months before.

"South of the Border Again," I answered, officially adopting the only song I had even begun to come up with verses to as my soon-to-be title track.

Minutes later, it was a done deal. Flight reserved. Studio time booked. Band hired. Only one thing left to do. Write ten songs.

Sitting poolside in Kino Bay on a hot June day, three were now finished. Another three were halfway completed, and three more were basically "iffy" ideas that would need to be rewritten again and again, if they were ever going to come together at all. That left one that would still have to be written completely from scratch. During our week-long trip, a lot of pages would be torn out of my notebook and thrown into the trash as I scrambled to come up with an idea.

There was a song about how some girl's imperfections made her perfect. Tossed. Another one about quitting your job and moving to the beach. Been there, done that. Tossed. There was a funny song that wasn't so funny. A cute song that wasn't so cute. A silly song that was just, well, stupid. All torn up and tossed in the trash, along with enough aluminum cans to start my own recycling plant.

Then, out of nowhere, it happened.

"Daddy, look me, look me!" Luis shouted across the pool in his trademark broken English. To his credit, approximately half the English my three year old boy had ever learned he had acquired this week alone, just from playing with Kody and Cooper. There he stood at the edge of the pool, waving his arms wildly to attract my attention.

"I going to jump! I going to jump!" he yelled.

"Hold on, Luis! Let me catch you!" I shouted back, jumping into the pool and wading toward him as quickly as I could. After all, he had just learned to swim two days before. Suddenly the dude's an Olympic diver.

Before I could get closer to him, there was a splash. He had gone in.

"Luis!" I shouted, racing to grab him.

A second later his head emerged from the water and there he was, grinning deviously as he dog-paddled towards the pool steps. Pulling himself out of the pool, he jumped up and down happily.

"I do it again, Daddy. I make cannonball like Marcos!"

The look of pure joy on little Luis's face said it all. Looking at him, I knew I had seen that smile before. It was Adela's.

Later that day I returned from paying a past-due electric bill in town, with lyrics of a partially written song scribbled on the green and white receipt after pulling off the road several times to write.

It's like Adela smiles at me
Every time I look into my little boys' eyes
If I had only known back then
I'd do it all again, and wouldn't think twice
When they ask "Daddy, how'd our family come to be"
I say it all began when Adela smiled at me

****

Standing there behind the microphone, I watched through the small window of my isolation booth as Kenny made a few last minute adjustments on the mixer. Finally, he turned to me and gave me a thumbs up.

"Ready?"

This was it. It was down to just us now. No band, no musicians. Just Kenny, me, and a microphone. And one last song to sing.

"Ready!" I answered, wiping the nervous sweat from my hands as Kenny cued up the pre-recorded band tracks. Before I knew it, the same guitar intro I had heard just a couple days before began to play through my headphones, only this time beautifully finger-picked by Pat and accompanied by Dennis Wage on piano.

Pat was right. He and the band had done more than get the song down right off the bat, as he had assured me they would. Instead, unlike the other nine songs we had tracked together for the project, they had nailed this one perfectly on the very first go-round, as if inspired by the meaning of every single individual lyric. What they had done on that first take days earlier was simply gorgeous, assuring me that I wouldn't have to sing the "scratch" vocal on a redo for a second time.

Of course, I'd now have to re-sing it for the actual main vocal track, but the very real emotion I wanted to convey in the song hadn't become "practiced" or watered-down by repetitious performances of it while the band was busy mastering their parts. In fact, from the moment the band finished their work after playing along to my one scratch vocal performance, I deliberately hadn't rehearsed along to their finished recording for that very reason.

Plus, there was another reality. The song was the most difficult song I've ever had to sing. So, just like I had told Pat while the band prepared to record their parts, I now only wanted to sing the actual "keeper" vocal for the song once. Unless I totally bombed, however it turned out on that first take is exactly how I would leave it.

The instrumental intro was over. It was time.

From across the market Adela smiled at me
With the prettiest grin this gringo had ever seen

Though I hadn't practiced to the band's recorded track, not even in my hotel room the night before, somehow the words flowed out of my soul with ease, wrapping themselves around the music like they hadn't on any other song the entire project. By the time I was halfway through the vocal track, I wasn't in some recording studio in Nashville. Instead, I was in some unheard of town called Guaymas in Sonora, Mexico, falling in love with the girl I would one day marry.

When Adela smiled at me
Just like that, suddenly
This boy fell in deep
Said adiós to my old ways
My wild and reckless days were history

I swear I felt my heart skip a beat
The first time Adela smiled at me

****

"Got it! That's a keeper!" Kenny exclaimed. "Let's listen to it again, but unless there are any changes you want to make…"

I was filled with relief. *The story's been told. I can actually die now,* I thought to myself, taking a deep breath as I removed the headphones. Before I knew it, I was adding the last harmony to the final line of the song, before walking out of Kenny Royster's Direct Image Recording studio and heading off into the Nashville night.

And tonight when I get down on my knees
I thank God Adela smiled at me

Chapter Twenty Seven

I've always hated roller coasters. When I was a child, they terrified me. And when I got older, not only did they still frighten the dickens out of me, but they usually left me dizzy and often sick to my stomach. Barfing after riding one of the scariest roller coasters in America, back in 2001 at Sandusky, Ohio's Cedar Point, didn't help to ease my reluctance.

The downhill runs are terrifyingly fast and unexpected curves seem to hit you out of nowhere. You have to hold on for dear life and at any given moment, it appears you might actually career off the tracks and die a horrific death, or at least puke on the unfortunate soul next to you.

But at least, unless you happen to be riding on a Mexican roller coaster operated by a *cerveza* swilling fourteen year old, you can rest assured that you're safely strapped in. No matter how fast the descent, you know that after a frightening free fall, the track will eventually even out. Then come the "ups" on the ride, which may take a while to climb, but the higher you get, the better perspective you gradually have of the entire track you're on. During that time the dizzying ride actually becomes comfortable, even peaceful for a few moments, allowing you to catch your breath, regain your composure, and enjoy the view. That is, until you hit another peak, come to a momentary near-halt, everyone screams, and you begin an even more chaotic, terrifying descent downward.

I used to be afraid of roller coasters. Now I was just plain sick and tired of riding them.

****

"What's wrong, Mark? I just don't recognize you lately. It's like every little thing that happens makes you angry. You've been like this since you got back from Nashville."

I had to admit, my sister-in-law was right. The second youngest in the Ruiz family, she had temporarily moved into our second bedroom, now that Eva had long since returned to her own home.

"What am I supposed to be so thrilled about, Katy?" I answered glumly. "My life has turned into one giant hassle."

"Don't you think you're overreacting just a bit?" she asked. "Some of this stuff is no big deal. Why are you suddenly taking everything so personally and getting upset about every little thing that comes up?"

She obviously didn't understand. Someone had to set her straight. I instantly volunteered for the job. "Katy, name me one thing that's gone right for me lately."

"Your boys are healthy," she answered. "And even though I'm helping out a bit around here, at least now you know now that you can raise them on your own. You've come a long way as a father since everything happened. That's something to be happy about."

"I should've never *had* to learn to be a single father in the first place," I began, "so it doesn't make me any happier knowing I'll be a good one for the rest of my life."

I shrugged my shoulders in frustration. "Face it, I'm screwed."

"*¿Por qué?*" Katy asked, puzzled.

"Because this is just the way it's gonna be from here on out," I shot back. "This is my life. I didn't want it to turn out this way, but there's no going back in time and changing it. I can't rewind the clock to the day before the accident. This is the way it's now gonna be. Forever."

Katy crossed her arms and listened as I began to rant.

"I had a wife. My kids had a mother. My family was complete just like everyone else's. Now look at me. I didn't even get a chance to say goodbye. What did I do to deserve being alone? Just a fraction of a second, and Adela would still be here. That bastard would have never hit her. If she had left the house just one second earlier or one second later, everything in life would be different!"

"I know you're lonely, Mark," Katy interjected. "But hey, look at me. The father of my little boy abandoned me before our baby was even born. He left me here to deal with raising him and just took off. It isn't easy for me, either. But, life goes on. There's no point in staying angry."

"Well, you should be angry," I retorted. "And so should I. I'm exhausted and sick of everything and everybody. People suck."

"No, they don't," she insisted.

"Really?" I asked. "How about the family of the guy who caused the wreck? Did they really have to put up a cross for their son right next to the one we put up for Adela on the highway? What an insult! He's the one who caused it, not her. This whole thing is his fault! There's a part of me that wants to take that cross of his, rip it out of the ground and throw it in the trash! And these worthless, so-called 'officials' who never had time to give me a straight answer about anything. They suck too!"

"What about your faith?" she persisted, undaunted by the meltdown she was witnessing. "Look, it's not like I ever claimed to have the strongest of faiths, but I at least admired you for yours. Now look at you. When things get the least bit difficult, you stop believing in God."

"Oh, I believe in God all right!" I snapped. "I just don't believe He likes me, OK? And come to think of it, I'm not exactly His biggest fan either."

"Mark, how can you say something like that? Don't you care at all what God thinks?"

"Why should I be afraid, Katy?" I asked. "If God's all-knowing, then He knows how I feel without me even saying it. He already knows it. I don't like Him. And He obviously doesn't like me!"

Katy just stood there, listening as I wallowed in depression and anger.

"God lets murderers and thieves live forever, but He lets Adela die when she barely even got a chance to live? What about her kids? What about me?" I continued bitterly. "Come on, He doesn't even give us a chance to say goodbye? I'm tired of this "angel looking out for us" crap. Look, I don't know what His plan is, and honestly I don't care anymore. Whatever it is, it's just plain stupid, this whole bit about having to send His son down to die on a cross. Really, is this ridiculous soap opera the best script God was able to write when He created this universe? Believe me, I've got a much better one. In mine, nobody invents some fallen angel who screws things up for everyone else. In mine, innocent people don't suffer and die. In mine, if I'm lonely and just want 'my children' to hang out with me in Heaven, I snap my fingers and put 'em there. Easy! I don't even a create a place called 'earth', just Heaven!"

Katy rolled her eyes. "You're being ridiculous. Nobody knows why God's plan is what it is except for him."

"Yeah?" I replied. "Well no offense, but I'm starting to think God just might turn out be a Mexican woman. 'Hmm, let's see. Today I'll invent a huge problem and then force you to solve it in order to prove you truly love me! Get on your knees! Worship me! Tell me you adore me!' Sorry, but I'm tired of that routine. I'm through getting on my knees! I'm done running around saying 'I adore you, I adore you!' I'm through!"

****

"You've gotta be kidding me!"

"*¿Qué pasó?*" Katy called out from the kitchen.

"After all the work I've put in on IslandFest, all of a sudden one of the main guys is bailing on me!" I exclaimed, staring at my laptop screen and reading the e-mail message as I spoke. "Just like that! He says he got an offer from another gig he can't afford to pass up. Whatever!"

"Who are you talking about?" Katy asked, now looking over my shoulder at an email written in English she couldn't decipher.

"Kelly McGuire," I answered, exasperated. "He couldn't have told me *before* I sold the tickets? *Before* I got all these folks in the States to reserve flights? *Before* I paid for the ads and sank my money and efforts into this? Doesn't my time mean one damn thing to any of these guys? Now what am I supposed to do? Part of the reason these people are coming is to see him! He's one of the main acts!"

"I don't know," Katy said, pausing before offering a suggestion. "Is it too late to hire a replacement?"

"This late in the game? It's doubtful!" I muttered, slamming my laptop closed. "Even if I do find someone, I shouldn't have to deal with these constant headaches. I swear, it's just one thing after another! Now I get to spend the next few days fixing this. That's the last thing I have the time for!"

You'd think my house had just burned down and I lost all my possessions. Or that I had been diagnosed with cancer. Or that Jimmy Carter had just been reelected president.

"I'm seriously getting tired of people having zero respect for what I do," I sighed in frustration. "I swear, I'm always the guy getting the shaft."

"It'll be fine, Mark" Katy reassured me. "Everything will be OK." Apparently she was unaware of how sick I was of people telling me everything was "going to be OK." I'd been hearing that tired line for the past two years. Besides, nothing is more annoying than somebody who has no clue what you're talking about, telling you "it's gonna be OK."

In case you haven't figured it out by now, that "I Be Smilin' Today," "Son of the Sunshine," "Even My Bad Days Are Good" guy can be quite the bastard.

Exhibit A. Subject line: IslandFest *Dear Kelly. Go ahead and bail on my event. I'll find someone else to replace you. But I just wanted you to know the difference between Gary Seiler and you. He let me know in advance he couldn't be here. And when he does make a commitment, he keeps it, even if someone else comes along and offers him more cash. That's the difference between you and him. He's a pro. Best of luck with your event.*

Seconds later I hit send.

And days later, when Kelly's explanation arrived to my inbox, I hit another button. Delete.

****

"Sure Mark, I'd love to come down and join you guys!"

I breathed a sigh of relief. "Thanks Bob, I really appreciate it!"

"Even if you *did* only call me because Kelly canceled on you!" he added. "But hey, that's OK, I'm happy to come off the bench. It's not like I have an ego or anything."

Would the real Bob Karwin please stand up? Man, this overly sensitive fellow I was talking to didn't sound much like the booming-voiced, brash, in-your-face former rugby player I thought I was dialing. Maybe inviting him down to Mexico wasn't the wisest thought, especially considering he'd be performing onstage alongside Brent Burns, something that would definitely require a thick skin. Come to think of it, perhaps I should have called Don Rickles. Was he still alive?

"I'm just messing with you, man!" Bob continued. "Hell yes, I can't wait!"

Cool. Just days after my biggest event of the year had been unexpectedly shaken up, things were back on course. At least I could let everyone know that yes, IslandFest would still feature three established, top-notch trop-rock singer-songwriters joining me from the States: Bob Karwin, Brent Burns, and Rob Mehl. Even without Kelly on board as advertised, it would still be an event worth traveling down to Mexico. My fears of being flooded with a wave of cancellations and a barrage of glass bottles disappeared. At least *that* problem was solved.

As if some singer bailing on some performance at some musical event was really ever the "problem" in the first place.

Chapter Twenty Eight

Landsharks 'n Lions!

Dave had always razzed me about the names of the "trop-rock" festivals I'd perform at: Laid-Back Attack, PHINS to the West, Parrot Grande, the list goes on. In our genre, festively-titled events often got their names from Jimmy Buffett songs, much like the fans who attended them.

"Hey, did you hear Twelve Volt Man got trashed at BlenderFest and hooked up with Blonde Stranger?" my brother would joke. "Little Miss Magic told me all about it!"

That kind of thing didn't happen in Americana music, Dave's adopted musical genre. While my brother had a sense of humor, others in that scene sometimes took themselves so downright seriously that it was somewhat comical. A respected artist engaging in lighthearted banter with his audiences wasn't considered cool. Smiling on stage? Forget it.

The genre was chock full of songs that would make Tony Robbins want to reach for a '45 and blow his brains out. In fact, Dave and I once pondered doing a show together, one where I would sing all positive songs about beaches and palm trees, and he'd sing only depressing ones about drug addicts and murder-suicides, and at the end of the night we'd poll the audience. If the majority were happy or felt like reaching for a frothy drink with a little umbrella in it, I won. If they were reaching for a shot of bad whiskey or a noose, he won.

Depressed as I had been for the past month you'd think I had listened to nothing but Americana icon Townes Van Zandt's songs, like the one he wrote soon after getting married, called "Waiting Around To Die." (Bet his new bride loved that cheery little number.) Needless to say, neither Dave nor Townes Van Zandt would be performing at August, 2008's festive, first ever Landsharks 'n Lions event, hosted by the Carpinteria, California Lions Club and the Santa Barbara Parrothead Club.

On the other hand, I'd be there, and so would Kelly McGuire. I hadn't spoken or written to him since firing off that nasty email, and knew with IslandFest looming around the corner soon after the California event, he'd be uncomfortable seeing me.

Good, I hope he is uncomfortable, I thought, both hands on the steering wheel as I sped up Highway 15 toward the Hermosillo airport. *Serves him right.*

As the radio signal out of Guaymas faded, I turned it off and took a deep breath, figuring I'd enjoy a rare moment of silence or two. After all, back home there still wasn't exactly a lot of peaceful "alone time" in which I could clear my mind. Not with Marcos and Luis running around, "the Jims" over night after night, and my sister-in law Katy now raising her own little boy under our roof. A three ring circus provides a more tranquil atmosphere than the interior of my residence.

So for the next fifty miles or so, I'd roll the windows down and enjoy some quiet time, by myself. Yep, me, and no one else. Except for some guy who kept looking at me from the rear view mirror.

****

There must be a million crosses that dot Highway 15 from Guaymas to Hermosillo, all marking a spot where some unfortunate traveler perished on his journey. If you've ever driven a Sonoran highway at night, you'll understand why the side of the road could easily be mistaken for a cemetery. Aside from the fact that a six year old can obtain a Mexican driver's license by merely paying the required fee, there are other factors that you don't often face in more developed countries. Imagine livestock on the highway, cars without working taillights, and eighteen wheelers with failing brakes and drivers who haven't slept in thirty-six hours. Add all that to a lack of highway shoulder lanes and you've got a recipe for frequent disaster.

Each time I passed one of those crosses was a split-second reminder of not only July 16th, 2006, but also a day that came weeks later, when I first saw another cross erected next to Adela's. One with a name inscribed on it, belonging to the very individual who caused all this misery. I thought of his family and why they would choose to erect that cross under the very same tree we had placed Adela's, instead of a hundred feet away where the accident had actually taken place. What were they doing, rubbing it in? Every time I thought of it, it angered me more.

What jerks! I thought. *At least they lost someone too.*

****

I turned the radio back on, but not yet getting decent reception from Hermosillo, I flipped it off again, turning my thoughts to my game plan once I got to the airport. My flight would take me to LAX, where I'd be picked up by my friends Tom and PJ Hankins, who were also headed to California to catch the show. Given the fact they had just returned from another year's worth of sailing adventures in the Caribbean aboard their 43' foot sloop, *Conch'd Out*, they'd surely have a lot of stories to tell. Undoubtedly, they'd want to catch up on what was happening in my life too. I only hoped they would somehow sense I was happy, and not pick up on the fact that I had somehow hit my lowest point since Adela's death, feeling emptier than ever, exhausted, lonely, and increasingly bitter at the world.

After Tom and PJ picked me up, they'd take me to Nikki and Rodd's place up in Newbury Park, California, where I'd perform at a house concert in their backyard along with Kelly and Gary Seiler before heading up the coast to Carpinteria for the Landsharks 'n Lions event. Needless to say, I wasn't looking forward to that first show at Nikki and Rodd's. How was I supposed to smile and joke around publicly with Kelly, acting like nothing happened, when he had left me hanging like he did? Friends, much less professionals, don't do that. At least, not if they give a damn about the other person. Hanging out with Kelly, especially on a stage, was really the last thing I wanted to do.

But, just as I wanted to hide my other issues from Tom and PJ, I didn't want Nikki and Rodd to feel any unnecessary stress having to deal with any of my negative feelings toward Kelly. Better to just keep that to myself. This first night before Landsharks 'n Lions was their party, after all. And besides, Rodd had already helped me out in a way he didn't even realize.

"I'm hearing a lot about you, but not a lot about anyone else," he had once told me, following some self-pitying, largely alcohol-induced monologue of mine during an earlier depression the year before. "I'm not hearing about Adela. I'm not hearing about Marcos or Luis. Just you and how you feel. And this isn't about you."

That advice angered me when I first heard it. Who the hell was Rodd Landon to give me advice about anything? Only later down the road did I realized he was right. And although it didn't whip me into shape in many other areas, at the very least it was cause for thought, leading me to finally absorb something.

I didn't die. Adela did. I didn't miss out on so many years of life to come. Adela did. I didn't lose the chance to be a parent. Adela did. I didn't leave this world far too early. Adela did.

I didn't have to learn to walk again. Marcos did. I didn't nearly die at birth only to suffer traumatic injuries in a horrible car accident. Luis did. I didn't sit strapped into a car seat in the aftermath of a terrible wreck, frightened and alone, suffering in pain. My children did.

Occasionally throughout 2008, Rodd's words would pop into my head as I worked to become a better father. Little by little, Monopoly game by Monopoly game, plate of chicken with sauce after plate of chicken with sauce, I became one. If only that would have paved the way to me dealing with other issues that continued to demonize me. Some of them were real, like the loneliness, emptiness and exhaustion I desperately wanted to hide from anyone outside the four walls I called home. Some weren't really issues at all. Like singers who cancel performances at musical events.

****

I'm having major doubts about waterspouts
Somebody tell me what to do
I'm having major doubts about waterspouts
I wish I was home with you

"I love this song!" Adela told me, tapping her fingers on the dashboard. "And look at little Marcos! He's dancing in his car seat!"

It was the fifth time in a row we had listened to it. We had no choice. Every time the song off the *Redfish Island* CD would end and the next one would begin, little Marcos would cry. There was just something about that "Major Doubts About Waterspouts" song that had the boy enthralled. Kelly McGuire certainly had a new fan, even if it was a two year old Mexican kid bobbing up and down in a car seat.

"I can't explain it, Kelly. My kid loves your song!" I said over the phone. "He won't let me play anything else. It's driving me absolutely crazy!"

"Ha ha!" Kelly laughed. "That's funny! You know, some songs are just like that with little kids."

"Well, truth is it's a great song," I replied. "In fact, there's another one on that same CD that I myself really love, "Turn Around And Run.""

"Hey, that's great," he remarked. "Glad you like that one!"

"I do!" I continued. "It reminds me of so many people I see on vacation down in Mexico. Man, they would love that song. It's them!"

I paused for a moment. "Kelly, I wanted to run an idea by you. What would you think about me recording it?"

With Kelly living in Houston and me in Mexico, we had never met in person, and wouldn't until some time later when played a house concert together in Phoenix. His first invitation to perform at an IslandFest was still a couple years away. So it's not like I had done anything for Kelly McGuire before. A polite, diplomatic "no" would have been completely understandable, especially since it wasn't like he had George Strait or Toby Keith on the other end of the line.

But by the time I hung up the phone, the deal had been sealed. Unfortunately for Kelly, it wasn't a financial bonanza that would have him retiring early.

"Don't worry about royalties," he said. "Just go ahead and record it. And hey, if I get the chance to meet your fans and sing for them someday, it'll be worth it."

As I would learn in years to come, that was just typical Kelly McGuire. Generous to a fault.

Before he had the wits to summon a lawyer or retract his previous statement, plans were in the works to include "Turn Around And Run" on my upcoming *Life in a Beach Town* album. It would turn out to be the first song Kelly ever wrote *and* the first one I ever sang to get airplay on Radio Margaritaville. And it would become a crowd favorite for years.

****

"Lord?" Peter asked. "Why can't I follow you now? I will lay down my life for You!" Jesus replied, "Will you lay down your life for Me? I assure you: A rooster will not crow until you have denied me three times." John 13:37-38

Saint Peter. I hadn't thought of that guy in a long, long time. That Bible up on my shelf had collected quite a bit of dust, sitting there among a dozen unread "self-help" books intended to instruct me about how to deal with grief, find closure and all that crap. Yeah, like I had time to read.

My earlier stated feelings about Pete hadn't changed over the years. Put me down as "not impressed." To me, he was still that disloyal, carpetbagging friend who tags along for the ride but opts out as soon as the fun stops.

To be honest, I wasn't exactly impressed with Jesus' skills as a judge of character either. Of everyone you could choose to pick as your friend, why this clown? He's the first one you choose? I know a few *panga* fishermen. And believe me, they've got some annoying flaws, like leaving gutted triggerfish carcasses, beer cans and plastic bags all over your favorite beach. They drink too much, and aren't exactly known for being rocket scientists. But at least, your average fisherman will hang with you not just when the fish are biting, but when also when the nets are empty.

But you, already having a good handle on how things are going to go down, chose to hang out with this guy?

"...You aren't one of this man's disciples too, are you?"

"I am not!" he said. John 18: 17

That's guts, Pete. OK, look, I'm the first to admit I'm no longer a big fan of your friend's father. But as for your buddy Jesus, you've got to admit he was pretty darn good to you. Not only was he loyal to you and treated you like a friend, but come on, he even showed you firsthand a bunch of really cool miracles. He didn't just let you witness them, but actually participate in them, like when he taught you how to do that freaky "walking on water" trick. And you were actually rocking on it for a few moments! That is, until you panicked, took your eyes off of Jesus, and sank.

He had you believing in him when others around you weren't quite so convinced. When most didn't believe at all.

And Jesus went on with his disciples, to the villages of Caesare'a Philip'pi; and on the way he asked his disciples, "Who do men say that I am?" And they told him, "John the Baptist; and others say, Eli'jah; and others one of the prophets." And he asked them, "But who do you say that I am?" Peter answered him, "You are the Christ." Mark 8:27-29

How Pete? How could you go from a guy walking on water and believing Jesus was truly the Messiah to such a cowardly loser?

Now Peter was standing and warming himself. They said to him, "You aren't one of His disciples too, are you?" He denied it and said "I am not!" John 18:25

Seriously, Pete. How did Jesus stand hanging out with you when he knew all along you were this weak? That you'd cut and run and bail on him? That when pressured, you'd deny even having him in your life?

One of the high priests slaves, a relative of the man whose ear Peter had cut off, said, "Didn't I see you with Him in the garden?" Peter then denied it again. Immediately a rooster crowed. John 18:26-27

****

I couldn't avoid him, no matter how I tried. Every time I glanced up, there he was. It was him, alright. That guy up there, looking back at me from the rear view mirror.

Man, he had aged since I last took a real good look at him. What on earth had happened to make him look so old? So tired? So worn out? So bitter?

Leave me alone, I thought, quickly looking away and reaching for the radio knob.

A mile later, I glanced up just to see if he had found anything better to do than watch me. He hadn't.

****

"Son of a bitch!"

Couldn't I have just listened to the radio? Now look at me, berating myself in the rear view mirror. "You worthless, worthless piece of crap! *Loser!* You should have been the one who died that day, you sorry piece of trash! Hypocrite!"

There was no denying it. I was everything I had always hated about Peter. A coward. A traitor. A loser.

I pounded the steering wheel. "You son of a bitch! You *son of a bitch!*"

Twice, I had begged from the heart for God to intervene and save me. Twice I had insisted to him that I believed in him. Twice I had witnessed, within twenty-four hours, outright miracles beyond what I could have ever asked for.

Twice I had been caught up in the passion of the moment, feeling unshakably confident of God's grace and mercy.

Twice I had gotten on with my life.

And twice, I had let myself become absorbed back into the "reality" of this world. A world where God is an afterthought, an obligatory prayer or some thick set of rules someone hands you and instructs you to observe.

Twice I had been extended an invitation. And twice I had rejected it. I had treated Jesus like my personal errand boy. Give me what I want and get on your way.

Forget Peter. At least Judas had the conscience to go hang himself. I didn't even have the guts to do that.

I could almost hear a rooster crow.

Chapter Twenty Nine

"Katy, it's me."

"Mark! Where are you?"

"I'm at the airport in Hermosillo," I answered, my voice trembling as I spoke.

"Good, you made it!" Katy replied. "When I heard your voice, I thought you might have had car trouble, or worse. Are you OK? You don't sound too good."

I took a deep breath. Like Eva, living under our roof Katy had seen a lot of things over the past few months. She had seen a "me" that others hadn't, one I wasn't exactly proud of. "I'm OK, Katy, just really bummed."

"Mark, I know you're down, but I know things are going to get better," she began.

"It's not about that," I answered. "Things *did* get better. Look at the past year, how well the boys are doing, but still, look how I've spiraled again, this past month or so worse than ever. I don't know why, but I just can't beat this thing. I've let everybody, especially you guys, down."

"You haven't let us down, Mark," she reassured me. "We love you, you know that."

"Katy, if Adela could see me right now, she'd be embarrassed. And she ought to be."

"She would be proud of you, Mark," Katy insisted. "We all make mistakes. You're a good father."

"But I'm not a good person, even if everyone thinks I am," I continued. "Adela was. She would have honored my memory more than I ever did hers. I feel so guilty about that, but it's too late to take it back. And in spite of what you say about me being a good father, she would have done a much of a better job of raising the kids than I've done. We both know that, Katy." There was silence on the other end. Guess it was pretty hard to debate that point.

"I just called to apologize, Katy. Aside from all that, I feel bad that I've shaken whatever faith you had. Whatever issues I have with God, they're my problem, and I shouldn't say things that might affect how you feel. That's not fair, and I'm sorry for that."

"Mark, God knows you have faith," she interjected.

"Actually, He knows that I don't have faith, Katy," I sighed. "I talked a big game for a lot of my life. But the nasty things I said to you before about God, I meant them. He knows it. No matter how I try, I just can't fake positive feelings for God that I don't have. I don't know, maybe it's because He's known all along the way I really am, but I just don't feel like God loves me. To be honest, I don't blame Him. But I also have to be honest and say that I can't help it, I just don't feel love for Him either."

Katy was quiet, listening to every word.

"I just *wish* I did," I added wistfully. "I really *want* to feel that way about God again. Not some up and down thing where I love Him one moment and hate Him the next, but I wish I just believed enough to love Him once and for all. I'm so tired of all this, I just don't know what to do."

"So, what now?" Katy's question just hung there, suspended in the silence of a pause that seemed to last an eternity. I hadn't anticipated having to answer any questions. "What now?"

What now? Hang up the phone, get on a plane, fake some answers to Tom and PJ, treat Kelly like crap, make some money and come home? Book some more shows and go do it again?

What now? Pour stronger drinks? Go searching for satisfaction with the first pretty face that comes along? Find something or someone to cheer me up before something else gets me angry again?

What now? Feel great when something goes my way? Then plunge into the depths of self-pity when they don't? Was this life from here on out?

What about Jesus? Hadn't I once believed in Him so strongly that I'd never have dreamed of walking away? Had I now walked so far from Him that there was no turning back? Was my relationship with Him ever going to mend? Or come to think of it, even start? What now?

Before I could think of some answer that made logical sense, like actually reading one of those self help books my friends had given me or seeing a shrink, three words unexpectedly shot out of my mouth. "I forgive Kelly."

I know. It made no sense.

"What?" Katy asked. "I'm confused here. Forgive Kelly? What does that have to do with any of this?"

Excellent question. "I don't know, Katy. But I just decided, this very second, that I forgive Kelly for whatever stupid little thing he did that ticked me off. And you know what? I'm going to tell him!"

"Um, Mark, that's all admirable, but honestly you're confusing me here," a perplexed Katy responded. "I thought you were talking about mending your relationship with God, not Kelly."

"My relationship with God is exactly what I'm talking about, Katy," I answered. By now, Katy had surely broken into my liquor cabinet and poured herself a shot of whiskey just to make sense of this conversation.

"You know what? Maybe God is just as sick of my empty, meaningless words as I am. Maybe He's tired of this roller coaster ride too. Maybe just once, He'd like to know that words like '*as we forgive those who trespass against us*' aren't meaningless like the rest of my prayers. Look, I can't go die on some cross, but maybe I can do something smaller. Like forgiving a friend, and hoping He forgives me. Hey, it's a start. And maybe a small start matters to God."

"You're crazy, Mark," Katy chuckled. "I'm happy for you, but you're crazy. Go, forgive your friend."

****

"*¿Algo para tomar, señor?*" the flight attendant asked.

"Diet Coke, *gracias*."

Before she continued down the aisle, she glanced at the book laying open on my foldout tray: The New Testament. So much for flirting with the stewardess. But hey, I'm no dummy. If my plane goes down, I want to have something more than the *Sports Illustrated Swimsuit Edition* in my hand. Besides, I had already bored myself with a Mexican newspaper at the airport, done a crossword puzzle after boarding and scribbled some song lyrics down on the back of a barf bag. What else was there to do?

It had been quite a while since cracking open anything but a beer can, much less a book. And this wasn't exactly what you'd call a "light read." So, how does one know where to start when reading from the Bible? I have a simple answer, albeit one that may not strike you as the most logically based. Open it up, and let whatever random verse that appears on the page speak to you. Yes, Katy was right, I am crazy.

Here goes, I thought, closing my eyes and opening the cover.

Then Peter came to Jesus and asked, "Lord, how many times shall I forgive my brother or sister who sins against me? Up to seven times?" Jesus answered, "I tell you, not seven times, but seventy-seven times.

"Therefore, the kingdom of heaven is like a king who wanted to settle accounts with his servants. As he began the settlement, a man who owed him ten thousand bags of gold was brought to him. Since he was not

able to pay, the master ordered that he and his wife and his children and all that he had be sold to repay the debt.

At this the servant fell on his knees before him. 'Be patient with me,' he begged, 'and I will pay back everything.' The servant's master took pity on him, canceled the debt and let him go.

"But when that servant went out, he found one of his fellow servants who owed him a hundred silver coins. He grabbed him and began to choke him. 'Pay back what you owe me!' he demanded.

"His fellow servant fell to his knees and begged him, 'Be patient with me, and I will pay it back.'"But he refused. Instead, he went off and had the man thrown into prison until he could pay the debt. When the other servants saw what had happened, they were outraged and went and told their master everything that had happened.

"Then the master called the servant in. 'You wicked servant,' he said, 'I canceled all that debt of yours because you begged me to. Shouldn't you have had mercy on your fellow servant just as I had on you?' In anger his master handed him over to the jailers to be tortured, until he should pay back all he owed.

"This is how my heavenly Father will treat each of you unless you forgive your brother or sister from your heart." Matthew 18: 21-35 NIV

****

"Hey, Marco, good to see you!" Kelly approached me, noticeably a bit nervous, before reaching out and giving me a hug.

"Hey, Kelly!" Before the conversation in Nikki and Rodd's backyard could go any further, I heard another voice from behind.

"I'd recognize those skinny legs anywhere!"

Yep, it was Gary Seiler alright. A newly married Gary Seiler. "Good to see you buddy," he said, high-fiving me before wrapping me up in a bear hug.

It was good to see Gary. It had been way too long since the two of us had hung out without guitars in our hands. And that was my fault. Truth is, after all he did in going to bat for me in Seattle, I had somehow messed up as only I can find a way to do, at a spring show in Cave Creek, Arizona. It was during one of my worst emotional lows I had experienced up until then. Hours before taking the stage with Gary and, speak of the devil, Kelly McGuire that day, I had been in tears and considering pulling out of the show at the last minute, calling my mom on my dad's borrowed cell phone from the side of the road.

"I can't do this anymore Mom. I just can't keep faking being happy on stage," I sobbed. "It's wiping me out. I give up."

Mom did her best to cheer me up, her grown son crying like a baby on the phone. But as anyone who knows my mother would expect, she ended up in tears too, talking about Adela and all that had happened. Eventually, somehow, I decided to get back on the road and go sing at the show.

It ended up being a performance I wish I could take back. I was emotionally spent even before our host asked me to perform and dedicate "It's About Time" to his wife, who was undergoing serious health issues. Completely drained, my usual on-stage chatter with Gary was strained and unfriendly. Like the audience members, Gary didn't have a clue about what had happened just hours before, and understandably took it personally. He felt like it was deliberate, especially since I had already done a pretty damn good job of phasing him and nearly every other friend I had out of my life as my personal train wreck continued.

Luckily, in studying his Bible while preparing for his baptism, Gary must have read the same parable of the unforgiving servant too. It was good to laugh, talk, clink a couple bottles together and most of all, see my old friend again.

"Kelly's pretty nervous to see you, though. I think the little diva is scared of you!" he joked. "Anyway, he knows he messed up."

If we'd only had some hot, overly-dramatic women around, we could have actually filmed a Mexican soap opera on the premises.

"No worries, Gary. My turn to forgive," I replied. "Besides, in the grand scheme of things it's all no big deal. Last time I checked, there are starving people in this world. So once I get a chance with Kelly and no one else around, we'll talk."

That moment never came. As the event began and the night progressed, we were constantly surrounded by people before, during and after the show. Everyone was going in three directions at once, until suddenly, the post-show party was over and Kelly had disappeared.

****

"We're raising funds to help build a new bar for the Lions Club?"

"Yeah," Nikki's dad Randy admitted with a sheepish grin. "Told you it was a good cause!"

Welcome to Lions Park in Carpinteria, California. So much for curing cancer, eradicating malaria in third world nations, neutering stray dogs or wiping out world poverty that day. But hey, it was still going to be a great day. The skies were blue, weather was perfect, and for a thirty-five dollar donation the crowd would certainly get their money's worth of entertainment, beginning with Gary, Kelly, and me, then topping the day off with an evening show from Jerry Gontang and San Diego band, Stars on the Water.

"Welcome everybody to our first ever "Landsharks 'n Lions" festival!" event organizer Carol Ewald announced to a cheering crowd, as Gary grabbed his guitar and stepped up to the microphone to kick things off. Within minutes, Gary had the crowd revved up and rocking, singing along to every word.

Oh I love Mexico
Siesta, cerveza
Tan girls and blond strangers
I don't wanna go back home

The beer was flowing and Randy Graham was in his element, grinning broadly as the hours passed. On stage, the three of us were having a great time, joining together to lend each other harmony, rhythm and guitar leads. It was a special day, one where I forgot all about whatever stupid little problems kept the three of us from doing this more often. Like the crowd in front of us, we were enjoying ourselves and having a blast, right up until the moment I glanced at my watch and we only had time for a couple more songs. Already? Just like that, our show was coming to an end.

So were my hopes of having that planned conversation alone with Kelly. While I'd be sticking around with Nikki, Rodd, Tom and PJ to catch Stars on the Water, Kelly usually left shows soon after he was done playing.

Oh well, I thought. *No need to talk. Everything's cool and Kelly knows it.*

Oops. Guess God didn't get that memo. No sooner had the thought of casually blowing off what I had planned to say that trip crossed my mind, when I suddenly turned to see Kelly just a few feet to my left. He was just standing there with his guitar, right in the middle of a song, looking at me. With Gary smack-dab in the middle of rocking the crowd with a guitar lead, Kelly approached me nervously.

"Hey Marco!"

OK, this is kind of an odd time for us to strike up a conversation, I thought. "Yeah?" I answered, shouting over the music.

"Hey, man, I just wanted to tell you that I apologize. I know I let you down and I feel really badly..." he began.

"Hey Kelly!" I interrupted. "I forgive you!"

There it was, just as I concisely as I had hoped to say it, and exactly as Mom would have advised me to do it. Put a period on it. No commas. Don't screw it up with an "if", "and", "but", or even an "OK, but don't let it happen again". Simply, I forgive you. Period.

Kelly just stood there for a moment, gazing at me with a bizarre look on his face. It was a look I hadn't seen from him before, except for that time he accidentally consumed five shots of Mexican moonshine. It was almost as if he were expecting a different reaction, or was waiting for me to clarify with some kind of follow up. Shoot, if anything, I was going to ask him for his forgiveness, for being a judgmental, hypocritical jerk, aside from the nasty note I had written in momentary frustration. But I didn't get the chance. Gary's guitar solo was coming to an end, and it was time for Kelly to jump back up to the microphone and sing.

"Thanks Mark!" he shouted back as he approached the mike, still sporting a somewhat shocked look on his face.

Moments after Kelly turned his back to me, I inexplicably felt a huge weight leave my body. It was one I had been carrying since long before some singer named Kelly McGuire ever canceled an appearance at some stupid event of mine in Mexico. It was a heavy burden of anger, frustration, and pure negativity, at anything and everything. Kelly never had a single thing to do with any of it. He had simply been the straw that broke the camel's back. He was merely another in a long line of folks I could blame for my own emptiness and spite.

It was a weight I had lugged around for so long that I had actually forgotten what it was like *not* to carry it. But suddenly, in an instant, I was completely rid of it, freed of a burden I hadn't even realized I was carrying. As the show ended, I was light as a helium balloon, ready to lift off the stage and into the summer sky.

I was too busy feeling good to even grasp that in letting go of that weight by "forgiving" him, I was opening my heart to forgiving someone else. Someone who actually *had* done something to hurt me. Someone who had taken all I had from me. Someone who deserved to be held responsible for all he had done, not forgiven. Someone whose name was printed on a cross, in the median of a highway leading southbound into Guaymas, Sonora Mexico. Someone who in his thoughtless, selfish recklessness killed my wife and robbed my children of their mother.

But by the time I closed my eyes and fell asleep that night, it had happened. On August 23, 2008, I forgave Víctor Torres López, the man who took Adela's life.

Chapter Thirty

I can do this, Lord.

Oblivious to the flight attendant's detailed exhibition of how to correctly master fastening a seat belt, I sat there, eyes closed.

I can do this, but I can't do it alone. I need you. I realize it now, Lord, more than ever. You gave me the strength to forgive. You've lifted a weight from me, but I need something else.

Here I am, Lord, asking you to come through for me one more time. I need you to fill me with your Holy Spirit, and do for me what I can't do on my own.

If I were God, I'd be laughing my proverbial buns off. *Wait a second. Haven't we been through this before? Aren't you that guy who begs for my help when the chips are down, and then when I pull through with whatever favor you request, you bail on me? Your so-called faith comes and goes like the tides? And you're asking me to help you out again?*

Yep, some nerve, I admit. Especially considering the fact I was calling in God's big guns, the Holy Spirit. Yes, you heard me, the Holy Spirit.

OK, let's get real here. Does anybody with half a brain really buy that Holy Spirit business? Sure, the Old Testament talks about Moses being guided by the Holy Spirit, along with other heroic characters, like King David, Joshua, Gideon and Isaiah, just to name a few. And yes, in that Old Testament we see the Holy Spirit called into action when power, courage, and strength are desperately needed. And how with the help of the Holy Spirit, average everyday human beings were capable of accomplishing things no person could otherwise do. But that's the Old Testament. Isn't that just a collection of cute stories someone made up to guide a bunch of stupid, uneducated people into behaving civilly in ancient society?

Sure, except for one pesky little fact. Old Testament, Book of Isaiah prophecies are actually fulfilled, as some dude named Jesus comes along. Before he departs this earth, he sends the power of the Holy Spirit upon his disciples, who overnight go from being a bunch of terrified cowards fearing for their lives to becoming the gutsiest, bravest, most fearless group of men you'll ever see. Men who would change the world.

As for my old buddy Peter? You guessed it, he was transformed completely by the Holy Spirit. Although historians will likely debate Jesus' resurrection until the end of time, there is no doubt about Peter's death. It's fact. We know where, why and how it happened. The same terrified guy who would deny he even knew Jesus, became a fearless warrior for the Lord, roaming the earth to proclaim his gospel even though it would eventually cost him his life.

And when that final moment came, what did Peter do? Before being filled with the Holy Spirit, he would have run. He would have tried to hide, or simply denied the whole thing. Hired a liberal lawyer and claimed insanity. Or claimed he "misspoke" in preaching the gospel. Surely he would have tried to rescue himself.

But what did he actually do? When faced with the brutal punishment of crucifixion, Peter not only willingly accepted it, but demanded that he be crucified upside down. Kind of like my son Marcos asking for an extra ten minutes when being sentenced to "time out," he showed the powers that be that he wasn't afraid of them or their punishment. He did something that previously would have been impossible for him to do without the help of the Holy Spirit. He conquered fear.

Sitting there on that plane, I wanted to be Peter.

I'm tired, Lord. Tired of this whole ride I've been on. I'm tired of walking away from you, only to come back to you, only to walk away again. Loving you, then hating you. Believing in you, then not believing in you. If I were you I'd be tired of my act, too. But please, Lord, listen to my prayer. Bear with this hypocrite just one more time.

"Seat forward, sir," said the flight attendant.

Within moments, the engines roared, and we were taking off, heading thousands of feet into the sky above Los Angeles, bound for Mexico. A place where so much had happened over the past two years. A place where I found myself hopelessly mired in past tragedy, unable to escape, always appearing to break free of my shackles only to find myself trapped inside the walls of disappointment once again.

A place where tragedy, anger, fear, doubt, loneliness, sin, and bitterness dominated my life, coming back to haunt me each time I thought I had left them far behind. There was every reason to believe, once the emotional high of yesterday's event in Carpinteria faded into the past, the same forces would recapture me again. And they would once again defeat me.

It was time to face it. No matter how I tried, I was simply unable to conquer them on my own. All this time spent spinning my wheels, trying to recover and move on from the tragic events of July, 2006... it was wasted, every bit of it. It would all lead me nowhere. The peaks might get higher, but the valleys would only get lower. The cycle would merely keep repeating itself, over and over again, with no way to escape it.

I had spent two long, exhausting years, my hands on the wheel, gripping it as hard as I possibly could as if I were somehow in control of the vehicle. Acting as if I, myself, could determine the conditions of the road or the direction it would lead. Constrained by human logic, without a clue that the only way to get to where I truly needed to go was to let go of that wheel. Throw my hands up into the air and release it, with no fear whatsoever of crashing.

At my worst, I had ignored God completely. At my best, I had treated him as "my co-pilot." It was time to switch seats.

The rooster has crowed, Lord. I've got no right to ask you to accept me again after getting what I want, then rejecting you time after time. But I ask you to somehow forgive me. I ask for your grace. After yesterday, I'm reminded of the power of forgiveness. And I believe in your mercy.

I don't want to walk from you ever again, Lord, even though you know I'll always be a sinner. I want to be your friend, your child, for life. That's why I need something different than in the past. No, I don't need miracles, you've already shown me more than I ever deserved to see. What I need, more than anything, is to simply know that I'm capable of walking with you throughout the good and the bad, and not denying you even when things get tough. I need to free myself from the past and walk with you again.

Let me be Peter. Let me have the guts to walk with you. Give me the courage to be the person you want me to be. Fill me with your Holy Spirit and give me overflowing strength. Give me the guts to live for you, even die for you if I have to.

By this point the fellow sitting next to me in the aisle seat was likely thinking of requesting a seat change. Tears fell as I silently prayed, even more intensely than on that long-ago day when I begged for light at the end of the tunnel, or when I prayed myself to sleep asking for a message from Adela.

Lord, I'm bound to repeat the same mistakes. I know me, and you know me even better! But I need to know that I'm capable of standing on firm foundation, once and for all. That's why I'm asking you for something different than I've ever asked you before. Jesus, for my own sake, I'm asking you to give me a challenge so incredibly big that I couldn't possibly handle it. Put an obstacle in front me of me that's so big, I can't get around it. Give me a mountain I can't climb. Give me every opportunity to doubt you, to hate you, and to walk from you yet again.

And then Lord, give me the strength and the wisdom to put my faith in you. To put it whatever it may be in your hands, trusting in you rather than in myself. Test me like I've never been tested. Give me all you've got, more than I can handle. And then fill me with your Holy Spirit. Give me wisdom and all the strength I need to pass that test, whatever it may be. Do this Lord, I beg you, so that no matter what, this non-stop, up and down tumultuous ride finally ends. Do this so that I know in my heart that the weight you've lifted from me and the peace I've found aren't just temporary highs, bound to fade away like every other time before, but lasting. Let me know that I stand on firm, unshakable ground with you. I need to know I can do this Lord, not just for you but for me. Give me the opportunity to show you, and more importantly, to show myself, that I am that person and not this one I don't want to be. Put me to the test. Yes, give me a challenge too big for me to face. Give me the opportunity to walk away. And the strength to believe. It's all I ask, in Jesus' name."

****

"Welcome back, Mark!"

Putting my guitar down, I hugged Katy as she excitedly asked me about the trip.

"How did it go?"

"Great!" I replied. "Really, really great!" She sat down and I filled her in on the trip.

"You look happy!" she remarked. "Hey, did you forgive that Kelly guy?"

"I did!" I answered, pouring myself a glass of water.

"Good for you! And how do you feel now?"

"Katy, I haven't felt this good in a long time," I replied, "probably since before the accident. I can't explain it, but for the first time since I can remember, I feel like me again. I had forgotten what that felt like."

Katy smiled. "See? I knew you were in there somewhere. I told you everything would be fine."

"Everything is fine, Katy," I responded. "I've had some time to think, to really think about some stuff. Even more so than when I talked to you the other day. And I feel good."

"I'm happy for you," Katy replied.

"But, before you get too excited," I quickly added, "there's something you should probably know." Katy arched her eyebrows.

"When I boarded that plane yesterday, I knew something had to change. Not just for the moment, but for good. And I prayed to God with every ounce of energy I had."

"Okay, that's good," she remarked, appearing to be a bit confused. "But prayed for what?"

I looked Katy in the eye. "For something really, really bad to happen."

"What?" she exclaimed. "What on earth are you talking about?"

"Katy," I sighed. "I can't do this anymore. I can't continue the routine of believing in God when things go my way and then abandoning him when they don't. It's been over two years of that garbage now. Look at the person it's turned me into. Every time I think I'm riding high, I spiral downhill, falling lower each time. It's time to cut the crap. I either believe in God or I don't. So I prayed for something awful to happen, something so bad that I can't handle it."

"And then," I continued, "I prayed to be filled with the Holy Spirit. With the wisdom and strength to put whatever it is entirely in God's hands," I continued. "To not walk away, like I have every other time."

Katy sat there, bewildered. "I don't get you. You're finally happy again. Why can't you just leave good enough alone?" She shook her head. "You truly *are* crazy, and I don't know what to do with you."

Chapter Thirty One

It was a beautiful San Carlos morning. Sure, late August can be hot. Okay, hundred degree hot. And so humid you could suck water out of the air with a straw. But who cares? Quite simply, it just felt good to be me again.

When you've forgotten what it's like to feel good, feeling good feels great! I felt like a spokesman for the *HerbaLife* product, or some *"after"* picture from a Nutrisystem ad. Like I had somehow shed a hundred pounds in a mere instant.

In a statement that could potentially have me sentenced to fifteen years in a California state mental institution, I felt like the Holy Spirit was actually at work inside me. Like somehow the negative, cynical, angry person who had temporarily possessed my body had been evicted, and a new renter had signed a lease.

Unlike previous spiritual and emotional highs, instead of weakening with time, the feeling only grew stronger as each hour passed. By mid-afternoon, I was feeling a strength I hadn't felt in years. So much so, in fact, that I could barely contain my happiness.

"Hey, Katy, change of plans. You stay here, and I'll go into town to pick up Marcos from school today."

"Mark, there's no need for you to go all the way into Guaymas," Katy reassured me. "You've got a lot to catch up on after your trip. Just do what you need to do and don't worry about Marcos. I'll go get him."

"But really, I want to pick him up!" I insisted.

"You do?" Katy seemed surprised. "OK, have it your way. I just figured you were busy."

"I am, but this stuff can all wait." Closing my laptop, I picked up my keys and headed for the door. "Today, I want to pick up my kid from school."

****

"Hi Dad! What are you doing here?"

"*¡Hola, Marcos!* Hey, I just thought I'd pick you up today." I hugged him as he got in the car. "How was school?"

"Good. And I don't have any homework today!" he answered gleefully. "Want to play soccer when we get home?"

"You got it buddy!"

He buckled up his seatbelt and off we went, headed toward San Carlos. The way he chattered about his classes, I could tell he was happy I had been there to pick him up.

I should really do this more often, I thought, pulling up to a stoplight. We sat there at the intersection, talking about Marcos' day at school, when suddenly I heard a voice. *"¡Oye!"*

Quickly turning and looking out my driver's side window, I saw a black and white police pickup truck beside us in the left lane, with an officer hanging out the side, looking straight at me. *"¡Oye!"* he again shouted, whistling and signaling with his arms to get my attention.

What on earth...? I thought to myself, unaware of any traffic laws I might possibly be violating. It's not like I had been speeding, cut anyone off or made an illegal turn, so why would he be bothering me? Shutting off the air conditioning, I rolled my window down.

"Yes?"

"That boy next to you," the officer said, pointing to Marcos. "Is that Adela Ruiz Fuentes' kid?"

What the hell was this all about? How did this stranger know who Marcos was? And why in the world would he refer to him as *"Adela Ruiz Fuentes' kid"*?

"Who's that, Dad?" Marcos asked, puzzled by what was happening.

"I have no idea!" I answered, suddenly concerned.

Staring straight at me, he shouted out one the question once more, firmly and loudly. "Is that Adela Ruiz Fuentes' kid?"

"Who are you?" I shot back, just as the light turned green.

"Pull over!" the officer demanded. "Now!"

"What's going on Dad?" Marcos asked, frightened a bit by the tone of the officer's command.

"Honestly Marcos, I don't know," I answered, calmly as I could so he wouldn't be alarmed. Just stay in the car, OK?" With that, I pulled over and parked at the entrance to a dusty used car lot on the side of the road as the police pickup followed me, lights flashing. "I'll be right back, Marcos" I assured him, as I got out of the car. "Don't worry buddy, everything's going to be fine."

The police vehicle came to a stop and as the driver shut off the flashing lights, the passenger door opened and a uniformed officer stepped out. *"¿Quién es?"* he demanded as he pointed toward Marcos, wanting to know who he was.

"He's my son, Marcos and yes, he's Adela's kid," I answered. "Who are you and why do you care?"

He smiled slightly. "Because I'm the one who pulled him out of the car the day his mama died."

Oh, my God. Here he was. The man Marcos had spoken about in his dreams. The one I remembered looking for right after the accident. Here he was, standing right in front of my eyes. All I could do was stand there in stunned silence, finally gathering my wits.

"I… I came looking for you…" I stammered.

"I left Guaymas for a little while right after it happened," he interjected, as if he knew where my conversation was leading. "That accident, it was the worst I've seen ever since becoming a cop. It was bad."

"But how did you know who Marcos…?"

"I'll never forget that kid's face, even after all this time," he answered. "Not after that day. How old is he now?"

"Seven. And his brother is three."

"Unbelievable!" the officer said. "But Marcos looks like he's doing well. That's great. I was worried about the kid."

"He's fully recovered now," I answered, still in disbelief at this fellow's sudden appearance. "Want to say hi to him?" Quickly I motioned inside the car. "Marcos, come on out buddy. I want you to meet someone."

The door opened and Marcos popped out. *"Sí, papá?"*

I took a deep breath and knelt down on one knee. "Marcos, I want you to meet somebody. This is the man who pulled you out of the car after the accident," I said softly, pointing toward the officer. "It was him."

Marcos looked at me, then up at the uniformed cop standing beside me. "Is there anything you want to say to him?" I asked, nudging him a bit.

Marcos just stood there, looking up at the officer's face. Finally, he stuck his hand out. *"Gracias, señor.* Thanks for helping me that day."

"Hey Marcos, I'm just glad you're OK," the officer reassured him. "I've always been worried about you and your brother."

"I'm doing good. I even play soccer!" Marcos said with a big smile.

"That's good, amigo, you be a good boy for your Dad, OK?" the officer said, patting Marcos on the head.

I looked at Marcos, quickly switching from Spanish to English. "Hey buddy, how 'bout you wait for me inside the car?"

"OK, Dad. *¡Adiós señor!"* Marcos waved as he closed the door behind him and turned the radio on.

"Sure is a cute kid you've got there," the officer remarked. "Glad to know you guys are all doing well."

I just stood there, amazed that this fellow had appeared out of the blue, a flood of thoughts racing through my head. How on earth had he actually recognized my son? In traffic? Was this really happening? All I could do was look at him in disbelief, for some reason finding myself unable to speak. Before I knew it, the officer was reaching for the door handle of the pickup, opening it as he turned to leave.

Don't go! I thought to myself, my mind racing. *I don't even know who you are!* Before I could say a single word, he turned back around and faced me.

"You know, every single time I pass that cross on the highway, I think about that awful day. And ever since then, I've felt some kind of responsibility to your kids because of the words your wife said to me."

What? I stood there, dumbfounded. *Because of the words your wife said to me?* Did I hear him correctly?

I cleared my throat. "Excuse me, but what did you just say?"

The officer shrugged. "You know, that I've always felt responsibility toward your kids. Because what your wife said to me," he answered, unaware that my heart had suddenly begun to race.

"What do you mean, what my wife said to you?" I asked, my voice beginning to tremble. "She was conscious? My wife was *conscious* when you found her?"

The officer backed up a bit, nervously, apparently sensing he had struck a nerve. "Hey, amigo, that was all a long time ago. Look, I wish I could stay, but we've really got to go, my partner here is waiting." Suspecting he had said something he shouldn't have, he quickly reached for the passenger door handle of his truck.

"Don't go anywhere!" I shot back. Letting go of the handle, he turned and looked at me, startled by the tone of my voice.

"Look, *señor*," I continued, my voice shaking uncontrollably. "It's been two years! All this time believing Adela was unconscious throughout it all, that she was knocked out seconds after the wreck. But now you tell me my wife spoke? She *spoke?*"

The officer just stood there, a helpless look on his face. I took a step and staggered, overcome with emotion. As I leaned against the car, we stood there for a moment, looking at each other. Neither of us knew what to say.

Finally, I gathered the courage to speak. "What happened? I need you to tell me the truth, right now. Tell me the whole truth, even if it kills me!"

The officer looked at his waiting partner in the pickup and motioned for him to wait a moment. Then he patted me on the shoulder. "*Señor,* what is it you want to know?"

Here we go, I thought. *It's time.*

"She *was* conscious when you found her?"

The officer paused. *"Sí señor,* she was conscious when I got to her. She was awake and knew what was happening around her."

"How long?" I pressed, eyes closed as I forced the words out of my own mouth. "How long was she conscious?"

"For just a few minutes," he replied. "She had some things she wanted to say. It wasn't easy for her, but I held her up as she spoke."

I just stood there, still in disbelief at what was actually happening. Finally I gathered the strength to continue. "Did she mention me?"

"Sí señor," he answered. "She told me you were on the other side of the border, far away, and to have someone find you. To tell you that she was going to die that day and she wouldn't see you again."

I raised my hands to my forehead, trying with every ounce of my might to keep my composure. "The pain..." I continued. "Was she numb to it... or did she suffer?"

The officer hesitated, looking away as he kicked a little dust with his boot.

'The truth, *señor,* I need it now," I insisted. *"Por favor, dime la verdad."*

He turned back to once again look me in the eye. "I don't want to tell you this," he reluctantly replied. "But you asked. Yes, she was in a lot of pain. Really, she tried to be strong. But *señor,* the truth is, yes, your wife suffered. She suffered greatly."

Clenching my fists I raised my hand to my face. Quickly, the officer grabbed my arm as I leaned against the car for support, momentarily speechless.

"So she knew she was going to die?" I finally asked, my voice reduced to a bare whisper.

"Sí señor," he answered, sadness in his voice. "She knew." He struggled for words, motioning with his hands as he spoke. "The steering wheel was... her body... her head... The injuries were just too severe. She knew she wouldn't survive."

There was a long silence. "Did she have any last words?" I finally whispered.

"Sí," he replied.

"What were they?"

"Take care of my kids," he answered. "She just said it over and over until she finally lost consciousness. 'Please, take care of my kids.'"

****

The black and white pickup truck rolled out of the parking lot and disappeared into traffic, leaving me standing there alone, shell shocked. After two years of somehow deluding myself, the truth had finally come like a blow to the gut. Adela was conscious, awake through it all. The impact of the oncoming car hadn't knocked her out, like I had somehow come to accept. She knew I wasn't there with her. She was in pain, suffering in her final moments. And she knew she was going to die. Everything that had comforted me in the days, weeks, months and years following her death was just an illusion, one that somehow fell apart within a matter of seconds. Doubts that had once lingered in the back of my mind had been falsely cast aside. How had I let that happen?

I never even asked his name. But the stranger's words tore through me like nothing ever had before. As I stood there, at last picturing Adela's painful final moments on this earth, it was like getting the phone call in Moore's Hill, Indiana all over again.

Chapter Thirty Two

"Where's Marcos?" Katy sounded alarmed. "You didn't forget to pick him up, did you?"

"No, Katy," I answered wearily, closing the kitchen door behind me. "I dropped him off at a friend's house so he could play for a while."

"Good, you had me worried for a moment," she laughed, relieved as she turned her back to me and resumed washing dishes. "So, what will you guys want for dinner tonight?"

I had already sat down behind her, lost in a fog. Images of Adela swirled through my mind like a terrible storm. Of her waiting to die in that car, bloodied behind a steering wheel that crumpled around her body. Of her consciously hearing the sounds of Luis crying and Marcos calling out to her, knowing she'd never be there for her little boys again.

"Mark, are you listening? I was asking you…" she began, turning to face me. "*Dios mío,* Mark! You look horrible! Are you okay?"

I sat there, dazed.

"Mark!"

Finally, I gathered the courage to speak. "Katy, there's something I've got to tell you. I don't want to, really, but I have to. You need to know. About the accident. About your sister."

She instantly put the wash rag down.

"But you have to first swear to me that you won't share it with your mother," I continued, my voice trembling.

"What are you talking about?" Katy asked nervously, her own voice beginning to shake. "Why can't I share whatever you're about to tell me with my mom?"

"Because Katy," I answered, hesitating a bit before continuing, "no mother wants to hear that her child suffered."

"*Suffered?* What do you mean, suffered? Mark, tell me!" Katy suddenly looked terrified.

I just sat there, choking up, unable to speak.

"She was unconscious wasn't she?" Katy cried. "Don't tell me my sister suffered! My beautiful sister!"

"I'm sorry Katy," I said softly. "We believed it because we wanted to believe it. We just didn't want to think otherwise. Your sister never was unconscious on impact. She felt the hit. She suffered, badly, Katy. It's time we all knew the truth. And that's the truth."

Katy had already lost it, sobbing uncontrollably as she listened to the entire story about that tragic day, and the truth we had managed to avoid about her sister's final moments. The comforting, reassuring, "she didn't feel a thing" illusion was over. I held Katy up as she wept, my own tears falling on her shoulders.

"My sister! *¡Mi hermana!*"

Even though it might make no sense to an outsider, just hearing that truth spoken for the first time, two years later, was like taking a knife and opening those very same wounds Katy thought had healed. I knew exactly how she felt. We stood there and cried, thinking of the wife and sister neither of us ever got a chance to say goodbye to.

Suddenly, Katy pushed me away. "And you!" she cried, pointing to me. "*You!*"

I was utterly confused. *What did I do?*

"Just when you truly believed!" she exclaimed. "Just when you finally found faith in God again! She buried her face in her hands and sobbed.

I was helpless, watching her struggle with emotions that overwhelmed her, until suddenly it dawned on me, hitting me out of the blue. How could I not have known? *What an idiot!* In the midst of the chaos, I hadn't even realized it. But it was clear as the light of day!

"Katy!"

"What?" she answered, lifting her head as the tears continued to fall.

"Katy!" I whispered. "Listen to what you just said!"

As so often happened when I'd open my mouth and speak, a look of confusion came across Katy's face.

"Just when I put my faith in God again. Just when I believed," I continued. 'You're absolutely right!"

"What are you talking about?" she asked, exasperated.

"Katy, what did I tell you twenty-four hours ago right here on this very spot?"

"I don't know, something about forgiving your friend…" she began, wiping her eyes as she spoke.

"And?" I pressed.

"*¡No sé!*" Katy stood there for a moment, shaking her head.

"Don't you remember? I told you I got on that plane yesterday and prayed as hard as I ever have in my entire life. For something awful to happen," I continued, my heart racing as I spoke. "For a test too big for me to pass. A challenge that's too big for me to handle. I prayed for the chance to hate God, to lose whatever trust I have in Him, and to walk away like I do every single time things get tough."

Katy jaw dropped.

"*This* is too big for me to handle! This hurts! Katy, don't you see, God gave me exactly what I begged Him for!"

Katy just stood there, wide eyed.

"And you know what Katy?" I declared, my voice rising. "This time… *THIS TIME*… I'm not walking away! I refuse! I'm not going anywhere! My faith is in the Lord and I am *NOT* walking!"

She stood there, shocked at what she was witnessing. The words flowed out of my mouth before I could even stop them.

"I don't understand one bit of this, or why any of it happened! I'm just as confused as ever, if not more! But I no longer need to understand!"

Katy was speechless, hanging onto every word.

"You know what I'm gonna do right now? This very instant? I'm taking every bit of my confusion and anger, and putting it all in His hands, period! He doesn't need me to understand, He just wants me to turn it over to Him. Look at Luis! Look at the message from Adela! And look how He answered me today, with the truth, finally, after all this time! Maybe He knew I wasn't ready for it before, but He heard me yesterday and knows I'm ready for it now. So listen to me, Katy… I trust in Jesus!"

A river of tears streamed down Katy's face, but this time, they were tears of joy.

"You've seen the weak, worthless human being I am, Katy" I declared. "You've seen me abandon God every single time things get rough. OK, we know the truth now, and it's not what we wanted it to be. But listen to me and make no mistake about it. My faith is in Jesus Christ! And I'm *NOT* walking away from Him!"

Chapter Thirty Three

Víctor Torres López was a year and a half older than Adela. A job working for an American-based employer had brought him to San Carlos, much closer to the border than his home well to the south in Michoacán. When he hopped into his faraway boss's car on July 16th, 2006 and pulled out of the driveway, he had no idea it would be his last day on this earth.

He never knew that on his way back from Guaymas, shortly before 6 p.m., he would come across a random police checkpoint, manned by officers on the lookout for so-called *"carros chuecos,"* or illegally imported, American plated vehicles being driven by Mexican citizens. Police had authority to seize automobiles on the spot if documentation could not be produced.

Cars just like the maroon Mercedes sedan he was driving that day.

It was too late to turn around. An officer at the checkpoint had already noticed Nevada plates on the car, and a Mexican driver behind the wheel. He approached the vehicle to demand papers. Víctor Torres had none. He panicked, making what would turn out to be the most selfish decision of his life. Hitting the gas, he blew through the checkpoint. Seconds later a high speed chase began. The driver weaved recklessly in and out of traffic, desperately trying to avoid the pursuing squad car, nearly colliding with another northbound vehicle as he approached the *"maquiladoras"* on the edge of town. The chase continued, reaching speeds of ninety miles per hour.

No one will ever know if the fleeing driver had heard the local rumors about a few corrupt cops who, rather than turning seized vehicles into the proper authorities, were allegedly keeping them for themselves or taking them to illegally-run chop-shops to sell for a profit.

It's a secret he took to the grave, as he finally lost control of his vehicle, swerving across the median at kilometer 131 and slamming head-on into an oncoming southbound car, driven by a young wife and mother of two. Víctor Torres López died upon impact.

The pursuing police officer hit the brakes, slowing down as he witnessed the horrific crash on the opposite side of the highway.

Then, as the dust settled and a parade of motorists stopped their cars, rushing to help, the officer gunned it. His squad car disappeared into the distance, never returning to the scene of the accident.

There was no record of a police checkpoint that day in Guaymas.

****

You will know the truth, and the truth will make you free. John 8:32

PART TWO

Chapter Thirty Four

Now Adela's looking down from up above
Her little Marcos and Luis, they're growing up

"Remember, Luis?"

Who was I kidding? Of course he didn't remember. But for some reason, I held on to a faint hope that somehow, years later, a light might come on inside his head.

"Remember how mama used to say *'hola bebé'* to you every time she'd walk into the room?"

Luis just looked at me, puzzled. He didn't have a clue what I was talking about. After all, he was all of one and a half years old when he last saw his mother or felt her cradle him in her arms. Sure, he knew what her voice had sounded like, but only from watching a few short videos on our VCR that Adela and I had filmed on her old camcorder. Those movies were the only ones we had of his mother. Were it not for them, he wouldn't recognize Adela from a stranger if she were to walk into the room. His first-hand memories of his mother had disappeared. Quickly, I turned to his older brother.

"Marcos, you remember, right? Remember how she used to walk into his room and…?"

Marcos stared at me blankly.

"OK, but you remember how she used to sing you that song, right? The one that goes like this?" I began to sing. "*No se que tienen tus ojos. No se que tiene tu boca…*"

Marcos just shook his head.

Oh no, I thought, panicking as it slowly dawned on me. *He's forgetting too!*

****

"Kick it Luis, kick it!"

Watching my boy as he dribbled the ball down the street past Marcos and prepared to shoot, I couldn't believe it. In just a few months, Luis Antonio Mulligan would turn four years old. *Four!* What happened to that tiny infant I had watched struggle for life, connected to a bunch of tubes in an incubator?

And Marcos? Where was that baby whose chin looked just like mine the day he was born? Would he really soon be turning eight? Where had the time gone?

"*Goal!*" Luis shrieked, jumping up and down with his arms raised into the air as the ball sailed into the makeshift goal.

"Way to go Luis!" I shouted as Marcos ran to fetch the ball. "You just smoked your older brother!"

Marcos turned and frowned. "Come on Dad," he yelled back. "You know I let him score that on purpose!"

"No you didn't!" Luis insisted. "I make the goal! I make the goal!"

"I let you make it!" Marcos retorted.

As Marcos's teammate Jim Scheidler jumped into the fray, attempting unsuccessfully to arbitrate the sudden controversy, I turned for a moment and gazed back at our house. The light was on in the kitchen, as if someone were inside cooking dinner. It was as if any moment, the door would open and Adela would call out "dinner's ready!" For a split second, I half expected us to walk in, wash our hands and sit down to some of her famous chicken *mole*, made with her mother's secret recipe. Or maybe her mouthwatering *carne asada* tacos.

She had made that house into a home.

****

It was time.

Some of her possessions I had already given to her family. Older sister Katy got her phone. Eva, her wedding dress. Her mother, copies of some of Adela's old photos.

There were other things that sat on those shelves. Some were personal items I had hung on to for sentimental reasons, like that shoe box full of old letters.

Adela never did have an email address. Back when we dated, I didn't have one either. Whenever a trip took me far away from her, we communicated the old fashioned way. Aside from international phone calls, which were expensive in those days before Skype or Magic Jack, we wrote letters. Yes, words scribbled on paper, placed in envelopes, addressed and mailed.

Occasionally, I would take them down from the closet shelf and read them, their words evoking tears, laughter and smiles. I could now see things in retrospect. Some I had outright forgotten about. Like an early letter I read from Adela, discussing her issues with jealousy.

Wow, she really had warned me about it right from the start, I thought, reading her hand-written promise that as I earned her trust, her jealousies would gradually disappear. It should have never been a surprise, though in my mind I had somehow re-invented that huge obstacle between us as a sudden, unexpected occurrence. Memories can be "creative," having us remember things precisely the way we prefer to, instead of how they really were. I was often reminded of that when reading those old cards and letters.

Behind the shoe box full of letters was another box, far back in the corner, filled to the top with old cassette tapes. Not only did Adela not have an email address, or a computer for that matter, but most of her music she had was on tape, not CD. The box was stuffed with those old music cassettes, piled up in no particular order, most not even in a case. Some were pre-recorded and store-bought, but most were simply copies recorded by Adela onto old TDK tapes and labeled herself.

Rummaging through the old cassettes brought back to mind all her old favorite groups. She loved old fashioned accordion-laced *música norteña,* as evidenced by her *"Ramón Ayala y Los Bravos del Norte"* and *"Los Invasores de Nuevo León"* tapes. She loved to dance to *"banda"* music, with its huge horn sections complete with tubas and trombones. She enjoyed the *bachata* style of the Dominican Republic's Juan Luis Guerra. She also liked established Mexican artists like José José and classic groups from the 60's, preferring those to the sounds of more modern pop. But aside from *música norteña,* the music she played the most was *"ranchera,"* featuring well-known performers like Juan Gabriel and Vicente Fernández, otherwise known as *"El Rey,"* or "The King." A legend in Mexico, Fernandez was known as "The Mexican Elvis." As I reached in the box and pulled out a homemade recording of his greatest hits, with the *"Éxitos de Vicente Fernández"* title scribbled on a thin strip of masking tape, I smiled. After all, Vicente Fernandez caused the first "disagreement" Adela and I ever had.

"This guy is so sappy! My God, listen to him. He's actually crying!" I had remarked, rolling my eyes. "This is ridiculous! What kind of loser is this dude?"

Adela wasn't happy. She didn't care if it was one of our first dates. She would set the record straight, right then, about my critique of an authentic Mexican legend.

"Don't you ever insult Vicente Fernández again!" she fired back, glaring at me from across the table. I naturally assumed she was joking.

She wasn't. "He's *El Rey*. And a lot more famous than you are. If you don't like his music, maybe that's your problem!"

Wow. This chick was definitely a Vicente Fernández fan. My bad.

****

"Whose voice is that, Dad?"

"It's your mama, Marcos," I answered, smiling as the cassette tape played on our living room boom box. "That's her, talking to you when you were just a tiny baby!"

"Hola mi bebé! You sure are a handsome little man! Aren't you?"

Marcos was incredulous. "That's my mama?"

Adela's voice cooed softly as the tape played. *"What's that, baby? You have a secret? Tell your mama all about it!"*

Marcos was wide-eyed. "Is that really me saying *ba ba ba*?"

"*Sí*, Marcos, that's you! Talking with your mama!"

"But what was I trying to say?" he asked, perplexed.

"I don't know, those noises were the only sounds you could make,"I answered "Other than farts!"

"*Papá!*" Marcos slugged me playfully.

"But mama knew exactly what you were saying. Listen to that conversation you guys were having, just the two of you!"

Marcos beamed as the tape played on, giggling at the sounds of baby talk interspersed with Adela's loving voice.

"Oh, really? Hmm... really? I see... yes... you don't say!"

"Wow! That's my mama!" he exclaimed. "Where did you get this, Daddy?"

"I just found it today, Marcos," I replied, "while I was cleaning out the closet."

Truth is, it had almost gone in the trash, along with a worn out *José José* cassette and a bunch of others. After all, unlike her other items I had stored up on the shelf, no one would be able to make use of them anymore. They were old, worn out, and besides, nobody I knew even had a cassette player anymore. Her family had all swapped theirs for CD players. Sure, I still had one, but since it barely worked and had a nasty habit of eating tapes, it too was destined for the trash can along with the box of cassettes. Why hang on to a bunch of worn out old tapes no one would ever hear? Half of them weren't even labeled anyway. Like the one we were listening to now.

"Can we play it again, Dad?" Marcos pleaded.

Who knows what possessed Adela to record that random moment with her and her little boy. She probably never expected anyone else to listen to it. She likely never dreamed that one day, long after she was gone, it would suddenly bring her back to us in an unexpected moment, her voice filling our home and gently reminding her oldest son how much she loved him.

****

They point at pictures and say 'that's my Mom'
And when I see them smile her memory lives on

Chapter Thirty Five

What a beautiful, miserable afternoon

Oh, no! I thought. *Not again!*

Lifting one foot up out of bed and onto the floor, I tried to stand. Seconds later, wobbling and leaning one hand against the wall for support, I knew it.

Vertigo! Seemingly like clockwork, I'd get nailed with a nasty bout of it every two years. And when it hit, it really hit. Any slight head movement to either side would bring on a head rush that would send my entire world into a sudden, seemingly never-ending spin. Walking? Forget it. I might as well be Otis, the town drunk from *The Andy Griffith Show*, trying to walk a straight line. And driving? Joseph Hazelwood was safer behind the wheel of the *Exxon Valdez* than me attempting to navigate a motor vehicle from one point to another.

Vertigo rendered me useless. All I could do was lay there, out of focus, unable to read, write, send emails, or do any work whatsoever on my computer. When stricken with a bout, I was about as productive as your average federal government employee.

Great, there goes my next few days! I thought. After staggering to the bathroom to slap some cold water on my face and brush my teeth, I laid back down and picked up the phone next to the bed.

"Eva, can you take Marcos and Luis for a day or two?" I asked, explaining to her the situation. Since Katy had just moved out, returning to her mother's home to live, Eva volunteered to take the boys to her house and care for them there.

I'd have to cancel my gig that night too, one of my first shows of the season. Even if I were sitting on a bar stool rather than standing, it'd be impossible entertaining a crowd in my condition. Not unless I were completely motionless and staring straight ahead, with no audience interaction whatsoever for a full three hour show. Maybe Bob Dylan had successfully pulled off that stunt for the last thirty years of his career, but given the energetic nature of my shows, I couldn't get through half a song performing like that without being hit by a Corona bottle. Besides, chances are that with one inadvertent glance to either side of me, I'd be falling off my bar stool. True, I might not be the first fellow in history with the Mulligan surname to fall off a bar stool, but nonetheless, I knew from prior experience that rest was what the doctor ordered. In bed was where I'd be spending the rest of my day.

What a wasted day, I muttered to myself.

****

"So what exactly is going on when you turn your head?" My brother, being a doctor, was curious about my symptoms.

"Just like every other time, John," I replied. "If I move my head to either side, I feel dizzy, kind of like I just stepped off a merry-go-round after drinking a bottle of vodka."

"Interesting," he observed, as I pressed the receiver to my ear. "Man, this is crazy you keep getting this as often as you do. Let me tell you what I think may be going on."

I listened as my brother began to describe the various factors that contribute to occurrences of balance issues. John always had a way of making otherwise complicated things simple and understandable to complete idiots like me. It's one reason why his patients love him so much. Plus, other than Jack Kevorkian, he was the only doctor I knew of who would make actual house calls. Only difference is, rather than showing up to kill you, my brother was known to show after work hours to check on a patient's recovery, bringing with him a six pack of India Pale Ale or Imperial Stout he had personally brewed himself.

Lousy as I was feeling, Kevorkian actually sounded like the more appealing option.

"Now, there's also this thing called Meniere's Disease," he continued. "It's an inner ear disorder. I don't think that's what you've got, though, and here's why."

I listened intently. Suddenly, my focus on John's explanation was interrupted by a loud knock on the kitchen door. Before I could ask my brother to hang on so I could stagger to my feet and check who was outside, I heard the door open and footsteps in my kitchen.

"Eva?" I called out, covering the receiver with my hand as to not interrupt my brother's train of thought. "Is that you?"

Seconds later, I heard the sound of my bedroom door creaking open. Gingerly, doing my best to avoid a movement-induced head rush, I turned my head.

Elsa?

What in the world was she doing here? Was this a dream? Or possibly a nightmare, one where I inexplicably found myself in the state of New Jersey?

Before I could even uncover the receiver to ask John if I could call him back, Elsa came to my bedside, taking the phone out of my hand and laying it on the bed beside me. Without saying a word, she put her hands on my face, pulling it close to hers. Softly, she kissed me.

Talk about making my head spin. Forget vertigo, Elsa looked absolutely beautiful, in a blue dress I had never seen her wear before. She was simply stunning. I, on the other hand, must have looked like a Nick Nolte mug shot at that very moment. Why on earth Elsa didn't turn around and flee for the hills is beyond me. But she didn't. She just kissed me, over and over and over again, with my brother's voice still audible from a phone receiver that lay on the bed just inches away.

I quickly motioned for her to stop for a second, reached for the phone and held it up to my ear. "So the Meniere's thing is unlikely, bro," he was saying. "But, what it could be…"

"Uh-huh," I answered, grinning back at Elsa as I once again set the phone back down on the bed. She leaned over, turned the receiver away from us, and kissed me again.

Now what a beautiful, miserable afternoon
Ain't it awful, awful perfect for a party of two
The kids are gone, it's just me and you
What a beautiful, miserable afternoon

****

"What are you doing here anyway, Elsa? I thought you weren't flying back to visit your folks until Christmas!"

"Don't you remember?" She grinned. "My best friend Irazema is getting married this weekend down in Navojoa. I'm one of her bridesmaids! I just got into Hermosillo a couple hours ago, and am on my way down right now."

I didn't remember. It's not like Elsa and I had kept in constant contact after she left for New Jersey. In fact, during the entire six months she had been gone, we had only talked once, over the summer when I called her from my hotel room in Nashville.

"It's really beautiful back here," she had told me then. "The people I'm working for are really nice. Their house is huge! And everything back here is so green and pretty."

New Jersey? Pretty? Just wait until winter comes and let's see how pretty it is, I thought at the time.

It wasn't just my notorious dislike for conversing on phones that kept us from keeping in touch. We were both busy, and the truth is, there really was no reason for us to keep in touch like we otherwise would have. Sure, the program she was participating in technically involved a one year commitment, but chances were likely it would be extended to two, or even more. After that, with Elsa's background as a event planner and the fact that she was bilingual, there would surely be extraordinary demand for her up in the United States, especially being that close to New York City.

Aside from all that, I also knew there would be no shortage of guys back east who would be falling all over themselves to get a girl like Elsa. Put it all together, and there wasn't a doubt in my mind she wouldn't be coming back to Mexico, other than to visit now and then. So in my mind, I nostalgically looked back at that unexpected springtime kiss we had shared as a moment that would never be repeated. As a one-time, out of the blue moment that would remain a special memory for both of us, but never go further.

Apparently, given the fact that my phone wasn't exactly ringing off the hook either, she felt the same way. Maybe that was due to the fact that one of my predictions had indeed come true already.

"Are you dating anyone?" I asked curiously.

"Oh, I've gone out on dates with a few different guys," she replied. "One of them really likes me a lot." She filled me in a bit, and from the sounds of things, were she to give it a shot, it might actually go somewhere.

"But with my new job, I just want to keep all my doors open right now, and not commit to anything serious with anyone," she added. "It's just not the right time in my life."

Probably a smart strategy. Elsa had nowhere to go but up in this world. With a future like hers, why limit herself?

"How about you?" she asked, turning the same question on me. "Have you gone out with anyone?"

"No, not since way before you left," I replied. "I've officially decided this is my year to regroup. To finally get my act together. So I've pretty much taken this whole year and spent it with the boys. I know it might sound pathetic, but a big night for me these days is watching Luis kick Bomberg's butt in *Candy Land*."

"But you know what?" I added. "It actually has been great. I feel like

God's given me this strength and sense of peace I didn't even know I had. Maybe a little wisdom and patience, too. And it's brought the boys and me closer. Who knows? I think Adela might actually be proud of me now."

"Do Marcos and Luis ever ask about her?" Elsa asked curiously.

"Unfortunately, less and less," I answered. "At least with Marcos, I'm trying to keep her memory alive so that he remembers whatever details he still can. But I don't think it's working. I can tell, he's starting to forget. We watch old videos now and then, and he enjoys them, but I think inside he doesn't actually remember much about those days."

"That's probably normal," she surmised. "He was only five when this all happened. And really, how much do you remember from when you were five?"

"Me? I don't remember what I had for lunch," I remarked, wishing I were more than just half-joking.

"What about Luis?" she asked. "Does he ever ask about Adela?"

"You know, I think he probably forgot her within a year or so," I answered. "I doubt he has any recollections of her at all. He's just got those videos and pictures to show him who she was."

"What's kind of sad," I added, "is that he calls any woman who spends time with him 'mamá'. It can be any random person, as long as it's a female and she spends time with him. I'm not just talking about back when I was actually dating. It can be anybody, like Cristina, Eva, Katy, babysitters, any woman who pays him any attention. To Luis, she's 'mamá'."

"That *is* sad," Elsa commented, frowning a bit.

"But it doesn't seem to bother him when they leave," I remarked. "It's like he's gotten used to women disappearing on him. If I hire a babysitter one week and a different one the next, it doesn't affect him like it might other kids. It's almost like he expects them to leave, right from the start. So he never really bonds with any of them."

We continued catching up on all that had happened over the past six months, talking for hours about life on the East Coast, her experience working as a nanny, the two children she cared for, and how she missed her own family. After a while, she closed her eyes and fell asleep, exhausted from her trip. She dozed peacefully, until waking suddenly and glancing at her watch.

"Oh no, look at the time! My bus for Navojoa leaves in less than an hour!" She pulled out her cell phone and quickly dialed Tony, the taxi driver.

"I'll be there in five minutes," answered Tony. "Wait for me outside."

Snapping her phone closed, Elsa looked at me and gently took my hand. "I'm really glad I could catch you here, Mark. Other than this vertigo thing, I'm so glad things are going well for you and that you're happy. Most of all, that you're spending this time with your kids. You won't regret it and they won't either."

She leaned over and hugged me tightly. "Guess I won't see you at Christmas, since you say you're going to up in Phoenix to be with your family. That's my only trip back here. Wow, who knows when I'll see you again?"

Moments later, a horn honked out on the street and Elsa stood up, picking up her purse. Leaning down, she kissed me one more time. It was a long kiss, one I didn't want to end.

"Adiós Marcos."

Seconds later, staggering to my feet, I stumbled to the window and watched as she got in the cab and closed the door. Just like that, Elsa was gone.

Chapter Thirty Six

"We know what was going on in there!" Jim Bomberg flashed a guilty grin.

"Nothing happened, guys!" I insisted. "Really, she was only in my room 'cause I was laid up in bed with vertigo."

"Yeah, right!" Scheidler laughed. "I bet you were feeling just fine!"

Great. Couldn't these two clowns have popped by my house any other time than the one precise moment Elsa happened to drop by?

"*Elsa! Elsa!*" Bomberg mocked, exhibiting his trademark sophisticated sense of humor.

"Get a life, Bomberg," I retorted. For some strange reason, a song came to mind, one called "Jesus Loves You, The Rest of Us Think You're a Jerk."

Scheidler just stood there, chuckling, eyebrows arched curiously.

I pointed to the door. "Out, guys. Get out of my house!"

****

"*Papá*, do we have to stay with a babysitter again?" Marcos looked at the floor dejectedly as I snapped my guitar case shut.

"Buddy, what do you expect me to do?" I stopped, put my guitar case down, knelt in front of him and looked at his sad face. "I've got to work, Marcos. Not just for me, but for you and your brother. And I'm going to have to do it more often now. It's the start of another season, and I've got to make money while I can. Especially after losing that gig the other night when I was sick. Man, I wish I could stay home with you and Luis tonight, but we've got to eat! Come on buddy, you like chicken with sauce, right?"

He nodded.

"Then let your Dad go out and earn the money to buy it, OK?" I pleaded, trying my best to cheer him up. "Otherwise, you'll just have to eat vegetables like carrots and zucchini all the time!"

"*Yuck!*" he exclaimed, grinning.

"You guys will have fun with Cristina, I promise. Just be good for her, don't fight and go to bed on time. OK?" I stole a quick hug from each of the boys and closed the door behind me.

Several hours later, my tip jar was overflowing and the crowd was hopping down the beach at La Palapa Griega. I glanced at the clock. Eight o'clock. Cristina would be tucking the kids into bed right about now. Maybe she was telling them a story at that very moment. Or perhaps they were saying their bedtime prayers.

Meanwhile, I still had a couple more requests to get to, plus I'd need at least another hour to spend with the customers, get paid, and talk to the owner Raphael about a few things. After that, I'd still have to haul my sound system and lights out to the car to load up. I wouldn't see either of my kids that night nor the next, since I had a private event scheduled, followed by a trip to Phoenix for weekend shows.

But that's life. And unless I was going to win the lottery, things weren't going to change. Fact is, looking toward the future, after spending most of their daytime hours at school, my kids would likely be tucked in many a night by a babysitter rather than an actual parent. Sometimes it would be Cristina. Sometimes Katy, whenever she was free to help. Sometimes, if neither were available, it might be a total stranger. And that was just how it was going to be, from here on out.

But things were different now. I wasn't about to jump back onto that tumultuous road I had walked before. No more letting emotions take me down paths of destruction I had been already been down too many times, and no more dwelling on negatives. It was time to focus on positives. My boys were healthy. They were happy. We were together.

And most of all, God was with me, right by my side, guiding me and giving me wisdom I never had before. Sure, I might mess up here and there like every human being, but I had a newfound strength, one that would keep me from walking away from Him again. He had answered my requests. Now, I was determined to answer His.

****

"Kelly, like I told you, everything's cool, bud. No need to apologize again!"

"I know, Marco," said the voice on the other line. "But hear me out. I never did get a chance to ever really explain to you why I had to bail on you like I did. Believe me, it's not how I do things. But unfortunately, it was something I just felt I didn't have a choice in."

I listened as he explained in detail why he had to take that corporate gig he ended up canceling his IslandFest agreement for.

"You see, I was working with an agent that sent me a contract on a date I thought was dead. It showed up right after I told you 'yes' to Mexico. It's the kind of thing that almost never happens, like maybe every six or seven hundred gigs. But it left me no choice, especially since it was an agent that sent me tons of work. I wasn't worried about passing up that one event for yours, but what it likely would have cost me is a ton of work outside of that since that agent wouldn't have booked me again."

It was something he had already touched on by email previously, but Kelly seemed determined to explain it personally.

"Regardless of all that," he added, "I should have been more careful when I committed to you and I feel bad about that, 'cause I know how these kind of events need to be planned. Plus, truth is, of all the artists on this circuit, you're literally the only one who's gone out of his way to include me in an event like this. I really do appreciate it Marco, won't let something like that happen again, and I hope you and I can be friends. I just wanted to tell you that."

I realized it at that very moment, something that would be proven again and again as we'd tour five countries and countless states in years to come. When it came to friends, you won't find them any more loyal than Kelly McGuire.

"I get it, Kelly," I replied. "Just please know that none of that crap ever had anything to do with you anyway. It was my own messed up head dealing with other issues. You just happened to walk in on it all at a bad time."

"But Kelly," I continued, "even though you have no idea what I'm talking about, you played a role in me moving beyond all that. Crazy as it sounds, without even knowing it, you helped lead me to a turning point. And I'm not going back, ever again."

****

"Mi hijo," Doña Telma exclaimed, greeting me her front door with a big hug. *"¡Que gusto verte!"*

"It's good to see you too," I answered, noticing how beautiful she looked. Especially considering how difficult things had been for Doña Telma these past couple years. Losing her husband and her daughter in a span of eighteen months left her fending for herself, doing whatever she could do just to earn enough money to get by. From selling her famous banana leaf tamales door to door around the neighborhood, to giving therapeutic massages to ailing neighbors, to selling homemade popsicles directly out of her kitchen, somehow she managed to get by daily in the face of financial challenges others would have succumbed to. Never complaining, she always did it with a smile.

"Siéntate, mi hijo," she insisted, motioning for me to come in and sit. "Let's talk a bit."

Within seconds, we were catching up on all that had happened since I had last visited months earlier. Truth is, I had been somewhat of a lousy son-in law since Adela's death, visiting Doña Telma far less than I should have given the loss we both shared. I wished I could blame it all on having my hands full with the kids. But I couldn't.

Luckily, unlike me, she had managed to keep her head together through it all, growing stronger and wiser as a result of all the tragedy that had befallen her. Her faith may have been simple, but unlike mine, it had remained strong, never wavering.

As we chatted, I glanced up at the large framed photo of Adela and me that hung in her living room. It was our wedding picture. Next to it was a black and white picture of Doña Telma when she just a young girl of perhaps seventeen or eighteen. She was stunning, with those same gorgeous eyes her daughter would one day inherit.

"My daughter was beautiful, wasn't she?" Doña Telma noticed my gaze at the pictures on the wall.

"Yes, she was," I said wistfully. "And you know what? She got her looks from you." Doña Telma blushed a bit. "She sure loved you."

"She was a special girl, Marcos. She was perfect in every way except one. And between you and me, we both know what I'm talking about. She had only one fault, and it was definitely jealousy." Doña Telma chuckled. "Well, maybe she had a little vanity too. We all know she wanted to be the prettiest girl in the room."

"And she was!" I interjected.

"Yes, she was," Doña Telma said. She smiled, although it seemed to be somewhat of a sad smile.

"Mi hijo, it's time. "

"Time for what?" I asked.

"Time for you to open your doors to someone new," she gently replied.

"Doña Telma," I began. "As much as I hate to say it, I've been there and done that. Just ask your daughters and they'll tell you. I blew off my kids and thought only about myself. I don't want that to happen again. I've got Marcos and Luis, and I really want to be a good father for them."

"I know what you've done, Marcos. But that's in the past," she said, shaking her head a bit. "Time's gone by. Yes, you've made mistakes, but you've learned. And you're a better father because of it. But now you're afraid it's going to hurt me if you move on. That it'll make me sad, or somehow betray my daughter."

"But you're a good man," she continued. "You'll always be my son, no matter what happens. But God has somebody else in mind for you. He wants you to be happy"

"And *mi hijo*," she said, taking my hand, "I want you to love again."

Chapter Thirty Seven

This is gonna sound crazy
Don't freak out
I probably shouldn't tell you
But last night I dreamed of you

One late November day, my cell phone rang. Yes. I said "cell phone." And I prefaced it with the word "my." Someone alert the press.

"Ugh!" I muttered, fumbling around in my pocket with one hand as I kept the other on the steering wheel. Finally, I pulled it out, glancing quickly at the number displaying on the screen. *Oh, my God...*

That particular ten digit number hadn't shown up on my "calls received" list in a long time. In fact, at one point I had actually deleted it from my directory, just to avoid the temptation of dialing it in a moment of weakness. After all, I knew myself.

Should I take the call? I placed the phone on the passenger seat and gripped the wheel with both hands for what seemed like an eternity, just letting it ring. Finally, I took a breath and picked it up.

"Mark?"

There was a long, lonely period after Adela when the sound of that voice would have caused my heart to beat faster. When anything it would have asked me to do, I would have done without a second thought. When just a few words spoken by it would have convinced me to cast aside every unpleasant reality my closest friends and loved ones were trying to get me to see. Realities I had once ignored, in blindness, weakness, and fear. Oh, and stupidity, many might add.

And now, after what seemed like ages, that voice was back, asking me what I'd been up to and how I'd been. Suddenly dropping hints that things might be different were we to give things another shot. And offering me a chance to return to a place from my past.

It was a turbulent place, full of ups and downs and bad decisions, where momentary voids were filled easily, but always temporarily. Where my desires led me down roads I wasn't prepared to be on.

That voice was back. And I'm a weak person. A person who missed companionship. A person who missed love.

A very weak person.

****

Remember that old TV show, *Love Connection*? Admit it, you watched it, late at night while scarfing an entire bag of Nacho Cheese Doritos on the couch. Anyway, the basic idea was that singles would choose among other contestants of the opposite sex, in the hope of finding a compatible romantic partner. After making the choice, they'd go out on a date. Then, they'd come back after the date and relate their experiences to the host, Chuck Woolery. He'd pepper each of them with questions about how their experience went. If all went well, you'd hear "*oohs*" and "*aahs*" from the crowd, along with a hearty round of applause as the couple agreed to a, get this, second date. (In current pop culture this is known as a "long term relationship")

Of course, if the participants had a not-so good experience, Chuck would wince.

"He took me to Burger King!"

"She brought her ex-boyfriend along on the date!"

"He dressed as a chick!"

You get the picture. The studio audience would emit boos as the guilty party hopelessly defended himself, with Chuck finally wrapping things up, stating the obvious.

"It doesn't sound like things went so well."

Of course, Chuck had seen this routine before. With over two thousand shows filmed, by now he was an expert. He could likely tell before the couple ever even agreed to go out on a date whether things were going to work out or not. In fact, with experience like his, he had a pretty good handle on who each contestant *ought* to choose for the ideal partner. In fact, he knew better than they did.

But hey, in this game, people had to choose for themselves. Chuck's job wasn't to make that choice, but instead to sit back, moderate the show, ask a few questions, and occasionally chuckle along with the rest of us at some of the stupid things contestants would do in the hope of finding love. Oh, and to try to keep himself from choking the loser who didn't realize his prospective love interest was "just a bit too much of a partier" when she asked him to pick her up at a bar at nine thirty in the morning instead of at her home.

So Chuck would wait until the end of the show, after the laughter had died down, to offer his words of wisdom, perhaps "sounds like maybe next time you ought to go out with someone you meet at the library instead of morning happy hour." Then, he'd invite the contestant to come back when he got act together and give it another shot.

You sensed he really wanted that unlucky contestant to eventually get his dignity back and have a second chance. To learn from his mistakes and be with someone he was actually meant to be with.

Call me blasphemous, but did the Holy Spirit ever derive His inspiration from syndicated television re-runs? Could He secretly long to be some kind of spiritual Chuck Woolery, offering this hapless loser a chance to vindicate himself and finally love the one he ought to be with?

****

"I just can't."

What? I couldn't believe the words were actually coming out of my own mouth. But I couldn't stop them. They just kept coming.

"Look, I know this sounds crazy, but I've finally got my head together. I'm finally focused on being the father I need to be. God knows, it took a long time and a lot of mistakes. But I'm finally there. I'm on solid ground now. I can't go back. Not now."

There was a surprised silence on the other end of the phone. Likely, she was just as shocked as me at my own reaction, at the unexpected strength in my voice, and a self-confidence she had never witnessed in me before. I was a different person now. Even I realized it at that very moment.

All of a sudden, in the midst of lingering silence, a word came to me, unexpectedly and from out of the blue. One word, flashing in my mind like a big, neon, Las Vegas sign.

Elsa!

What in the world? I had spoken with Elsa only twice over the past nearly eight months, first on that long-ago call from Nashville, and last when she surprised me at my house on her way to her friend's wedding. When that cab pulled away from my driveway that day, I knew I'd likely not see her again for a long time, if ever. Hell, she might be married to that new dude she told me about, or settled down in New York City by the time I picked up a phone and called her. So why was her name suddenly coming to me?

Finally the voice on the other end of the phone began to speak. But I was too busy listening to another voice. One that came from within.

Elsa, I thought, my mind suddenly racing. *How I'd love to be talking to Elsa right now!*

****

And if only dreams came true
I wouldn't have to close my eyes

Calling New Jersey from a TelCel phone in Mexico is bad enough. Aside from rates that actually make ObamaCare premiums look reasonable, you've invariably got to attempt several dialing options in vain before stumbling upon one that works. Do I dial 01 or 001? Do I have to put another 1 before the U.S. area code? What about that 044 thing? Or is it 045? Or is that only for domestic Mexican calls?

Each failed attempt left you listening to that annoying woman's voice saying "I'm sorry, your call can't be completed as dialed." If I ever locate that woman's address, I'm going to drive to her home, knock on her door, and slap her.

As you can probably guess, I didn't make a lot of long distance calls from cell phones. In fact, in all my years of living in Mexico, I don't think I ever once had made a call from my Mexican cell phone to a United States number. That was about to change.

I would so love to hear Elsa's voice. Right now! The thought grew louder in my head with each passing moment.

What was the deal here? Hadn't I barely hung up from some call that anyone from my past would have expected to last a *lot* longer? Shouldn't I be making a U-turn and heading north on Highway 15 right about now?

Life ain't a game show. But maybe that friendly, previously mentioned game show host and the Holy Spirit do share something in common. Maybe when they witness some pitiful, laughable idiot of a contestant actually learn from his mistakes, come back and take a leap of real faith, they want to see him rewarded. No, the Chuckster can't intervene. But the Holy Spirit can.

****

Don't be embarrassed
Come on, it's worth a laugh
'Cause we've been friends forever

This is ridiculous. Why am I so nervous? I thought, dialing an endless set of digits. Why would I be nervous? Elsa was my friend. Sure, we had kissed. But even that was innocent, not having led to anything more. So why were my hands sweating like they were?

Maybe she's talking to that guy she's dating? I wondered, waiting impatiently as the call was processed.

One ring of her land line phone is all it took.

"Hello?"

"Elsa, is that you?"

"Mark!" she exclaimed. "I can't believe this. I was just, this very moment, picking up the phone to call you!"

What? Wait a minute, she was trying to call *me*? At that same precise moment?

"Oh, my God!" I exclaimed, incredulous. "Are you serious?"

"Yes! I tried a little while ago, but your line was occupied," she said, in disbelief at the sound of my voice. "This is so strange, I can't believe it's actually you!"

She was trying to call me? Precisely when her name came to me? At the very same time I realized I longed for her voice?

Blame it on exorbitant TelCel rates, but I decided to cut right to the chase. "Elsa there's something I called you to tell you," I began.

She quickly interrupted. "Before you say anything, there's something I was calling *you* to say."

"Really?" What was this, *The Twilight Zone?* "OK, you go first."

"No you go first!" she insisted.

"No, Elsa you go..." I stopped myself. This sounded like one of Marco's crazy ideas for a game. Unfortunately, quite an expensive game to play while communicating on any given phone connection owned and operated by billionaire Carlos Slim.

"Elsa, I just called to tell you something. Something I didn't really know until today."

She listened intently.

"I just got off the phone a few minutes ago," I explained, telling her about the unexpected call that had come in from out of the blue moments earlier.

"Let me guess! You're getting back together," she interrupted. Evidently, Elsa knew "the old me" pretty darn well.

"No, Elsa. She actually told me she missed me. She hinted at giving it another shot. But I told her I wouldn't."

"You didn't?" she asked, surprised. "But why not?"

"Because something hit me out of the blue while she was talking to me. I realize it now, Elsa."

"Realize what?" She sounded perplexed.

"I realized I would so much rather be talking to you."

There was a stunned silence on the other end of the line. It was too late to stop now.

"I don't know how and I don't know why, but in one split second it was all so clear. It was like their was this voice inside of me, speaking your name. And I know it now. I would rather talk to you. Elsa. I'd rather talk with you than anyone else!"

More silence. *Uh-oh*, I thought. *Did I just mess up big time?*

"Now what was it you wanted to tell me, Elsa?" I asked.

The pause seemed to last an eternity. Finally, she spoke.

"About an hour ago, the mother of the kids I care for pulled me aside, to let me know that some things have happened in their family. She told me they won't be needing me anymore as a nanny. Mark, I'm coming back to Guaymas!"

****

Then you told me that you wanted me too
Last night I dreamed of you

Chapter Thirty Eight

"This is the worst wedding *ever!*"

There she stood, in the middle of the Guaymas Civil Registry. Beautiful as an angel. And madder than hell.

The day had started out just like any other. Oh, except for one small detail.

"I can't believe it. We're actually getting married today!" Elsa stood there at my kitchen door, smiling as I greeted her with a kiss. She looked so happy, even if today was just the required legal ceremony in front of a judge at Guaymas's Civil Registry, with the church ceremony still a month off. In Mexico, it's every guy's nightmare and every girl's dream come true: *Two* weddings!

"I can't believe it either, Elsa. How did this all happen so fast?"

Wow! It really *had* happened fast.

Wasn't it only yesterday that I was at my brother Tom's house, another Christmas party coming to an end, catching Dave before he walked out the door?

****

"Dave, don't go yet. Let's have a beer together!"

"Bro, it's almost midnight!" Dave exclaimed, as if that ever stopped my younger brother from consuming an alcoholic beverage before.

"I know. But how many times do we get to talk? Come on, stick around a bit longer. Let's have one more cold one," I insisted. "Oh, and take a walk," I added.

Dave looked at me like I was crazy. *Take a walk?* he thought to himself. *Like, around the neighborhood? At midnight?*

I reached in the refrigerator and grabbed four beers.

Four? Dave raised his eyebrows, looking at me curiously as I turned to him, beers in hand. "Come on, Dave, let's go for a walk."

****

"I'm sorry, the judge isn't here today," the secretary responded dryly, barely looking at us as she typed away on her keyboard.

"Excuse me, but what do you mean, the judge isn't here?" Elsa asked. "Where is he? And what time will he *be* here?"

The secretary looked up from her desk. "He won't. He's got a meeting out of town and won't get back to Guaymas until Monday. You'll have to come back then."

OK, this may have been my second time around the block, and I don't claim to be an expert on the civil matrimonial process. But, call it a gut feeling, this wasn't looking good.

"He's out of town until Monday?" Elsa exclaimed, in disbelief at what she was hearing. "And we'll have to come back? Um, pardon me, but in case you haven't noticed, I'm wearing a dress! And him, he's wearing a suit!" she said angrily, pointing to me. "And those people, they're all dressed up because they're here as legal witnesses! To a wedding ceremony! *Our* wedding ceremony! A ceremony the judge himself scheduled for this morning!"

"*Lo siento,*" the secretary said nervously, rifling through a folder and pulling out the judge's itinerary. "He forgot he had you scheduled today. You'll have to come back Monday."

Monday? Elsa wasn't about to take that for an answer.

"No, we're *not* coming back Monday! One of the witnesses took today off of work to be here, and she can't get off a second time. And besides, my husband won't even be in town next week. I'd kind of like to have my witness, *and* my husband, here for my wedding ceremony!"

Yes, things were getting a bit uncomfortable.

"I'm not sure what I can do," the secretary responded with a helpless look on her face.

"Find another judge!" Elsa demanded.

"There aren't any others available," she replied. "Not today. They're all at the meeting."

Great! What now? No judge, our civil wedding reception planned for just an hour later, Elsa dressed up to get married, and me standing there in a suit. Forget Elsa's dress. Think I'm putting that damn suit on a second time?

Maybe it was the fact that the line behind us was getting restless. Or that my lovely bride was on the verge of going postal. Or maybe that woman behind the desk took one look at me in a suit and prayed to God I'd never have to put it on again. But she seemed to suddenly realize the urgency of our situation.

"Look," she said, lowering her voice to a near whisper. "If you really need to do this right now, I think there's a way I might be able to handle this for you."

****

"So that's it, Dave." I stood there, an empty beer bottle in one hand and a full one in the other. "That's how it happened. I never expected it to. But it just did."

My little brother was speechless. The story he had heard over the past fifteen minutes hit him out of nowhere. He stood there, gradually absorbing all he had heard. Finally, he spoke.

"Wow, I really don't know what to say."

Maybe I shouldn't have told him, I thought, instantly regretting my decision. *Maybe it was wrong to ever kiss her in the first place. Even if he himself had told me we'd make a good couple, maybe this whole thing is wrong.*

"Dave," I interjected. "Elsa and I both want you to know something. If on second thought, in any way if this is *not* what you'd want for us, or if it makes you uncomfortable in the least, we don't have to go there. Elsa and I can remain friends and never take it further. I mean that. It's not like we've crossed some line we can't cross back again."

"In fact, the only reason I'm even talking to you about this now is that I wouldn't want to start something I couldn't finish," I added. "It's just that with everything that's happened, from that first kiss to that last phone call, we just have this strange feeling that for some reason, we're meant to be together."

Dave just nodded his head, appearing somewhat pensive.

"Mark," he finally replied, popping open his last beer. "I'm going to tell you something, bro. First of all, I really appreciate you being honest with me. Man, it's crazy stuff you're talking about here. And I'll admit, even though I had kind of thought you guys would make a good couple, now that you're actually pursuing it, it's kind of a shock!"

He paused for a moment. "But you know what? This is exactly how things ought to be handled by brothers."

Good, he's not angry at me, I thought to myself, momentarily relieved. *No matter whether or not he wants Elsa and me to give our relationship a shot, at least he's not mad!*

"Listen, bro, you know I love Elsa," he continued.

OK, here it comes, I thought, bracing myself for a letdown.

"But most of all I want you to be happy." Raising his bottle to mine, Dave grinned. "Elsa is incredible. The only thing that'll ever upset me is if you love that awesome girl and don't give it a shot."

****

"OK, I've got everything else. Now I just need to see your friend's passport," the secretary said, motioning toward Jim Bomberg.

"Why is she pointing to me?" Jim asked, a bewildered look on his face.

"Just hand her your passport," I instructed him.

Jim reached into his pockets, then panicked. "I don't have it!" he exclaimed. "I must have left it in San Carlos!"

I rolled my eyes and turned to the woman behind the desk, explaining to her that my gringo friend wasn't exactly on the ball, and that he had forgotten to bring his passport with him.

"Is it really necessary?" I added.

She frowned. "I'm afraid it is. I can't complete the necessary forms without his passport number. It's required of any foreign witness."

Damn! Just then a thought crossed my mind. "Hey, do you actually need to make a copy of the passport, or is it just the passport number you need?"

"Just the number," she answered, "along with date and place of birth."

"Well, if that's the case," I informed her, "he happens to know his passport number."

"He does?" she asked, surprised. "Off the top of his head?"

Yeah, right, Jim Bomberg memorizing a passport number? On a good day he's lucky if he remembers his own birthday.

"Yeah, he travels a lot." I turned to Jim, winking. "Tell her your passport number."

"What? My passport number? I have no idea..." Jim retorted.

"Jim! Do you understand what I'm saying? The lady needs your passport number in order to fill out the documents." I winked again. The next guy in line must have suspected that I was not only gay, but had horrible taste in men.

"Oh, *mi pasaporte número!*" Jim exclaimed, suddenly beaming at the chance to assault another innocent victim with his Spanish. "Let's see, it's *siete cinco tres...*"

After Jim recited a ninth random digit, I quickly jumped in. "OK, *gracias* Jim, that's all!"

To my amazement, the clerk filled in the number, asked him the place and year of his birth, then handed him the document and a pen.

"Sign here," she instructed him.

Jim reached for the pen, then hesitated. "Can you ask her if this is under oath?" he asked, apparently terrified by the prospect of spending his waning days in a Mexican prison, practicing his flirtatious Spanish phrases with a lonely cellmate instead of Doña Telma.

"Just sign it, Bomberg!" I demanded impatiently. He took the pen from her, scribbled his name on the dotted line, then handed it back.

Jim looked at me, lowering his voice to a whisper. "Ever tick me off and I can get this whole thing annulled!"

Meanwhile, Elsa continued to pace back and forth, occasionally making frantic calls on the phone to explain our unexpected dilemma to friends and family down in Navojoa, who would be waiting until the church wedding to come up.

"OK *señor*," the secretary said, handing me a small stack of documents. "Take these originals, along with the copies, and your identification over to window three. Then come back and see me."

Sounded easy to me. "OK, *gracias*. I'll be right back!"

Soon I was standing in a line, apparently one that also included people paying for birth certificates and permits to operate heavy machinery. Before I had a chance to thoroughly examine the papers in my hand, I had reached the window.

"Yes, that woman over there told me to bring these to you?" I said, pointing to the secretary who had sent me and handing over the documents.

The cashier glanced at the papers. "One moment, please." Taking the documents, he disappeared from the window, moments later reappearing across the room. Speaking with the woman who had sent me over, he appeared to be concerned about something. After several minutes, he returned.

"Five hundred thirty-three pesos, please."

I reached into my pocket, grabbed my wallet and pulled out a wad of pesos. Counting out the correct amount, I handed it to the man, who recounted it and grabbed a rubber stamp. *Bam!* As we all know, there's nothing that turns a Mexican government official on more than slapping a rubber stamp on things. *Bam! Bam!* Whatever this part of the process this was, it was certainly very, very official. A few seconds later, he handed the documents back to me.

"*¡Felicidades!*" he said with a big smile.

Hmm. Why was this fellow working behind window three congratulating me?

"Hey, what's the deal…?" I began. He simply pointed, directing me back to the secretary's desk. Hurriedly, I grabbed the papers and made my way across the crowded, chaotic room.

"Excuse me *señora*," I said, "but that guy over there at the window just congratulated me. What's that all about? That wasn't it, was it? We're not, by any chance, legally married now, are we?"

"*Married?*" Elsa had heard my voice, and was now hurriedly approaching the desk "Wait just a minute! He's across the room standing in a line, I'm over here talking on the phone, and suddenly we're married? That was it? What's going on?"

The woman behind the desk fidgeted nervously. "Well, the documents have all been approved. The only thing lacking was the judge's signature, but I signed for him as a temporary measure. He can sign off on it all when he gets back, but for now, I believe everything is good and you're set to go."

"Set to go? You *believe*?" Elsa asked, puzzled. "What do you mean? Forget 'set to go'! Are we married, or not?"

There was nowhere for the secretary to hide. "Look, to tell you the truth, I'm not exactly sure. I've never done it like this before without the judge actually being physically present. Just call us Monday, he'll be back and can okay everything, and there won't be any confusion."

Elsa was livid. "You've got to be kidding! You don't know if we're married. What are we supposed to do until the judge gets back?" she demanded. "Seriously, when my husband goes to the United States this weekend and people ask him if he's a married man, should he say yes or no?"

The reply from the secretary wasn't exactly the vote of confidence we were hoping for, as she simply raised her eyebrows and haplessly shrugged.

Elsa lost it. "You're telling me I got all dressed up, convinced my husband to wear a suit, got all these witnesses to arrange their schedules… for *this*?" Exasperated, she turned around to face the rest of the crowd that filled the lobby. "This is positively the worst wedding in history!" she shouted, her face red with anger, as a roomful of amused onlookers chuckled. "This is typical Guaymas! This is stupid! This is…"

"Elsa, it's OK," I interrupted softly, realizing that if anyone were filming this debacle we'd soon be garnering millions of hits on YouTube. I grabbed her arm and pulled her toward me, reassuringly. "Come on. It's just the civil ceremony. Who cares? The only one that really matters is the church wedding next month."

It took a few moments but she finally calmed down.

"You're right," she grudgingly admitted. "This doesn't really matter. Not like the church wedding. Whatever. I guess we'll just wait 'til Monday to find out if we're actually legally husband and wife."

"There you go, much better," I consoled her. "And besides, after a wedding like we just had, think of the odds. Things can only go up from here!"

I was right. Things went up from there. Three days later, I got a long distance call from Elsa.

"Mark, I just called the secretary downtown at the *Registro Civil*. Good news! The judge showed up. He signed the papers. We're legally married!"

Chapter Thirty Nine

"I found it. The perfect spot! This is where our adventure is gonna begin!"

Welcome to Puerto Morelos, Quintana Roo Mexico. "Just wait until you see this place!" I excitedly said. "The beach is incredible, the water is turquoise blue, the town's beautiful, the people are friendly... this place is us!"

"Sure, Playa del Carmen would have been nice too," I acknowledged, realizing this was another last minute change to our hastily thrown together, so-called "plans." "But it's not far away, and besides, as mellow at this place is, it's just way more our style than that crazy scene down there."

"Look, if we're going to travel this far and spend a year away from San Carlos, I want it to be in the very best spot possible," I added."After all, who knows, this could be my last real adventure!"

There was a sudden silence on the other end of the line, until finally Elsa spoke. "What did you say?"

"That Playa del Carmen would have been nice, but..."

"No, not that," she interrupted. "The very last thing you said."

I thought for a moment. "That this might be my last adventure?"

"Yeah, that," she shot back. "I don't ever want to hear you say that again! Do you hear me? We've got a whole lot of adventures in front of us. They're just beginning!"

As she scolded me, I breathed a silent sigh of relief. After all, as a married man, there are things you obligatorily utter to make your wife happy. Like, *"sure I'd love to catch that new Meryl Streep flick,"* or *"Yes, I do think it's time to end life's adventures and settle down."* Maybe that first one would have made her happy, but thank God the last one ticked her off!

****

North, south, east, west
Which direction do you think is best

Elsa's always been a "go for it" girl, never quite fitting the stereotypical image of a wheat farmer's daughter in small town Sonora.

Though she loved growing up in the town of Navojoa, she definitely wanted to see more of this world, dreaming about places like Costa Rica and Cuba. Independent as she was, she'd find a way to get there, even if it was on her own. She never realized that one day, she'd stand on the altar with a guy whose favorite book was a *Rand McNally Atlas*.

Or that her honeymoon would find her in Costa Rica, sitting in a pool with that fellow, talking about where life had so far led.

"Do you ever get tired of San Carlos?" she asked, sipping on a cinnamon spiced piña colada.

"I love San Carlos. It's a great place," I replied, a bit surprised by the question. "But I have to admit, it's been almost seventeen years since I first moved to Sonora. That's a long time in one place."

"Do you ever think about going somewhere else?" she asked.

I paused for a moment. "I guess every time I've ever thought about it, I've deliberately put it out of my mind. Look, aside from the good work situation I've got, Adela always wanted to be near her family, and she loved our home. Even later, except for going to Phoenix that one school semester for Marcos, I've just figured that the kids needed stability. To be home, in one place, where I can work and they can be near cousins and friends."

"What about you?" she persisted. "What do you want?"

Now that's a different question. *What do I want?*

"Wow, if it were it up to me, I wouldn't even own a home at all," I answered, barely hesitating. "I'd probably invest in a piece of dirt somewhere and travel somewhere totally different, at least while the boys are small. I'd pack up whatever we need, leave the rest behind, and let my guitar take us some place we've never been. If it were just up to me, that's what I'd do."

Elsa took another sip of her piña colada and gazed around at the beautiful Costa Rica scenery, with its lush green hills that rolled endlessly into the distance off to the east. To the west, the sun shone down on the beautiful Pacific ocean, where we had taken a surf lesson earlier that morning. A howler monkey swung playfully in the branches up above the pool. Suddenly, Elsa turned to me and smiled.

"Why don't we do that? Why don't we just take off and try something different for a while? Disappear for six months? Who knows, maybe a year?"

Was it just the piña coladas talking? That bartender *was* mixing 'em kind of strong.

Apparently not. The next morning found us on a couple of rented standup paddle boards, making our way toward Playa Grande, just north across the inlet from the town of Tamarindo where we were staying. Two hours later, a barefoot Elsa was standing in a one room schoolhouse, talking with the principal about what it would take to enroll our kids in the Costa Rican school system. From there, we checked out a two bedroom house for rent, along with a couple apartments.

I couldn't believe it. We were actually looking at taking off, along with our kids, on a brand new "adventure." To Costa Rica! Funny, when most Mexican women marry a gringo, their inclination is to move north, not south. But that's what I love about Elsa. She unpredictable. She defies the norm. She's unlike any other woman I know.

For starters, and this was a biggie, she wasn't consumed by jealousy, a trait that ran culturally rampant among most Mexican women. Yes, yes, I know, it's not politically correct to embrace stereotypes, and I can just hear some crazed MSNBC News anchor calling for this book to be banned. But ask any Mexican guy if he'd take his spouse to see a subtitled version of *Fatal Attraction* and you'll get my point. Dinner at Hooters isn't such a wise idea either. Being the particular trait that nearly destroyed my first marriage, I thanked God every single day after marrying Elsa that I didn't constantly have to deal with the destructive jealousy issue.

But aside from that, and nearly equally as important to me, she had a gypsy soul. She didn't allow herself to be held back, by expectations of others or self-created obligations. She was a person who would be ready to pack up and go anywhere in an instant if an opportunity arose, as evidenced first by her move to Guaymas, then to the East Coast. Her willingness to marry some rambling gringo musician instead of a stable, corporate New Yorker underscores the kind of person I fell in love with.

Now here she was, willing to leave a comfortable home in San Carlos to take off and go somewhere else on a whim? And even crazier, was I actually the one infusing some degree of logic into the conversation? That doesn't happen often. But after a couple days of Elsa excitedly investigating our options, I gave it an obligatory shot.

"Elsa, as much as I'd love to live like some carefree tourist in Costa Rica, don't forget that wherever we go, I've got to work. Plus, remember another small detail. We've got two kids. For us, there's a lot more involved than just packing up and going. Believe me, I've done this before. I'd have to not only lineup work, and a lot of it, but get a work permit too. In foreign countries, that can be a real hassle. And if this is anything like Mexico, it can mean a lot of bribes too. It also takes connections. Connections that I may have up there, but not down here."

She listened attentively as I continued. "Then there's the whole issue of the kids. Like the teacher told you, the Costa Rican school system may be great, but it's not guaranteed that they wouldn't have to repeat a year of school when they get back to Mexico. And Marcos already had to repeat a full year after the accident."

God, talk about a vibe-killer. Was this me? For one terrifying moment I sounded like a rational human being.

But killing the vibe wasn't the point. I certainly was game if she was. I just wanted her to be aware of the hassles involved, including a list of other things I hadn't even mentioned. Like the fact I'd have to cancel most American shows I couldn't afford to fly to from Costa Rica, then gamble on being accepted by that nation's union as legally required, getting our vehicles legally imported or buying/leasing one, acquiring a sound system, etc, all on a shoestring budget. It's no fun to go anywhere on a limited time adventure and then spend half your time on hassles. You cruisers out there can vouch for me on this one.

So I at least wanted to give her another option, one that might provide an equal amount of fun with a lot less hassles.

"Elsa, Mexico is a huge country. It would take me days to drive across it. I've never been to most of it, and neither have you. The kids are already in the school system *and* I've got the only "independent artist" work permit for a foreigner in the whole country. My sound system, our vehicles, my union permit, they're all there. What if we took off on an adventure and went somewhere totally different within Mexico, with all those hassles already dealt with, so we could really enjoy every minute of our time away to the max?"

"What do you mean?" she asked. "Do you want to go somewhere nearby in Sonora like Rocky Point? Or over to Baja?"

"We can go anywhere we want! I'm up for it,." I assured her. "In fact, just find a map and pick out any random spot you'd want to go, no matter how far away. Then, just give me a little time to check things out, and I'll see if I can line up enough work to get us down there. What do you think?"

Maybe I should have been alarmed by the fact that this otherwise sane individual trusted my advice, about anything. It's truthfully the only thing that had given me doubts on the altar. But she agreed. And in true Elsa fashion, within minutes she had already decided on where.

"The Riviera Maya!" she happily exclaimed. "It's totally different than anything we've ever experienced! We could experience the

Caribbean, but right in Mexico!"

She was right. It'd be like living in the Caribbean, but without the dreadlocks and seven dollar beers.

"Cool!" I responded. "Let me check it out." Who was I kidding? I already knew we were gone. It's just that now and then, I like to momentarily think that God gave me a head to use for more than a hat rack, as my brother Tom would say. And at least I could now check the box that says "planned things out logically."

Barely a month later, we sat on the patio at San Carlos' Hotel Fiesta, a world away from where that conversation took place, enjoying a live band and a beautiful sunset over the Sea of Cortez.

"OK," I said, "I've read that *Lonely Planet* book cover to cover, along with every Riviera Maya guide book I could get my hands on. We've checked out as many things as we can on-line. I've called bar and restaurant owners, emailed resort managers, and done basically everything I can to check out what it would be like to live down there. We've talked endlessly about this, and now you know exactly as much as I do. We've come to that moment. It's time."

"Your *cervezas*, señor," the waiter interrupted, dropping off a couple cold Pacificos.

"It's time to walk the walk, or quit talking the talk," I continued. "Whatever we decide, it's cool with me. If we say 'go', we go, and let the chips fall where they may. And if we say 'no', that's OK too. We can talk about some other dream, and not waste time talking about this one."

She agreed, lifting her beer to mine.

"By the time we get to the bottom of these two bottles, we make the final call," I declared. "No going back, no matter what."

We got one sip into the deal, when she put her beer down. Smiling, she looked me right in the eyes. "Let's go."

Yep. That's why I love my girl.

****

Don't tell me I don't know where I'm going
My ticket says any way the wind is blowin'

Uh-oh.

"$750 per *week*?" I asked, aghast at the number I had just heard. In San Carlos I could rent the entire west wing of Paradiso Resort for that amount. And shoot, this wasn't even on the beach.

After several days of meeting with rental agents, then finally resorting to knocking on doors up and down the streets of Puerto Morelos, asking complete strangers if they knew of anyone with a place for rent, I had learned something I hadn't discovered in the *Lonely Planet* book.

Rents are expensive in Mexico's Riviera Maya! OK, maybe not if you're renting something in slower season months, but our problem was we needed something year-round. Unfortunately, "year-round" happens to include peak winter months when snowbirds from all over the world flock to the region. When that happens, prices soar out of reach for anything within sight of sand and salty water.

I was out of time. My exploratory mission was coming to an end. If I didn't find something quickly, I'd fly home empty-handed and we'd eventually be forced to rent something on-line, sight unseen, which made both Elsa and me nervous. One of the very reasons I had spent four hundred fifty bucks on a round trip Volaris Airlines ticket to Cancun was to personally find "that perfect place" for our family *and* to negotiate something reasonable.

No doubt, this second floor apartment was the best one I had seen so far. Though it wasn't on the beach, it was only a block away, and the porch had a view of the ocean and offshore reef. Sure, it was small, but with two bedrooms, we could stick the boys in one and us in the other. Besides, it's not like we needed a ton of space. After all, since I'd have to fit everything, including my sound system and guitar, into a relatively small four cylinder SUV, we'd only be bringing our clothes and a few board games for the kids.

"I can easily book this place solid at $750 *per week* during January and February," the landlord informed me, showing me the second bedroom as he spoke.

I was dismayed, but holding out hope, this being my favorite place I had seen the entire trip. "So $850 per month, on a longer lease, is completely out of the question?"

The landlord chuckled. "I'm sorry, amigo, but I can't pass up those weekly winter rents," he responded firmly. "If you need to be here during those months too, the best I can do is drop you to $1300 per month on a six month to annual lease. You won't find anything this nice, this close to the water, *and* with a pool, for less than that."

"Bummer!" I shrugged, realizing it was simply beyond what we could afford. "Oh well, can't say I didn't try. Thanks so much for showing me your place," I said, shaking his hand. "Hey, by the way, how's that little bar down on the beach?"

Ten minutes later, I was ordering him a cold beer.

OK, I may not have skills when it comes to plumbing, auto mechanics, masking politically incorrect views, or logging on to my own email account, but I do have somewhat of a knack for negotiating. Don't confuse me with some French-Canadian tourist haggling with a street kid over a pack of Chiclets. I only utilize my skills when I truly don't have the money to complete the desired transaction.

"It's Thomas, right?" I asked. He nodded. "Thomas, I gotta tell you, you would absolutely *love* my wife and kids. They're great! Oh, and did I mention? They're really clean too."

"I bet they are," he replied. "And buddy, I really wish I could let you guys live in that apartment below me, but I just can't. You understand, right?"

"Sure I do," I answered. As I watched Thomas take his first swig of dark *Leon* beer, I noticed a couple things about him. First of all, his English and Spanish were both perfect, even though he was from Austria. Second, he was a dead-ringer for Alec Baldwin. Though an incredible actor, I never liked Alec Baldwin. Most flight attendants reportedly don't either. Third, Thomas had his eye on a beautiful girl sitting behind me at the bar. She was apparently there with a few friends.

"Hey!" Thomas perked up. "I know her!"

Suddenly, I was sitting at the bar alone while Thomas conversed with a pretty *señorita*. Apparently he had been friends with her years back, maybe even gone on a date or two, before both had moved on. I wasn't sure about the details, but didn't have time to care. There were other pressing things to worry about. Like signing a lease. And quickly.

"Bartender, can you send that couple over there a round?"

It was the first of several rounds Thomas and his lovely acquaintance received, complimentary of some inexplicably generous fellow visiting from Sonora, Mexico.

"Mark, do you want to join us?" Thomas said, popping over momentarily to see how I was doing.

"Thanks Thomas, you guys do your catching up. I'm fine over here. But how about another beer?" I motioned the bartender to bring Thomas another cold one.

"*¡Gracias!*" he said, grabbing the beer and turning to head back to talk with his long-lost friend. Suddenly he stopped and turned to me. "Hey, I shouldn't do this, but you seem like a really nice guy. Tell you what. How 'bout if I were to drop the rent down to eleven hundred bucks per month? Six months?"

"Thomas, I appreciate that," I replied with a smile. "But like I told you back at the apartment, all we can afford is $850 per month. I wish it was more. But $850 is all we can do."

"It's too bad," I added. "My wife and kids would love that place. And I know you would really like them too."

Once again Thomas disappeared, heading back over to talk with his newfound friend from the past. They seemed to be hitting it off quite well by now.

"Bartender, please send another round to that couple, on me. If he wants a shot, give it to him."

The Lord works in mysterious ways. Maybe even through beer and beautiful girls.

"What if I drop it to a thousand bucks a month, winter months included?" Thomas was back, this time his eyes a tad bit glazed.

"Thomas, like I said, I really wish we could," I answered. "I'm truly not trying to weasel you down. I just don't want to get into a rent situation where I can't pay, lose my deposit and also leave you hanging in the slow months without a renter. Check any of the references I gave you and they'll tell you I'm not the kind of guy to do that. I pay on time, every time, in fact have never missed a payment of any kind in my life. But that's 'cause I only buy or rent what I can afford. And this is all I can afford, really. I'm not a tourist, just a musician. If you can't rent it to me, it'll bum me out, but I understand. Now, hey, how about one more beer?"

The bartender was already on it, setting a cold *Leon* in front of Thomas, well aware by now of the implicit instruction that a beer was to be served every time Thomas's bottle was empty.

Thomas looked straight into my eyes. Well, at least as straight as you can look into someone's eyes after several shots and beers. Nevertheless, it was strange. I felt like Alec Baldwin was about to kiss me.

Suddenly, he grinned widely. "Son of a bitch, I'm gonna regret this tomorrow," Thomas exclaimed, slapping me on the shoulder. "You got it. $850! But minimum six month lease, and you pay utilities! Deal?"

"Deal!" I excitedly replied. Realizing that a good buzz doesn't last forever, I hurriedly added, "How soon can we sign the contract?"

A couple hours later the ink had dried on a hastily arranged contract. "Welcome to Puerto Morelos!" Thomas said, slurring his words a bit as he shook my hand.

The adventure had begun.

Do you ever wander, I wander sometimes
Don't it make you wander

Chapter Forty

It's safe to say, when you leave on a trip with two kids and return with three and a half, fun has been had! In our case, the "adventure" started before we ever even pulled out of the driveway, with two unexpected words. Two *very* unexpected words.

"I'm pregnant!"

OK, a lot of folks may not quite understand a common reaction experienced by fathers of two or more children, the precise moment they learn they're going to have yet another.

In the span of approximately six point three seconds, an entire unspoken, internal thought process hurriedly takes place, starting with *"Did she just say what I thought she just said?"* Followed typically by a *"No! This can't be true!"* Stage three: *"Come on, is she messing with me?"* Then, *"My God, she's serious!"* Then comes your choice of the split-second *"What the $%^! was I thinking?,"* or perhaps a *"How in the #%! am I going to afford another child?"* Then comes the moment you look at the beautiful smile on your wife's face and slowly glance down at her belly as she asks, "Well, aren't you gonna say anything?" The process typically comes to a conclusion with an *"I can't believe it... it's incredible... awesome... I'm gonna be a Dad again!"*

It's a particular, insane joy experienced by men who have fathered multiple kids, Terrell Owens and the Octomom's husband excluded.

"What do you think, Elsa?" I asked. "Think we'll have a boy or a girl?" No offense to Marcos or Luis, but when it came to the whole *"it's a boy!"* thing, I'd been there and done that. Sure, another boy would be fun, but wouldn't it be something to have a little girl?

"I don't know," she said. "I have this feeling God wants us to have a girl."

Luckily, Elsa was still early enough along in her pregnancy to fly. Luis would accompany his pregnant mother in the friendly skies all the way to Cancun, where Marcos and I would meet up with them in the X-Trail after driving cross country for four days.

If it didn't fit in the car, it didn't come. Considering the fact that Marcos would have the front passenger seat and my sound system most of the rear of the vehicle, that didn't leave a lot of room for much else. Good thing is, when faced with limited space and lots to pack, musicians are experts. Come on, who else could somehow fit two 15 inch JBL speakers, a Mackie amplifier, a guitar, a full size keyboard, a half-eaten pizza, two speaker stands and a duffel bag stuffed full of cables into the back seat of a used Ford Escort? A musician, of course!

And lucky for me, I had recently traded in my big gear for a new, more compact Bose L1 Tower system, one that could break apart into four manageably-sized pieces and leave room for other necessities, such as my oldest kid. And even though the X-Trail wasn't big, it still could fit a lot of crap, especially when you occupied every square centimeter of space.

I practically had to wrap a bungee cord around the entire vehicle to keep the doors from popping open, we were so jammed. But somehow, we did it. Everything a family of five would need to survive on for the next year was miraculously packed into a four cylinder vehicle. OK, maybe that act didn't quite compare with Luis responding to his father again or Adela sending me messages from Heaven, but it was quite a miracle in itself.

****

"Look at this place! It's incredible!" Elsa couldn't believe her eyes as she stared out at the vast, never ending expanse of turquoise water. "Let's get in!"

Puerto Morelos was exactly as I had described to her. It was a hidden paradise, unknown to the swarms of tourists that flocked thirty minutes north to Cancun or Playa del Carmen, a half hour to the south.

"I love it!" she exclaimed, wading waist-deep into the water while Marcos and Luis kicked a ball in the sugary white sand. "I think I want to stay here forever!"

There's something to be said about a simple change of scenery in life. Even if the place where you reside is wonderful, it's great to get out and see the world, as much of it as you can. Me, I've always thought about this world as one big amusement park. Who'd want to simply ride the same ride over and over again? No matter how fun that ride is, wouldn't you be tempted to ride another? Better yet, as many as you possibly could? Isn't that what your tickets are for? What's the point of going home with any? It's not like they're any good to you once the park closes. This is it, your one visit.

Just as in life. Contrary to what Hollywood idiot Shirley MacClaine will tell you, you're not coming back again, not as a human being, a butterfly, an eagle or a cow. The tickets that have been given to you are to be used or shared with others while the park remains open, not piled up or stashed away, hoping there's time to spend them before the park closes.

Elsa and I wanted to do just that. Use up every ticket we could, ride every ride possible, share with our children our allotted stash of tickets, and then go home empty-handed at the end of the day. After all, no one knows what time the park is going to close. It may close unexpectedly early, or if you're lucky, late in the day. But one thing is certain. It *is* going to close.

For some, letting go of those tickets is scary. They've convinced themselves they know when the park is going to close. They assured themselves it won't be tomorrow.

If they could only ask Adela Ruiz Fuentes what she would think of that philosophy.

Sometimes it takes the death of another to remind us to live. To challenge us to make each day count, rather than count each day.

People often look at us doing that and ask me, "how do you guys do it?" The answer is simple. You do it.

Chapter Forty One

"*Lo siento, señor,* we appreciate you coming by, but we're not interested in an audition at this time."

Reality quickly sank in. The big, all-inclusive resorts that lined the Riviera Maya weren't at all interested in having someone encourage their customers to consume more by entertaining them. Why do that when they could pull a random Mexican guy off the street, hand him a guitar and tell him to sing for a bunch of foreign tourists who think "La Bamba" was the only Latin song ever written? Especially when management can pay him the equivalent of four bucks an hour, a six pack of Bud Light, and a bus ride home?

In that beer-swilling moment when Elsa and I threw all caution to the wind and decided to go wherever the wind took us, I hadn't quite pictured that glaring, unfortunate reality. In fact, by the time we showed up in Puerto Morelos, I had lined up in advance a grand total of one paid performance, at a tiny place called Posada Amor.

Fact is, no one on this side of Mexico had ever heard of me. Unlike back home in San Carlos, down here Mark Mulligan was a nobody. I'd basically be starting over, not much differently than when I walked into some cowboy bar in Kirkland Junction, Arizona twenty years before. But there was one big difference. Now, I wasn't playing for beer money. This time, I had mouths to feed, and another on the way!

So I couldn't afford to simply play at one of the little local Puerto Morelos bars for the fifty bucks they'd be willing to offer. I'd have to make several times that, at least, and hope for a big crowd so I could add to that with CD sales and tips.

Somehow I finagled a couple periodic gigs here and there, but I couldn't afford to spend all my time hitting the pavement, day after day, week after week, just trying to line up enough shows to get by each week. I had to find something steady, and build up a following. Otherwise, our adventure would be short-lived. Luckily, across the country in San Carlos, my good friends Bruce and Jeanie "Giggles" Tilley had been worried about this very same thing.

Bruce and Giggles were about as loyal friends and fans that a musician could ever have, attending every show I'd play in San Carlos, sitting in the front row each time, even naming their festively decorated home in San Carlos's Loma del Mar Trailer Park "A Bar Down in Mexico."

After all, the outside patio looked and felt so much like an actual bar that passer-bys would often stop in for a few drinks, then ask for their tab before finding out they were sitting in someone's home!

He's not gonna know anybody on the other side of Mexico, Giggles thought, when she heard of my plans to pack up the family and head off on our adventure. *We've got to help him out!*

That's all it took. Next thing anyone knew, they had packed up their motorhome and left, traveling across Mexico for nearly a week, pulling into a town they had never even heard of, days before Marcos and I made it down ourselves. They spent those days before I showed up getting the word out about a gringo singer coming down from northern Mexico who played beach songs.

"You gotta see him!" Giggles would say as she walked her dogs down the beach, filling in total strangers about that first and only show I had lined up.

Meanwhile, Bruce made himself right at home on a bar stool at a little local joint called Cantina Habanero. It was kind of the Froggys of Puerto Morelos, a place where the locals and expats would hang out and enjoy live music, cheap beer and pizza. It looked like the ideal place to sing.

But Ed Hoffman, the surly owner of the establishment, would have no part of it.

"He's that guy playing over at Posada Amor? He can forget about playing here!" Ed growled. "My musicians work cheap and they work exclusively for me. Once a week here and nowhere else locally. I'm not about to waste money promoting someone, and then find out they want to play other places too."

Ed was a stubborn guy who let his opinions be known, no doubt about it. So much so that I never even asked him for a gig before getting rejected. Instead, he outright informed me right off the bat that I would never have one, the first time I ever stopped in for a beer.

By this time, Bruce and Giggles were living at Cantina Habanero. No, I don't just mean that figuratively. They were literally *living* there, their motorhome parked on the curb and plugged into Ed's place for electricity and internet. With the vast quantity of beer Bruce consumed on a daily basis, the free rent deal was a win-win for both bar owner and customer.

If folks thought Ed was stubborn, they hadn't seen anything yet. Giggles is definitely not a gal who takes "no" for an answer or simply give up as Ed would find out. I'm not sure exactly how it happened, but one thing I know. Had Bruce and Giggles not hopped in that motorhome and crisscrossed the country, I would have never sung a single song at Ed's place. Needless to say, he broke down.

Soon I was singing not once, but twice a week at the best little bar along the Riviera Maya. It was almost like "Tuesday Nights at Froggys" all over again, the patio packed and my music getting into the hands of new listeners night after night. Although Ed didn't exactly write me a blank check, he took good care of me and my family too.

"Tell your kids I'm going to make them Hawaiian pizza tonight," his wife Naty would say, as she'd spot Elsa and me around town together.

As for Ed, turns out he wasn't such a surly guy underneath. When he heard about the Castaway Kid project up in San Carlos, he came to me with an idea.

"Mark, I hear there are these families living out in the dump outside town, eating from whatever trash falls out of the garbage truck. Little kids, man! It breaks my heart. We gotta do something!"

And he did. After personally matching my donations raised from CD sales with profits from pizza sales, Ed hopped in the passenger seat of my X-Trail and off we went. Soon, Ed was a popular guy among the families out there, bringing them food, clothing, and tons of batteries he'd collect so those who scavenged at night could actually see with small flashlights.

As time went by, I learned what had made Ed so rough around the edges. It was the sudden, unexpected death of his daughter years earlier that embittered him. I could sense he didn't want to feel that way, especially after hearing about my own past experience over a few beers.

"Son of a bitch, I'm not a believer, but you're probably gonna convert me!" he'd mutter as I'd sing "Jesus Loves You, The Rest of Us Think You're a Jerk." Soon, it became the grumpy bar owner's favorite request. He wouldn't let me finish a gig without singing it.

It didn't take long for Cantina Habanero to become our home away from home. A year later, when we left Thomas's place for a bigger place not far from the bar, I could actually put my kids to bed *during* my gig.

"Marcos and Luis, one more song. Then it's time to hit the sack!" I'd shout from the microphone, knowing they could hear the sound of my voice carrying through their open bedroom window just down the street. *"¡Buenas noches, boys!"*

Naty loved our kids and we loved hers. Ed, in spite of financial troubles at the bar, always had a big smile for us when we walked in the door, usually sending a pizza to our table about fifteen minutes after we'd arrive. Not only was every single pizza he ever gave us on the house, but he never once let me pay for a drink in his bar.

"Until I can someday pay you what you're really worth, you're not paying for one damn drink!" he insisted. There was no arguing with Ed. And there never would be, up until the day we stood in a hospital waiting room, holding Naty up as the doctor broke the news.

"He's passed away."

The news was sudden. It had happened overnight, when Ed fell ill at the bar, suffering what appeared to be a stroke. When the ambulance took him away, Naty had a sinking feeling her husband would never return to his beloved bar.

"It's not a bar, it's a *restaurant!*" I can almost hear Ed growl, as he did every time someone referred to Cantina Habanero as a mere drinking establishment.

Restaurant, bar, whatever, folks were worried it would disappear forever with Ed suddenly gone. His personality, gruff as it was, had helped make the Cantina what it was. Little did patrons know, Naty had not only learned quite a few things from her older husband, but also had some ideas of her own. Cantina Habanero survived, the spirit of Ed Hoffman continuing to sing along with me to "Jesus Loves You" right up to the day I played my last show there, eighteen months after arriving in town.

We pulled out of town with a lifetime's worth of memories we'd never forget. Zip-lining and water parks, snorkeling on the reef, boat trips to Belize, visits to 'cenotes" and Mayan Ruins, endless walks down gorgeous beaches, and countless experiences unlike any we had ever imagined before. Oh, and one more thing.

"It's a boy!"

Chapter Forty Two

I guess I never really dreamed that somebody new
Would ever come into your life
Now it simply blows my mind
To look at you holding on to him
The girl I love and my next of kin

OK, he wasn't my first kid, or even my second. But the arrival of Jose Miguel Mulligan Osuna was just as thrilling. And for Elsa, who had never experienced the joy of bringing a child into the world, it was a happiness beyond words. With the perfect name to one day own a sports bar, it was obvious from the start that Jose Mulligan would turn out to be an amazing little guy.

Just one look at those Osuna eyebrows, and you knew he was Elsa's kid. But when it came to his personality, you could tell he was mine. Music? Right off the bat, he loved it. In fact, before he was even born, Elsa could calm him in the womb by playing obscure solo tunes by Colin Hay, former lead singer 80's group Men At Work. By the time he was two, he was rockin' to Peter Frampton's "Baby I Love Your Way," strumming along with daddy on a toy guitar. "Guacamole?" His favorite song of all.

At my gigs, we could keep him occupied for three straight hours simply by giving him a Matchbox toy car. He'd play with it for a while, then set it down and focus on the stage, watching my left hand curiously as it formed chords on the neck of my guitar. Forget that strumming thing other little kids were fascinated by, he was actually interested in how to form the chords. He'd sit there, watching intently, never making a sound until the song was over.

"*¡Bravo!*" he'd exclaim clapping his hands as he grinned widely at his dad on stage. It was the third word he learned, right after "*mama*" and "*papa.*"

You could also tell, he was going to be one good natured, happy go lucky boy. Always smiling and quick to give you a hug, we knew we had somehow lucked out and avoided the child from hell we were statistically likely to get. The kid was as easy to please as they come. Even on his third birthday, when Elsa woke him up with a kiss, offering him *anything* he wanted to eat that day.

"Tortillas!" he shouted, beaming with joy.

That August day we took him home for the first time, we still weren't even a full year into our trip, an adventure we knew couldn't last forever, unless we somehow scored a winning PowerBall ticket. Though my shows at Cantina Habanero were paying the rent, we had plenty of other bills piling up, especially now that we had a new arrival on the scene.

I guess there's a reason I would have flunked out of school as an accounting major.

"Let's stay, Elsa! I don't want this adventure to end when New Years Day rolls around. Do you?"

Stupid question.

****

Those additional six months were well worth staying for. I had gotten to open a charity fundraiser event for country music star Phil Vassar on Isla Mujeres, a gorgeous little island right off Cancun. We had even pulled off another IslandFest, this time on an actual island! We had kayaked in beautiful Bacalar, visited the world famous X-Caret park, experienced the wonderful city of Mérida, seen alligators and monkeys and every tropical beast imaginable.

We had delayed and delayed as long as we could, but it was obvious. Our "adventure funds" had been depleted, and I'd need every one of those upcoming U.S. summer tour dates to catch back up. After those shows, though, then what?

We had learned one thing about the Riviera Maya. Tourist season may boom, but it's short. Shorter than San Carlos, for example, where Americans and Canadians begin arriving in mid-October and stay well through May, June or even the Fourth of July, before finally fleeing the summer heat. In Puerto Morelos, however, things were basically dead until early January, when they'd suddenly take off until Easter. Then suddenly, the town would become a ghost town again, except for the few year-rounders that actually stayed. Unfortunately, after two seasons, those people all had my CDs by now. It was tourists and new faces I needed to sing for, and the fact that they wouldn't be back in large numbers until January presented a challenge we finally had to face.

"It's been a great time, an experience we'll never forget" I remarked sentimentally, shouting over the engine roar of the ferry boat, carting us back to the mainland following our final visit to Isla Mujeres. "We're so lucky we were able to extend this little adventure for as long as we did."

Elsa agreed. "Who would have ever thought when we took off for a year that it would have turned into eighteen months?"

We were wistful, but thankful. Part of us was really looking forward to getting back to San Carlos, seeing all our friends, getting my gigs going again, and settling back into our home.

But part of us wasn't. At least, not quite yet.

Funny how history repeats itself, in more ways than one.

****

"Elsa!" I said, holding the cell phone to my ear as I walked down a sandy Rocky Point beach. "I just had a crazy idea!"

I had just gotten to Sonora three days ago, leaving the family behind in Puerto Morelos to play Memorial Day Weekend shows in San Carlos and then Rocky Point. There had been a huge turnout at Hotel Fiesta event that first night, giving me a hopeful glimpse of what things would be like in autumn, when we'd come back to San Carlos for good.

"We're sure looking forward to having you guys back!" our old friends remarked, greeting me with handshakes and hugs.

No doubt, it was nice to be back in San Carlos, even if it was only for one show before heading up the coast to Rocky Point. Looking out over the Sea of Cortez as I sang, I thought of how soon it would be the backdrop to our lives again. In spite of all the fun we'd had in our travels, it sure would be great to be back on that Cortez again.

But I couldn't help but wonder, was that it? Was our adventure really *over?* I thought of all the experiences we never would have had, if we'd simply stayed in San Carlos a year and a half earlier. Those experiences were priceless. The time and money we put into them were "tickets" well spent.

A crazy thought hit me as soon as I got to Rocky Point. Could we still do that? Could we still experience something completely new, together as a family, even if we couldn't afford to do it in Puerto Morelos?

I looked out at the Sea of Cortez again. *What about here?*

My mind began to race. *What if before San Carlos, we came HERE for while? Elsa's never been up the coast before, so it would all be exciting and new to her! I could play for the visiting gringos on weekends, get down to San Carlos for weekday shows once or twice a month, plus get up to Arizona and California easily...*

Best of all, I thought, aside from replenishing the bank account, we could cram another ride into our "day at the amusement park." We had the tickets. Why not spend 'em?

Within minutes, Elsa's phone was ringing in Puerto Morelos.

Chapter Forty Three

I could leave, but I've learned why even bother
I'd just come back to these Cortez waters

"We lucked out again!" Gazing out over the ocean from our front porch, a silhouette of Baja California in the distance, Elsa couldn't believe her eyes.

"Welcome to Rocky Point, Elsa! I know it's not the Riviera Maya or Puerto Morelos, but hey, at least we get to keep this adventure going just a bit longer!" Looking at the big smile on her face, I could tell she agreed.

Thanks to my friend Steve Schwab, owner of Rocky Point's Seaside Reservations, we had set up a mutually beneficial swap. It was one that would find me promoting the company and performing at the resort properties he managed, in exchange for accommodations at his own beautiful, two bedroom, beachfront unit at Princesa Condominiums. Located on gorgeous Sandy Beach, it was more than we could have ever asked for.

Three pools? A jacuzzi? A gym? And the Sea of Cortez as our front yard? A fellow could definitely get used to this.

Within days, Marcos and Luis were enrolled in public school, where they'd quickly make new friends. Little Jose was keeping Elsa hands full, and I was busy organizing performances up and down Sandy Beach at Seaside's host resorts, as well as laying the groundwork for a larger IslandFest-style musical festival, scheduled for October. For a family that had gotten used to unpredictability and winds that constantly changed, we actually looked forward to settling in a bit and taking a breath.

That was the game plan. Right?

****

I swear, I spend more time on buses than most bus drivers do. This particular journey, barely a month after getting to Rocky Point, was my second trip to Hermosillo in a matter of days. It all started when we saw a used Ford Focus for sale there. After much debate, Elsa and I had decided that, given my frequent road trips to perform elsewhere and the cost of fuel, we needed to have something that got at least thirty miles per gallon.

With just four thousand miles on the engine, the Focus appeared to be the perfect answer. Though it was small, my guitar and entire Bose sound system still fit into it for any trips I'd make alone. And with room for five, the whole family could still get around town.

When Elsa's dad offered to buy our old pickup, it sealed the deal. I took the five hour bus trip to Hermosillo, test drove it, and put down a partial cash deposit. I immediately boarded another bus, this one northbound, where one hundred seventy eight miles later I'd cross the border into Nogales and arrange a few wire transfers through my U.S. bank account.

Soon I was crossing back across the border into Mexico by foot, wads of bills stuffed into a crumpled Burger King bag. (Blame it on stories about international drug smuggler Joaquin *"El Chapo"* Guzmán, but I figured even if I were to get the dreaded "red light" requiring a search of my duffel bag, customs officials wouldn't think to delve beneath a half-eaten burger in a fast food bag.) Twenty minutes later I was back on a southbound bus, headed once again toward Hermosillo, too tired to sleep, passing the time reading a book a friend had given me.

The book was *The Father's Guide to Birth, Babies and Loud Children,* written by a wacky, Wisconsin based sportswriter turned trop-rock artist named Jim Hoehn. Just as the subtitle described, it was "the absolutely, positively essential guy guide to pregnancy, diapers, car seats, pre-school… and living through it." The frazzled, terrified guy on the cover could have easily been me. I chuckled out loud reading about the utter, non-stop chaos he subjected himself to in raising three kids at a later age. Needless to say, as a fellow who had his first of three boys at thirty four years old, his second at thirty-eight, and his last at forty-four, I related to every situation he recounted, from sleepless nights to diaper changes to battles with car seats.

At least after Jose, I won't ever have to buckle one of those things again, I thought to myself, closing the book and fantasizing about a future without car seats, Huggies, baby wipes or Barney.

The following day, the ink had dried on the contract and I was the proud owner of a Ford Focus. All I had to do was register and insure it. Unfortunately, that meant yet another trip, this one a hundred thirty kilometers down to Guaymas, where I would spend another hour and a half waiting in lines, relishing the joys that can only be fully appreciated when dealing with the bureaucracy of a governmental motor vehicle agency.

From there, on to San Carlos, where I shelled out another seven hundred fifty bucks on an annual insurance policy. (Luckily President Obama had decided against invading Mexico and forcing "relief" on the uninsured, or my rates would have likely been triple.)

Finally, after two days of running around like a madman test driving, buying, transporting the cash for, registering, and insuring our new vehicle, it was time to head back to Rocky Point. I couldn't wait to show Elsa the car and let her take it for a drive! After driving bigger vehicles, I knew she'd get a kick out of the handling of a small car. To top it off, the spotless interior even had that "new car" smell. Usually the vehicles we drive smell more like an overheated engine or someone's dirty diaper than a new car.

I couldn't wait to get home. But just as I was about to pull out of San Carlos and get on the road, my phone rang. "Mark!"

"Hi Elsa!" I exclaimed. "Is something wrong? You sound a bit excited."

"Did you finish paying for the car yet?" she asked, hurriedly.

"Yep. Just moments ago got it all finalized." For some reason, the tone of her question seemed a bit odd. What struck me as even more strange was the bizarre silence that followed on the other end of the line. Finally she spoke.

"Mark..." *Why on earth did she sound so nervous?*

Suddenly, out of nowhere, it hit me. *Oh, my God. It can't be.* Before I could stop myself, I blurted it out.

"You're pregnant!"

The terrifying silence on the other end continued, as I waited in vain for Elsa to either laugh out loud or issue some sort of indignant denial. After what seemed like an eternity, I heard Elsa's voice.

"How did you know?"

WHAT? How did I know?

This was not the reply I had been hoping for.

You've got to be kidding! She's pregnant! But how... when... what?

Forget that multi-step, eventually exhilarating, *"you're what?"* process of grasping this type of heart-stopping announcement that I walked you through earlier. After a previous trifecta of boys, that process had long ago worn out its welcome. Trying to muster up the required energy for a positive, heartwarming response was beyond me.

Her voice cut through the silence. "How did you know?" she repeated cheerily.

She sounded *happy!*

"Believe me, Elsa," I sighed. "If there's anybody who knows the 'I'm pregnant' voice, it's me."

"Well?" she prodded. "Aren't you happy?"

I stood there, too shocked to answer, trying to absorb the blow I had just received. Evander Holyfield got lighter jabs from Mike Tyson, and he only lost an ear. I was about to lose my ass.

She's pregnant? As in, *having another kid?* A baby? *Bebé? Bambino?* In whatever particular phrasing you choose, this was not news I was expecting, nor honestly hoping for.

Until it dawned on me. This is Elsa. Wasn't this the same girl who weeks before had played a practical joke on her own mother, upsetting the poor woman by calling her and insisting that I had dumped her to run off with a younger gal? The same girl who, after dressing to the nines to go out on the town, likes to color one of her incisors black so it looks like she's missing a tooth? The same girl who once walked around the town plaza with a basketball under her blouse, pretending to drink from an empty quart of beer, just to shock onlookers into thinking she was the expectant mother from hell?

That's it! She was messing with me! And I wasn't about to fall for it.

"You're not pregnant!" I declared, confidently.

"What? Elsa responded, confused. "I just told you…"

"Yeah, yeah, I know what you told me," I interrupted. "But you're not fooling me one bit. You're not pregnant!"

"Yes, I am!" she insisted.

"No, no, you're not!" I stammered haplessly.

"Yes, I am!" she retorted, somewhat indignant at this point.

My newfound confidence was quickly waning.

"You are?" I feebly replied. "You really, really are?"

"Mark, I'm pregnant," she calmly replied. From the slight chuckle I detected on the other end of the line, she was either extending one heck of a cruel joke, or completely oblivious to the fact that on a musician's income we couldn't afford extra ingredients on our pizza, much less hospital delivery bills, baby clothes, diapers and formula, eighteen years of additional expenses and a future college education for yet another child.

"So, you're seriously not kidding around here?" Hell, it was worth one last shot. At this point, what did I have to lose?

"I'm not joking, I promise," she said, as if those words somehow reassured me.

I stood there, stunned, holding the phone to my ear, then slowly dropping it to my waist as I drifted off into a momentary fog. Seconds later, I heard her voice calling to me through the receiver.

"Mark? Are you there? Mark?"

Slowly I pulled the phone back up to my ear. "Yeah, I'm here."

"Are you OK?" Elsa asked, apparently worried I had pulled a Kurt Cobain on her.

I eked out a reply. "Sure, I'm fine, Elsa."

"Do you need some time alone?" she gingerly asked.

I thought for a moment before answering, slowly resigning myself to the situation. "Just give me a little extra time to get home."

"For what?"

"I need to pick up a 'For Sale' sign for this damn car we just bought," I replied. "Looks like we're gonna need a van."

Apparently she thought I was trying to be comical. People do say I'm at my funniest when I'm miserable. No wonder I'm so darn hilarious.

After a good laugh, her voice softened. "Mark, I know this is a shock," she said. "I didn't expect it either. But it is what it is. We'll be fine! And best of all, we're going to have another baby!"

You asked for my reaction
There it is, I can't lie
So how can it be
That somehow, suddenly
All I do is think of you and smile

Chapter Forty Four

I could tell it had been on her mind.

"I have to admit, with the baby coming in April, I'd kind of like to get back home to San Carlos again," Elsa commented one afternoon, gazing out over the ocean. "As fun as this has all been, it really would be nice to be closer to my family again."

She was right. When Jose was born, her mom had flown all the way down to Puerto Morelos to be with her, but just for a few days before having to return. Even though we were now back in the state of Sonora, we were still a good nine hour drive from her parents' home. San Carlos, on the other hand, was a mere three hours away from Navojoa, quite a difference if her parents wanted to make frequent visits to see the baby.

We had enjoyed our stay and were grateful to Steve Schwab for the opportunity he had given us in Rocky Point. Over five months, I had sung for countless new faces, met wonderful new friends, and gotten my CDs into lots of new hands. Elsa herself got to experience a part of Sonora she had never even been to. Living in a beachfront condo had been quite an experience for all of us, one we otherwise could have never afforded. Most of all, we had gotten to stretch our trip out to the fullest, enjoying every moment we could along the way.

But finally, nearly two years after heading out on our so-called "adventure," it was time to go home. With two kids in school, a baby in diapers and another on the way, the moment had arrived. Come New Years Day, the adventure would be coming to an end.

****

It's all so predictable
So safe, so sensible
So logical, it's driving him insane

"*¡Marcos, eres completamente loco!*"

Admittedly, it wasn't the first time I'd heard those words from Elsa's mouth. But this time, they seemed a bit more emphatic than usual.

Guess I couldn't blame the girl for thinking I was off my rocker. After all, just weeks before, we had finalized "plans." No, not our typical, crazy, "let's take off and go where the wind takes us" kind of plans like previous ones. Instead, they were plans to go home, settle down, and raise four kids in a stable, normal "home" environment, rather than out of a suitcase in some rented apartment or borrowed condo. They were plans to remodel the kitchen, put an addition on to our house, buy all new furniture, and to invest in a permanent future in San Carlos.

They were safe, smart plans. Ones that anyone with half a brain would endorse. Of course. They made perfect sense.

That's precisely what scared the hell out of me.

It's not that I wasn't happy to return to San Carlos. Heck, it's hard to find a more beautiful place. I missed my friends, sailing my Hobie Cat, kayaking in and out of beautiful coves, spearfishing, singing for the wonderful San Carlos crowd, and all kinds of things I had been far away from for the past couple years.

And true, my kids would certainly benefit from a more stable home environment, having their old friends to play with, and not being uprooted from schools whenever some opportunity arose for us to chase some crazy new adventure.

True, the kitchen could probably use remodeling. Yes, an additional bedroom would be nice with another kid on the way.

And I definitely agreed with Elsa when it came to being closer to her family in Navojoa so they could visit more often.

So it wasn't the desire to extend our "adventure," or head off to some other far-off spot to begin a new one, that had me second guessing our future plans. It was something else. Something that had begun gnawing at me as far back as our days in Puerto Morelos, in the middle of some of the most fun moments we had during our time away.

Something that took me back to when I first met Elsa.

****

"I think that's so cool what you're doing with the Castaway Kids. I'd love to help out too!"

Not only was this new assistant at MarinaTerra Hotel friendly, but she had a maturity and spiritual depth to her well beyond her age.

"You know, there's a part of me that sees myself working in another country one day, maybe in Haiti or Central America or even Africa," Elsa continued. "I can really envision myself doing some work with the poor, in a mission or as part of a Christian volunteer group."

"You'll never believe this," she confided with a shy smile, "but there was a time in my life I actually considered being a nun. I even went to a Catholic retreat with other girls to learn more, before I eventually decided against it."

Funny, as a child my mom had actually hoped I'd one day be the Franciscan priest in the family. Had Elsa and I somehow met later in life as priest and nun, wouldn't *that* have been interesting. And folks thought marrying my younger brother's ex-girlfriend was scandalous!

Anyway, it's not like both of us hadn't ever messed up in life. As a single girl, Elsa had definitely enjoyed her share of good times, especially after leaving the farm country of Navojoa and getting out on her own for the first time.

Me, I had killed any chance at a Supreme Court nomination years before, starting with when I first poured a beer down my throat around age sixteen. And while politicians get away with claiming that they "didn't inhale", when it comes to my past life, I make no similar assertions.

Matthew 5:27 had presented its own set of problems. Just looking at a woman lustfully is adulterous? Throw the book at me. Throughout my life, both before and after Adela, I had done way more than look. .

Well, at least I could partially blame the fact that my list of transgressions was quite extensive compared to Elsa's on the reality that I had seventeen years on her. After all, there's a lot a fellow like me can pack into seventeen years he might later regret. Especially when he's single until age thirty-three.

In spite of all that, as we became friends, I learned how similar our beliefs had eventually turned out to be with the passing of time. Until Elsa, I had never really met anyone who didn't make me feel like a lunatic for thinking the way I did. Someone who wouldn't squirm uncomfortably when Bible verses were quoted, or when "Jesus" and "Savior" were mentioned in the same sentence, yet didn't believe she had purchased herself some kind of insurance policy of salvation by simply uttering her stated acceptance of Him and moving on. Someone who believed that Jesus was anything but a fan of technicalities, wanting more than memorized words, checked boxes, or obligatory compliance with man-made rules. Someone who believed that Christ wanted her life, and nothing less.

I'm sure our conversations bored her co-workers to tears, but we enjoyed them immensely. And for some reason, every time I left her office after one of those kinds of conversations, my own faith seemed recharged. I'd leave with a desire to be a better person, and with a hunger to "raise the bar" and challenge myself to something beyond what I had previously expected from me.

Years later, I missed that.

****

"Who are we, Elsa?"

My wife lifted her head from the pillow and rubbed her eyes. "Who *are* we? I'll tell you who we are. Parents. Parents raising three kids with another on the way. Parents who have to get up early tomorrow morning. That's who we are."

"But beyond that, really, who are we?" I asked, apparently under some illusion that 1:30 a.m. is an ideal time to hit your wife with a barrage of philosophical questions. "Remember what we used to dream of doing, back when we first met? Where we thought we might one day find ourselves? Has that all just faded away with time? Did those dreams just disappear?"

If only I had recorded those words and put them to music, Air Supply might have finally had that long awaited comeback hit.

"If you're talking about who we were before I married you, took in two boys, had a baby and got pregnant again, sure I remember," she tiredly replied. "Africa… Haiti… Central America… I recall all that. But give me a break! Those dreams of going out and living the gospel in some far off place were nice, but they're not reality right now. Don't you see? This is a crazy time in our life!"

For some reason, I never could accept sensible answers to stupid questions.

"Elsa, let's be honest with ourselves. When is it *not* going to be a crazy time in our life? Think about it. Right now our kids are small, so we can't do anything. Then, there's high school. After that, college to put them through. By then our parents, if they're still living, will be old, and who knows what health they'll be in. Then, someday when they're not around and assuming we are, *we'll* be old. Hospital bills, maybe a nursing home, and then they shove you in a box. Sure, we'll have had a fun life. We'll have gone to some cool places, met some interesting folks, and been generally good to them. They'll speak at our funerals about how we were 'nice people' while we walked this planet. But didn't you used to think your purpose amounted to something more than simply 'being nice'? Remember what used to inspire you when we barely even knew each other?"

"You're forgetting something, Mark," Elsa responded. "Something called money. How on earth are we supposed to raise our family if we run off and save the world? Diapers cost money! So do formula, baby clothes, and hospitals! And a whole lot of other things you should have thought of a few months back, when you seemed to be a bit more interested in doing certain other things with me in this bedroom instead of having conversations like these!"

Well played, I had to admit.

"And besides," she added. "You haven't even told me exactly what it is you'd even like us to do if we did it. Where we'd go or how we'd get there. This 'plan' you keep waking me up for night after night isn't the most convincing!"

"Elsa, I don't have a plan," I interjected, as if that was somehow reassuring to a woman who had just been suddenly woken from badly needed sleep.

"Well, then? What's the deal here? Can we get some sleep?" she pleaded.

Unfortunately for Elsa, her husband is as persistent as a Jehovah's witness who also happens to sell vacation timeshares. "It's just that... I don't know, it's just..."

"What?" she demanded. "Say something intelligent, for God's sake!"

"I don't want to be one of those couples who looks back on all we would have done, if only we could have," I shot back. "Look at our friends who put things on hold. They never end up doing what they talk about. It's never the right time, and even if it were, they'd find a way to talk themselves out of it. OK, I know this isn't the ideal moment. But we need to realize, those moments are fictional. There's never going to be some 'ideal' moment."

Impatient as she could be, from the look on her face, Elsa seemed to grasp where this was going as I continued.

"That stuff we talked about years ago, is it supposed to become meaningless just because we have a family now? Does the gospel really not apply to people who have kids? Are families somehow exempt?"

"Look," I continued, "I'm not talking about selling our house, my guitar, Marcos' bike and Luis' toys and giving it all to the poor. But don't you kind of wish we had the guts to? To trust without fear? Are we that attached to this stuff? Come on, what's the most valuable material possession we have? Our house?"

She nodded. "I like our house! Anything wrong with that?"

"OK, we agree," I replied. "It's the only material possession I own, besides my guitar, that's worth a crap. But now that 'our adventure' is ending, I have this fear that we're going to go back to that house, build onto to it, fill it up with more and more stuff, and one day find ourselves so locked into a comfort zone that we can't break free."

My words were slowly beginning to resonate with her. After all, this was the woman who almost put my kids into a Costa Rican grade school two years before, and had bounced from one corner of Mexico to the other with me, pregnant, on the craziest of a whim.

"I guess I just want to know you're still on board with me, Elsa," I added. "That even when the baby is born and things are crazy, we'll still keep our doors in life open to doing what we were put here for. Shoot, it could be some small project out of our home in San Carlos, or something else far away in some place we've never even heard of. It could be the two of us helping fire victims locally, or raising funds for people who are truly starving. It could be anything! I just need to know that the girl I married is still in there, still believing in what she used to, and not letting the practical world somehow confiscate those dreams from her."

She listened intently, sitting up and leaning against the headboard as I spoke.

"I'm restless. I want us to get out of the bleachers. I want to us get in the game. And even if the coach isn't ready to put us on the field yet, I at least want us to be ready to be called in off the bench when he *does* need us. If we can't simply commit to that, seriously, who cares if our kids go to private schools or land great careers? All that's pointless if we can't guide them to a better place when this life we share is all over."

Elsa just sat there, taking it all in. I could tell from her face that she understood every word I was saying. But she's not an easy sell. I pity the telemarketer who dials her number.

"Mark, in my heart, I agree with everything you're saying, but look at us. We're going home to a two bedroom house that's got to fit all of us. We won't even be able to fit our kids in our car, with six of us and only five seat belts. How are we going to legally drive our kids to the store, much less school or anywhere else? Like it or not, we need to spend the next few years concentrating on making enough money to cover that kind of stuff, not getting into other areas."

She sure wasn't throwing me any softballs here. Still, like Barry Bonds minus the steroids, I took a swing for the outfield fence.

"Elsa, how much money do you think we need to cover our needs? Say, adding on to one of the bedrooms? Picking up a used van?"

She pondered my question for a while, adding in her head. "Wow,

I have no idea. But we can't even think about getting involved with anything whatsoever until we save up at least enough to get it all started. A car? An addition? Just a start, at a bare minimum, would be… I don't know, at *least* twenty-five thousand."

I prayed to God the girl was talking pesos. Unfortunately, she wasn't. Twenty-five thousand bucks! That's a lot of money for a guy whose first professional gig was for fifty dollars and a bar tab. But for some reason, as we continued talking, that number was stuck in her head, and she was insistent.

"OK, after I spend years trying to save up twenty-five thousand, then we finally set out to do whatever our purpose is in this world?" I pressed.

"Yes," she replied firmly. "I promise, at that point, we think about our larger purpose in this world. But first, before you say yes to some group in Uganda or even start to think about anything else, we add on to the house and pick up a used vehicle that fits us all."

OK, time to break out all the stops. Like the old Schlitz ad, go for the gusto. Another Doug Flutie "Hail Mary" into the end zone. You get the point.

"I have an even better idea, Elsa. Instead of delaying our purpose for who knows how long, trying to save up twenty-five grand, how about we bag remodeling the kitchen and buying new furniture? How about instead we simply commit to being open to any change God wants us to make, *whenever* he wants us to make it, whether that offer presents itself tomorrow or ten years from now? Whatever money we need for the necessary stuff, like a car or room addition, I say we ditch the fear and put it in God's hands. If He wants us to have it, He'll provide it. And if He doesn't, He won't. Plain and simple. Let's not be afraid to trust! Come on, what's the worst thing that can happen? We have to use Luis for a hood ornament when we go somewhere in the car? Or I have to ride a unicycle next to you guys when we drive to the store? As for the house, let's get real. In places like Uganda, fifteen people pile into one room with no running water or electricity. They'd kill to have the luxury of a two bedroom house and only six people sleeping in it."

Good chance there would be five people instead of six sleeping in *our* house if I kept talking. But there was one thing left to add.

"Elsa, I truly doubt it ever *will* come down to that. If it did though, as long as we're all together and trust in God, we'd be fine. The question really is, *do* we trust in God to take care of us? Or don't we?"

****

I'm sure after reading this chapter, every divorce lawyer in the continental United States will be trying to contact Elsa. Why she hasn't dumped my sorry butt is beyond me. Maybe it's simply because she felt the same thing deep inside, and just needed someone else to say it.

It's not like we're talking the Palestinians and the Jews here, but a life changing dialogue continued into the wee hours of the morning. We talked, just like we used to years before in her office. I'd love to say we figured out our entire game plan that night, but we didn't. However, something big happened, something that would affect our marriage and our future forever.

"I'm in," she said, startling me with an answer that came from out of the blue. "Whatever we do, whenever we do it, whether tomorrow or years from now, I'm in. One hundred per cent. No going back."

****

So if a brand new car never belongs to us
And if our house is kind of small, so what

Chapter Forty Five

"What time is it?" I asked, rubbing my eyes as the morning sun shone through the bedroom window.

"Time to get up, if we're going to get packed and make it up to Phoenix on time," Elsa responded. "Hey, next time you want to have a three hour discussion about our purpose in this world, could we begin it around, say, 8 p.m.?"

Yes, it had been somewhat of a long night, but it was well worth it. Several ideas had popped into our head during our lengthy discussion, everything from taking an old abandoned building in Guaymas and turning it into some kind of shelter to simply providing construction materials for fire victims. We'd follow up on our ideas once we got back to San Carlos.

With my final Rocky Point show coming up New Years Eve, that final move home would soon be upon us. But first, with Rocky Point much closer to the border than San Carlos, we wanted to sneak in a quick trip to Phoenix to see family.

"Rosita's sound perfect for dinner, Dad, see you there at 4 p.m." Yes, 4 p.m. And yes, "dinner." He and Mom definitely liked to eat early. In fact, I wouldn't be surprised if they frequently enjoyed an early bird dinner special about the same time my brother Dave was waking up for breakfast.

Not only did Dad like to enjoy supper anytime after 3:30 p.m., but he expected guests to be on time. And when it came to expected times, he was rather exact. Plan on meeting Dad for breakfast? "I'll be there at 7:37 a.m.," he just might inform you. Yes, he had his whole morning plan down to the precise minute, from the moment he woke up and did his pre-dawn exercises to his mile long walk and daily morning Mass.

Given his obsession for punctuality, the fact that he married a woman from Venezuela meant there were bound to be conflicts. He recognized it early on, back when they were dating. Let's just say Mom liked to keep Dad waiting, and not just in the way Catholics refer to. So, in a move that would enrage radical feminists even more than a pregnant woman choosing to have her baby, Dad set a condition for Mom that she would have to meet. Twenty-five dates of her choosing, she would have to be ready to go on time, or he would not propose. OK, not exactly the stuff Hallmark cards are made of, but hey, somehow Mom pulled the stunt off and they got married. As an interesting side note, she never once showed up for anything else on time again.

Dad had mellowed with age, but still I found myself glancing at my watch roughly every half minute as we headed for the United States.

"He'll be fine, don't worry," Elsa said. "He's so sweet."

"Yeah, he'll be fine with you because he thinks you're Miss Mexico!" I responded, flooring the gas pedal soon after we crossed the border. "For some strange reason, my brothers and I don't get away with that kind of stuff with Dad like you would."

Finally, a few hours later, we got to Phoenix and pulled into the parking lot of Rosita's Place. Damn, his car was already there!

"Get out!" I shouted to the kids. "Run!" Seconds later, we swung the front door of the restaurant open. Glancing at my watch one last time, I breathed a sigh of relief. Only seven minutes late, reasonably within the standard nine minute margin of error. (Ten or beyond and you're screwed.)

"*¡Hola abuela!*" Luis shouted, running toward my mom and greeting her with a big hug.

"Man alive, Marcos, look how big you've gotten!" Dad exclaimed, patting Marcos on the head as we piled into the building, instantly destroying all paying customers' hopes of enjoying a nice night out.

Yes, it was the normal chaos that ensued every time my gang walked into a building of any kind, be it a restaurant, shoe store or church. While Marcos shrieked over a *Los Tigres del Norte* song blaring at jet engine decibel level on the jukebox and Luis tossed a fork into the gaudy indoor goldfish pond, Elsa and Mom chattered and hugged.

"Let me hold that cute little boy!" Mom insisted, reaching for Jose. "And look at you, pregnant again! Don't you look darling?"

It was great to see everyone. Dad looked fit, having lost weight, and he seemed to be in a really happy mood.

Suddenly, he turned to me. "Hey, Mark," he whispered, tugging my arm before we sat down at our table. "Come over here with me for a second."

Knowing my Dad, I assumed I was in for a barrage of filthy nun jokes that he didn't want "Miss Mexico" or Mom to hear. With them busy talking, we quickly walked over to the corner.

"What's up, Dad?" I asked, motioning across the room for Marcos to quiet down before we got thrown out of the restaurant.

"Listen, buddy," he said. "I know you guys have got a lot going on right now with another baby on the way. And what the hell, I'm getting old! Instead of waiting until later, I want to see you guys enjoy yourselves a bit, before I die!"

Suddenly Dad reached into his pocket. "I want you and Elsa to have this."

He pulled out an envelope, handing it to me. I opened it up.

It was a check for twenty-five thousand dollars.

Chapter Forty Six

"This is unbelievable!" Elsa stood there, astonished, staring at the handwritten check with my father's signature on it. "I mean, to the very dollar, it's exactly what I told you we needed! Just last night!"

She couldn't believe it. "It hasn't even been twenty-four hours since we prayed about this!"

p   d reason to be stunned. Even I, who ought to be getting
c   , was taken aback, reflecting
                                                     ight.
)   twenty-five thousand dollars
]   ave no doubt, God heard you.
]   ven ask for it! So believe me,
                                                     rewarded for trusting in him.
                                                     of it."
                                                     nd asked me to pray with her
                                                     to sleep. Now here we were,
                                                     y-five thousand dollars in our

                                                     s of joy fell down Elsa's face.
                                                     ed me. Here's everything you

****

He does? I haven't got a clue. There are priests, p   scholars and all kinds of experts with all kinds of better answers than I've got. Me, I'm just a guy who bangs on a guitar and sings songs for a living, so what can I tell you?

But one thing I do know. The day I stood before an altar for a second time, with Elsa as my bride and Dave as my best man, I realized God didn't have a single thing to do with us being together. He had *everything* to do with us being together.

Elsa was a gift. A reward, for simply trusting in Him and finally putting my life in His hands. For relinquishing the wheel and letting Him drive.

For finally having the guts to stand up in my kitchen one day, the illusions of my former life shattered, and announcing that I want to walk *with* Him and not away from Him.

For turning to God when my life was spiraling and on the verge of destruction, so he could build it back up into something better. For letting the Holy Spirit go to work inside me, filling me with courage and strength I had never possessed before.

For having faith, accepting what I'll never fully understand. For realizing I don't *have* to understand, or have all "the answers." For simply believing.

Like a twenty-five thousand dollar check that my father wanted us to have sooner rather than later, Elsa was a gift God could hardly wait to give me. He hadn't even let me hang up that phone after finally rejecting past temptation when he had her dialing my number from New Jersey. He wanted me to be with her, and her with me. He just needed to know I was ready. Not only for her, but for Him.

No doubt about it, the arrival of Elsa after the loss of Adela was yet *another* miracle in this crazy, unbelievable chain of events. So why "The Three Miracles?"

What about that check? And our simultaneous phone call to each other? And a band playing me "Seven Bridges Road" while my dying wife was far away, unable to say goodbye?

How 'bout the fact that my Mom was actually on time for my Dad twenty-five times?

Why not "The Seven Miracles"? Or "The Fifteen Miracles?" Or "The Nine Hundred Forty-Eight Miracles?"

Plain and simple. It took a certain three of those suckers to slap me upside the head and wake me up. Three to free me from the constraints of human logic. Three to lead me to a place where I don't *need* to witness miracle after miracle to believe. Three to change my life forever.

And boy, would my life change forever.

****

So much for those other plans
Guess they were never meant to be
Instead I sit here and I wonder
Will you look like her or a little like me

Pacing back and forth impatiently in the waiting room, I couldn't help but wonder. Will it be a boy or a girl? For many months, we had resisted the temptation of finding out.

"I agree, let's milk this surprise for all we can," I had said early on. "After all, this is the last time we'll ever go through the experience of a pregnancy!" The words had barely escaped my lips when I turned to see Elsa looking at me, her eyebrows raised.

"Whatever," I sighed.

OK, even if past experience had proved I wasn't the best at predicting anything regarding the likelihood of pregnancies, I did know that I wanted the sex of our fourth child to be a surprise, just as it had been from the birth of Marcos through little Jose. After all, it's surprises that make life fun.

Like Christmas presents. Isn't it the thrill of spending days or even weeks wondering what's under that wrapping paper that makes opening the gift unforgettable? How about fishing? Who wants to know beforehand how many snapper or trout they're going to catch before they ever toss a line in the water? It's the thrill of not knowing whether or not you'll be skunked or land that big one that makes going fishing an adventure. But I again digress.

Any minute now, we'd find out just what gift was awaiting us under the wrapping paper. In fact, Elsa already knew. The baby had been born nearly thirty minutes earlier, but just like when my first three kids popped out of the womb, I hadn't been allowed in the delivery room with my wife. No men allowed, period. That was the policy, shocking as the enlightened world beyond the city limits of Guaymas might find it. So all I knew was that Elsa and the baby were both healthy, with doctors and nurses careful to avoid any inadvertent mention of the baby's sex.

"If it's a boy, we'll call him 'Jesus Adrian,'" Elsa had previously declared. Again, beyond the borders of the Spanish speaking world, naming your kid "Jesus" is a slightly brazen concept. But hey, what do you expect in a country like Mexico where mothers of nine children are frequently named after a virgin?

Anyway, aside from any similarities in name to a famous fellow who miraculously rose from the dead, "Jesus Adrian" also happens to be the name of an artist whose inspirational music Elsa and I love, a songwriter named Jesus Adrian Romero. He's one of our favorites, a performer whose lyrics, music and life have influenced us greatly. Given the fact that Elsa got to pick the name if the baby were a boy, that helped to inspire her choice.

On the other hand, if the baby were a girl, I got to choose. Years ago, my brother John had thrown an idea for a girl's name into my head without even realizing it. "Marisol."

"'*Mar*'" and '*sol*', like ocean and sun, two of my favorite things," he had casually remarked when mentioning potential girl names during his own wife's pregnancy. Although the literal translation for that would be three words, written as "*mar y sol*" rather than "*Marisol*," it was close enough for me. And given its popularity as a first name for girls throughout Latin America, it wasn't like she'd have some strange name, like the one rocker Frank Zappa chose for his daughter when he named her "Moon Unit," or actress Kate Winslet naming her kid "Bear." No, Marisol sounded nice. And beautiful, just like the ocean and the sun.

Suddenly the door to the waiting room swung open. "*Señor Mulligan*, you can come on back now!"

Seconds later, there I was with Elsa, as the doctor presented me with our newborn infant, wrapped in a blue blanket. Blue?

"*Jesus Adrian*!" I blurted out. Elsa shook her head and smiled. Little did I know, Guaymas Municipal hospital had no pink blankets. I opened the blue blanket and quickly realized, that ain't no Jesus!

No, you weren't supposed to be here
But thank God you came along
I can hardly wait to meet you
Soon I'll be singing you this song
And I can't wait to say welcome home

Chapter Forty Seven

The sun was barely on the rise as I sped up Highway 15 toward Hermosillo, sister in law Eva in the passenger seat beside me.

"*Gracias, Mark*" she said. "This really means a lot that you would drive me up to the hospital this early in the morning."

"I'm sure your son is fine," I assured her. "Especially since your husband is already there with him. Don't worry, the good thing is broken bones heal fast with little kids his age. Remember how quickly Marcos and Luis healed?"

She smiled and nodded. "Those were crazy times, weren't they? It all seems so long ago." She suddenly became a bit wistful. "Sometimes I still can't believe Adela is gone. It's been more than six years now, but it still doesn't seem real."

"I know what you mean, Eva," I replied. "But you know, we've all done OK, haven't we? Your family has grown, your Mom is doing well, I've got Elsa…"

"You're lucky, Mark" she agreed. "And so are the boys. It all turned out OK after all."

Passing the Kino Bay turnoff, we continued our journey north, revisiting the events of July 16, 2006 that had now shaped our lives forever. Events that might fade into the past with time, but would never be forgotten by any of us who knew Adela Ruiz Fuentes.

"Eva, there are things you never knew about your sister," I confided, "and things about this whole crazy story that I've shared with very few people. But you stepped in and took care of me when I needed it most. I think she'd want you to know." By the time we were within twenty miles of Hermosillo, she had heard the entire story, one I promised her I would one day share with others.

Eva sat there amazed, convinced too that this whole chain of crazy, against all odds, chance events was beyond coincidence. As she smiled, she looked so much like her older sister it was almost like Adela was sitting beside me.

"I don't know what to say, Mark, except *gracias*. I'm thankful that Adela was my sister, and I'm thankful that you married her." She took a breath. "Now there's something I want to tell you, something I never shared with you before. About Adela, and one of the last conversations I ever had with her, just before she died."

****

Standing there in the living room, Adela spread one last shirt out on the ironing board, smiling as her younger sister brought up yet another funny story from the past. "I can't believe you ever went out with that guy!" Eva exclaimed. Adela just laughed.

Before she ever met me, Adela had plenty of chances at other fellows. Guys fell all over themselves trying to get her to go out on a date. One look at that smile, and she was impossible not to fall in love with. Her father certainly had his work cut out for him, fending off eligible suitors.

"Sure, I dated, and I had boyfriends, but never serious," Adela replied, still smiling as she turned the iron off. "And thank God. Just think, I might have ended up with someone like our sister Katy's boyfriend. Remember what a winner we all thought he was, before he left her? But Mark, he was different."

"How did you know?" Eva asked.

"I just did," Adela replied. "Mark was my gift from God." Unplugging the iron and setting it to the side, she looked at her younger sister. "Eva, I want you to know something."

"What?"

Adela sat down, looked at her sister and smiled. "Listen to me. If God decides it's my time, I've had a good life…" she began.

Eva suddenly interrupted. "Adela, don't talk like that! Don't! I don't like it!"

"Just hear me out, Eva," Adela replied, gently calming her sister. "I wanted you to know. If God decides it's time for me to go, I've done everything in this life I ever wanted to."

Eva tried to interrupt, but Adela continued. "I wanted to go to school, and I got to go to school. I wanted to one day have a home, and I got to have a home. I wanted to marry a good man, and I married a good man. I wanted to raise a family, and I got to have two beautiful boys."

"Adela, please, stop talking like this! It makes me uncomfortable, like something is going to happen!" Eva insisted. "Whenever your final moment will be on this earth, that's all in God's hands. Why talk about it now?"

"I just wanted you to know," Adela answered, smiling peacefully. "If

God calls me from this world tomorrow, I've had more of a life than I ever dreamed I would. No one should ever feel sad for me. I'll die a happy person. A very happy person."

****

One month later, there she was in my rear view mirror, standing there in the driveway, waving goodbye as I slowly pulled our black Nissan X-Trail out on to the street...

Rest in peace Adela Ruiz Fuentes

At the author's request, all proceeds from
this book will go to charity,
including Castaway Kids, Inc., founded
by Mark and providing education to
underprivileged children in Mexico.

To learn more about Castaway Kids and
how you can help, please visit www.
castawaykidsmx.org   There is a permanent
link to Castaway Kids organization on Mark's
website at

www.markmulligan.net

76031755R00146

Made in the USA
San Bernardino, CA
09 May 2018